Playing by the Informal Rules

Growing protests in nondemocratic countries are often seen as signals of regime decline. China, however, has remained stable amid surging protests. *Playing by the Informal Rules* highlights the importance of informal norms in structuring state–protester interactions, mitigating conflict, and explaining regime resilience amid mounting unrest. Drawing on a nationwide dataset of protest and multisited ethnographic research, this book presents a bird's-eye view of Chinese contentious politics and illustrates the uneven application of informal norms across regions, social groups, and time. Through examining different types of protests and their distinct implications for regime stability, Li offers a novel theoretical framework suitable for monitoring the trajectory of political contention in China and beyond. Overall, this study sheds new light on contentious politics and authoritarian resilience and provides fresh perspectives on power, rules, legitimacy, and resistance in modern societies.

YAO LI is a postdoctoral fellow at Harvard University's Ash Center for Democratic Governance and Innovation. She earned her PhD in Sociology at Johns Hopkins University and was a lecturer in the Center for East Asian Studies at the University of Kansas. She was named an Exemplary Diversity Scholar by the University of Michigan's National Center for Institutional Diversity in 2015.

Studies of the Weatherhead East Asian Institute, Columbia University

The Studies of the Weatherhead East Asian Institute of Columbia University were inaugurated in 1962 to bring to a wider public the results of significant new research on modern and contemporary East Asia.

Cambridge Studies in Contentious Politics

(*continued after index*)

Playing by the Informal Rules

Why the Chinese Regime Remains Stable despite Rising Protests

YAO LI
Harvard University

CAMBRIDGE
UNIVERSITY PRESS

CAMBRIDGE
UNIVERSITY PRESS

University Printing House, Cambridge CB2 8BS, United Kingdom

One Liberty Plaza, 20th Floor, New York, NY 10006, USA

477 Williamstown Road, Port Melbourne, VIC 3207, Australia

314-321, 3rd Floor, Plot 3, Splendor Forum, Jasola District Centre, New Delhi - 110025, India

79 Anson Road, #06-04/06, Singapore 079906

Cambridge University Press is part of the University of Cambridge.

It furthers the University's mission by disseminating knowledge in the pursuit of education, learning and research at the highest international levels of excellence.

www.cambridge.org
Information on this title: www.cambridge.org/9781108456654
DOI: 10.1017/9781108557054

First published 2019
First paperback edition 2021

A catalogue record for this publication is available from the British Library

ISBN 978-1-108-47078-0 Hardback
ISBN 978-1-108-45665-4 Paperback

Cambridge University Press has no responsibility for the persistence or accuracy of URLs for external or third-party internet websites referred to in this publication, and does not guarantee that any content on such websites is, or will remain, accurate or appropriate.

To my parents, Yao Shuchun and Li Chensheng

Contents

Figures

Tables

Acknowledgments

This book started with a 2007 conversation with my mother's colleague, a retired doctor who was leading his colleagues in a fight against a government decision to privatize their hospital. At that point the struggle was close to victory. When the doctor described their protest experience, I was not only impressed by his eloquence, charisma, and wit, but also amazed at the protesters' ability to affect government decision-making and to push policy implementation in their favor. The first question that came to mind then was how they got there. The more I learned about this case, the more I was drawn into Chinese contentious politics and the more questions arose: What about other protest cases? How does the Chinese state handle protests in general? Are there regional differences? Does the state treat distinct social groups differently? What are the political implications of these protests? This book is the culmination of my efforts to answer these questions.

For their invaluable contributions to my work, I am grateful to many individuals. At Johns Hopkins, Joel Andreas, an incredibly devoted mentor, guided me at every turn and inspired me with his dedication, wisdom, and vision. I am deeply indebted to him for his insightful advice, valuable encouragement, and for reading countless drafts of this research project from its infancy. I am also thankful to Lingxin Hao, Erin Chung, Ho-fung Hung, Rina Agarwala, and William Rowe for their challenging questions and thoughtful feedback. Thanks also go to the late Giovanni Arrighi, Beverly Silver, Melvin Kohn, Stephan Plank, Kellee Tsai, and Michael Levien for providing wise counsel along the way.

In converting this research from a dissertation to a book, I benefited considerably from the tough questions and constructive suggestions of Tony Saich, Mary Gallagher, Steve Levitsky, Jessica Teets, Arne Westad, Elizabeth Perry, Edward Cunningham, Kaori Urayama, Manfred Elfstrom, Huirong Chen, Sara Newland, Chengpang Lee, Junpeng Li, and Yeling Tan, who read either the entire manuscript or parts of it. I would especially like to acknowledge Tony Saich for his close reading of the manuscript, sage advice, and inspiring comments during my time as a postdoctoral fellow at Harvard. I thank the Ash Center for providing financial and logistical support of a book workshop that greatly strengthened the final product. J. Megan Greene, So-Min Cheong, and John James Kennedy's support during my time at the University of Kansas is much appreciated as well.

For helpful comments at various stages of the project, I thank Mildred Schwartz, Karyn J. Wang, Dana Moss, Patricia Bromley, Anne Thurston, Ray Madoff, Rogers Smith, Chan S. Suh, Paul Y. Chang, Melissa Forbis, Woody Powell, Wayne Santoro, Neil Diamant, Lu Zhang, Evan Schofer, Yan Long, Ling Han, and Juan Wang. I thank Sahan Savas Karatasli for his excellent advice regarding data coding, and Charlie Mitchell and Daniel Pasciuti for their invaluable comments on my quantitative chapter. I am grateful to Burak Gurel, Sika Koudou, Nazish Zafar, Anne-Marie Livingstone, Erdem Yoruk, Mike Reese, Minchang You, Jing Li, Rachel Core, and Ben Scully for their intellectual and emotional support and their encouragement of my research.

I am thankful for feedback from audiences at various seminars and workshops at Johns Hopkins University, Stanford University, Harvard University, the University of Kansas, the University of Pennsylvania, Columbia University, and Stony Brook University as well as at annual meetings of the American Sociological Association, the Eastern Sociological Society, the North American Chinese Sociologists Association, the Association for Asian Studies, the International Studies Association (ISA), the ISA Midwest, and the American Political Science Association. Financial support from the Ash Center at Harvard and from the Program in East Asian Studies, the Department of Sociology, and the Program in Comparative Sociology and International Development at Johns Hopkins are greatly appreciated.

Two anonymous reviewers at Cambridge University Press put amazing effort into reading and commenting on this manuscript. Their insight and astute suggestions undoubtedly have helped me better achieve my goals. I am indebted to my editor, Robert Dreesen, for his support and to the whole team at Cambridge University Press who help this project come to fruition. Special thanks to Doug McAdam for his supportive comments and for including this book in the Cambridge Studies in Contentious Politics series. I am also grateful to editors at the Weatherhead East Asian Institute of Columbia University for including the book in their series. Randi Hacker's assistance in copy editing is much appreciated. Moreover, I thank Cambridge University Press for permission to reprint parts of my article, "A Zero-Sum Game? Repression and Protest in China," *Government and Opposition: An International Journal of Comparative Politics* (September 7, 2017; doi:10.1017/gov.2017.24), in Chapter 2 of this book.

Most importantly, I want to express my gratitude to my interviewees for their willingness to share their stories and thoughts with me. Special thanks go to friends of non-governmental organizations in China, who provided generous help in my fieldwork (who must remain anonymous to protect their privacy). I enjoyed the experience of doing interviews together with Chin-chih Wang (in Beijing in January 2013), who was doing his doctoral field research on environmental protests at the same time.

Finally, I thank my family for their patience and support on the road to this project's completion. My husband, Wu Huixuan, read numerous drafts of this manuscript and is always keen to discuss my research and give me inspiration. His resourceful advice and upbeat attitude have helped ease the writing process and bring sunshine into my life. I am also indebted to my parents, Yao Shuchun and Li Chensheng, for giving me a loving family, encouraging my intellectual exploration, and always offering me wholehearted support. In particular, my mother has instilled in me the belief that "a girl can do anything a boy can do" since I was young, and her participation in the hospital struggle inspired this research in the first place. Thus, it is to Mom and Dad that this book is dedicated.

Abbreviations

BLR	binary logistic regression
CAP	contradiction among the people
CBOE	contradiction between ourselves and the enemy
CCP	Chinese Communist Party
CDP	China Democracy Party
DCFTU	D City Federation of Trade Unions
DCPB	D City Petition Bureau
DCTB	D City Traffic Bureau
ICPC	Independent Chinese PEN Center
LAPD	*Law on Assemblies, Processions, and Demonstrations*
MLR	multinomial logistic regression
NGO	non-governmental organizations
NIABY	not in anyone's backyard
NIMBY	not in my backyard
NPB	National Petition Bureau
PEA	protest event analysis
PRC	People's Republic of China
PSAPL	*Public Security Administration Punishment Law*
PSB	public security bureau
SEPA	State Environmental Protection Administration
SOE	state-owned enterprise
WUC	World Uyghur Congress

Introduction

Rising Protests and Regime Stability

The Tunisian "Jasmine Revolution," the mass uprising that overthrew President Zine El-Abidine Ben Ali in January 2011, not only set off the "Arab Spring" in the Middle East and North Africa but also inspired anonymous calls for a Jasmine Revolution in China through the Internet. When the proposed revolution day (Sunday, February 20, 2011) arrived, it turned out that the online calls attracted far more police and journalists than would-be protesters. In Beijing, hundreds of uniformed and plain-clothed police along with a host of foreign journalists, some carrying television cameras, flooded the planned protest site – Wangfujing pedestrian mall, one of Beijing's busiest shopping centers.[1] A crowd of curious shoppers then milled around the site, wondering whether there was a celebrity in the area. The US Ambassador to China, Jon Huntsman, also appeared in the crowd.[2] At the scene, while everyone was waiting for something to happen, the only possible sign of protest came from a young man who attempted to lay down some jasmine flowers, although he claimed that he had come with friends to shop and was "just a normal citizen."[3] Foot traffic on weekends is always heavy at Wangfujing; therefore, it was difficult to discern protesters from onlookers. Likewise, in Shanghai, identifiable protesters were few, and it was reported that more journalists

---

[1] Wangfujing is located in the city center, 1.6 miles from Tiananmen Square. "'Jasmine' Protests in China Fall Flat." Jaime FlorCruz. *CNN.* February 21, 2011.
   www.cnn.com/2011/WORLD/asiapcf/02/20/china.protests/.

[2] But he quickly left after being identified by a crowd member. "Call for Protests Unnerves Beijing." Jeremy Page. *The Wall Street Journal.* February 21, 2011.
   www.wsj.com/articles/SB10001424052748703498804576156203874160350.

[3] "Chinese Steer Clear of 'Jasmine Revolution.'" Geoff Dyer, Kathrin Hille, and Patti Waldmeir. *Financial Times.* February 20, 2011.
   www.ft.com/content/b8495a56-3d1a-11e0-bbff-00144feabdco.

showed up at the designated protest spot than police.[4] There were no reports of demonstrations in other cities where people were also urged to protest.[5] This falling short of visible protest, thus, even led an anti-Chinese Communist Party (CCP) newspaper to suspect that the online appeals to action were a hoax staged by the CCP itself.[6]

Although nothing much came from the calls for China's Jasmine Revolution, authorities were on high alert. Security forces poured into the designated gathering locations, several suspected protesters were taken away, the websites and Internet searches relevant to the event were blocked, and more than 100 political activists across China were confined to their homes or went missing *ahead of* the planned demonstrations.[7] What's more, authorities even waged a war on jasmine, censoring the word "jasmine," issuing a jasmine ban at flower markets, and forcing the cancellation of events like the China International Jasmine Cultural Festival.[8]

Indeed, Chinese leaders had good reasons to be nervous. Popular protests typically pose a potential threat to the stability of authoritarian states. Contemporary history has witnessed breakdowns of authoritarianism in the face of mass protest: from the Iranian Revolution to the dissolution of the Soviet Union to the democratization in Africa and East Asia to the post-Communist color revolutions. A most recent lesson was the ousting of President Hosni Mubarak, who ruled Egypt for nearly thirty years but was toppled within just eighteen days after millions took to the streets in 2011. Within China, the traumatic ending of the 1989 Tiananmen movement is still not a distant memory.[9] In the past few decades, the country has witnessed a remarkable rise in popular mobilization. The number of "mass incidents"[10] – an official term for social protests – climbed from 8,700 in 1993 to 87,000 in 2005 to 172,000 in

---

[4] "Those Responding to the Jasmine Revolution Protest Call in Beijing and Shanghai Were Dispersed by the Police." *BBC News*. February 20, 2011.
    www.bbc.com/zhongwen/simp/china/2011/02/110220_china_jasmine_revolution.shtml.

[5] "China Tries to Stamp out 'Jasmine Revolution.'" Eugene Hoshiko. *AP*. February 20, 2011.
    http://usatoday30.usatoday.com/news/world/2011-02-20-china-jasmine-revolution_N.htm.

[6] "Jasmine Revolution in China a Trap, Say Analysts." Quincy Yu. *Epoch Times*. February 22, 2011. www.theepochtimes.com/n3/1501671-aborted-chinese-jasmine-revolution-a-trap-say-analysts/.

[7] "Call for Protests Unnerves Beijing." Jeremy Page. *The Wall Street Journal*. February 21, 2011.
    www.wsj.com/articles/SB10001424052748703498804576156203874160350.

[8] "Catching Scent of Revolution, China Moves to Snip Jasmine." Andrew Jacobs and Jonathan Ansfield. *The New York Times*. May 10, 2011.
    www.nytimes.com/2011/05/11/world/asia/11jasmine.html?mcubz=3.

[9] The state sent troops and tanks to put an end to the Tiananmen movement. See Chapter 5 for more details of the movement.

[10] It is a broad term that encompasses the full spectrum of group protests, including sit-ins, marches, rallies, strikes, demonstrations, building seizures, armed fighting, and riots (Tanner 2004).

2014 – an average of 471 protests per day in 2014.[11] Protesters, coming from various social classes and groups, have taken a wide range of collective actions to express their grievances. Examples include labor strikes for higher pay, peasant road blockages against land acquisitions, middle-class demonstrations opposing environment-threatening projects, resistance by pro-democracy dissidents, and armed insurgency by ethnic minorities. Hypersensitive to social protests, authorities, instead of crushing all of them, show leniency to many. Against this backdrop, one might wonder whether the Chinese regime is in danger of collapse.

Social scientists have tended to see growing unrest in authoritarian states as signals of regime decline. Unlike liberal democracies, authoritarian regimes lack effective institutions – such as a robust legal system – for peacefully containing conflicts, and they typically rely on repression to deal with protests. When authoritarian regimes face greater protests, as Charles Tilly (2008) claims, we expect that either the government is moving toward democracy or its capacity to use repression has been weakened, or both.

Nevertheless, a broad array of research suggests that this is not the case in China. Not only has the regime retained its fundamentally authoritarian character, without going through a democratization process (e.g., Human Rights Watch 2015; C. Li 2012; Perry 2007 and 2012), but also the state enjoys popular acceptance or support according to surveys (Chen 2004; Dickson 2016; Kennedy 2009a; Saich 2007 and 2011; Shi 2001 and 2015; Tang 2005 and 2016; Z. Wang 2006; Whyte 2010; Wright 2010; Yang 2007). This result is consistent with the general consensus among China scholars that the one-party state remains resilient and stable (e.g., Dickson 2008; Gallagher and Hanson 2013; Heilmann and Perry 2011; Naughton and Yang 2004; Perry 2014; Teets 2014; K. Tsai 2007; Walder 2009a; Zheng 2015; cf. Pei 2006 and 2016).

Then why does the Chinese regime remain resilient *despite mounting protests*? To explain this puzzle, some scholars stress that the improvement of *formal institutions* (such as the legal system) has created regime legitimacy and resilience by accommodating conflict and increasing the responsiveness of the Chinese state. However, despite this progress, the formal channels still have major limitations that impede effective management of conflict and satisfactory redress of citizen grievances.

A big part of the solution to the puzzle, I argue, lies in understanding the role of *informal norms* in managing contention. The Chinese regime has in place

---

[11] The number of mass incidents was sporadically reported. The figures for 2006, 2007, 2011, and 2013 were 90,000, 100,000, 139,000, and 165,000, respectively (see several volumes of the *Blue Book of Chinese Society* (e.g., Lu, Li, and Chen 2012) – edited by the Chinese Academy of Social Sciences, a large state-run think tank – and multiple volumes of *China Social and Public Security Research Reports* (Zhang and Peng 2012, 2014, and 2015) – edited by East China University of Politics and Law). For figures before 2006, see Tanner (2004) and Chung, Lai, and Xia (2006).

layers of institutional arrangements that prohibit social protests; in strict terms of law, most protests are illegal or extralegal. In reality, however, authorities routinely relax law enforcement and allow a greater space for protest than that stipulated by law. Protesters – while pushing the envelope – also enforce self-censorship. During the process, some unwritten rules, or what I call "accommodating informal norms of contention," play a vital part in shaping and constraining the actions of both the state and protesters. While China does not have the kind of robust institutions that exist in liberal democracies for handling conflict, I contend that accommodating informal norms work in this capacity by promoting conflict resolution through dialogue and building regime resilience. Focusing exclusively on formal institutions captures only a partial picture of politics and resistance in China.

Being informal, these unwritten rules are, by definition, not as visible or clear-cut as formal, written laws; neither are government officials bound to show leniency to dissenters, nor do aggrieved citizens always exercise self-discipline. Further, the application of informal norms can vary across social groups, places, and time. Yet investigating informal norms – the less detectable form of interactions between authorities and dissidents – is essential in unraveling the subtle, multifaceted character of Chinese contentious politics and casting light on its varied political implications. Drawing on extensive event data and in-depth ethnographic research, this book explores and analyzes what informal norms are in place, why they come into being, when and how they work, under what conditions they fail to work, and their political impacts. Since the 1989 Tiananmen uprising, the collapse or resilience of the Chinese regime has become a burning topic in academia, in the political sphere, and in public discourse; more recently, research on resistance and activism in China has flourished. Yet the puzzling coexistence of popular protests and authoritarian stability has remained largely unexplored. A systematic analysis of this issue not only can contribute to a better understanding of governance and society in China but has broader implications for the study of political mobilization and authoritarian politics in general.

FORMAL INSTITUTIONS AND REGIME RESILIENCE

The Arab Spring also inspired the upsurge of mass demonstrations in Western democracies. In fall 2011, the "Occupy movement" sprang up in the United States and then swiftly spread to other countries including France, Germany, and the United Kingdom. The movement even received support from the Egyptian activists who had helped overthrow the Mubarak government.[12] Nonetheless, rarely did observers associate the Occupy movement with

---

[12] "Tahrir Square Protesters Send Message of Solidarity to Occupy Wall Street." Jack Shenker and Adam Gabbatt. *The Guardian*. October 25, 2011. www.theguardian.com/world/2011/oct/25/egyptian-protesters-occupy-wall-street.

indications of regime decline or instability in the *democratic* world. This stands in stark contrast to considerable speculations about whether China or Jordan or Syria would be the next domino to fall on the heels of the Arab upheaval.

This contrast speaks to a common understanding of the drastic distinction between democracy and authoritarianism in the manner of contention management and in the configuration of contention. Democratic regimes offer many institutionalized forms of conflict resolution and mediation, such as electorates, parliaments, courts, and labor unions, all of which help prevent the escalation of contention (Koopmans 2004: 39; Tarrow and Tilly 2007: 449). Most contention in strong democratic regimes is channeled by these *institutions* created precisely to structure conflicts, and thus it is common to see relatively *contained* forms of contention in such regimes (Tilly 2006 and 2008; Tilly and Tarrow 2007: 60–61).[13] One example is the enormous concentration of social movements in the United States and Western Europe, which depend on regime-backed rights, notably rights of association, assembly, and speech (Tarrow 2011: 179; Tilly 2006: 188). Indeed, social movements have been regarded as an essential element of normal politics in Western democracies (Goldstone 2003 and 2004; Koopmans 1995; Tilly 1984), and a concept of "movement society" (Meyer and Tarrow 1998) has been coined to describe the *institutionalization* of movements in these countries (McAdam et al. 2005; McCarthy and McPhail 1998; Meyer 2015; Oliver and Myers 1999). When mature democratic states are able to channel contention into highly institutionalized expressions and to incorporate social movements and their organizations within the existing institutional arrangements, this can improve the flexibility and adaptability of regime responses to the complexity of society (Giugni and Passy 1998), preclude revolutions (Zhao 2010), and enhance regime resilience.

By contrast, authoritarian states lack effective institutional means to contain and channel protest, have a much weaker capacity for institutionalizing social conflicts, and they tilt towards the coercion of contention (Koopmans 2004; Tarrow 2011: 179). Contentious politics in these states tends to be in the form of clandestine opposition (or underground resistance) and *transgressive* contention (such as armed attacks) (Tilly 2006 and 2008; Tilly and Tarrow 2007). Since these contentious activities contest the regime's monopoly of power, repression is likely to be the main response; yet, if the repressive capacity of authoritarian regimes declines, such regimes are vulnerable to a massive eruption of protest (Goldstone and Tilly 2001: 193).

The coexistence of growing protests and authoritarian durability in China then makes the country a puzzling case. Seeking to make sense of this, a series of studies, in line with the institutionalist approach previously mentioned, have

---

[13] In Tilly's (1978: 106) earlier work, he does highlight that the repressiveness of a government is always selective: "Governments respond selectively to different sorts of groups, and to different sorts of actions." Yet, in his more recent works, Tilly is more concerned with analyzing distinctions *between* regimes than *within* a single government.

underscored the significant role of the institutionalization of conflict in strengthening regime resilience in China. Institutional adaptations and political reform – the improvement of channels for political participation including village elections, the legal system, the petition system (composed of a set of governmental agencies handling citizen requests, complaints, and suggestions), and the media – help bolster regime legitimacy and stability by directing discontent and contention into officially sanctioned channels, providing information about policy implementation, and increasing the responsiveness of leaders (Dimitrov 2013 and 2015; He and Thøgersen 2010; Kennedy 2009b; Landry, Davis, and Wang 2010; Y. Li 2013; Liebman 2011; Luehrmann 2003; Minzner 2006; Nathan 2003;[14] Schubert 2008). For instance, the legislation and judiciary system play a role in channeling grievances toward the institutionalized, bureaucratic system of labor arbitration and litigation, atomizing the working class and foreclosing labor movements in China (Chen and Xu 2012; Gallagher 2005; Lee 2007). Similarly, some peasants see the *Administrative Litigation Law* (ALL) as a useful if imperfect tool to combat official malfeasance (O'Brien and Li 2004). In this sense, the law leads to the final destination in a dispute's trajectory (Diamant, Lubman, and O'Brien 2005).

To be sure, since the reform era that began in 1978, the Chinese government has made considerable progress in restructuring and improving institutions for managing contention, and citizens are increasingly likely to use these institutions to press for demands (Cai 2008; Diamant, Lubman and O'Brien 2005; Hu et al. 2009).

Nevertheless, despite progress in institutionalization, China still does not have a highly effective institutional apparatus for managing grievances and conflicts (Gilley 2003; C. Li 2012; Liebman 2013; Michelson 2008; Pei 2006; Tang 2016; Van Rooij 2010). Due to complex local politics, village elections – even when they are free and fair, which is often not the case – can ensure neither democratic nor effective governance (O'Brien and Han 2009; Yao 2013). The legal institutions (the law and the courts), still lacking independence from government, are expected to be secondary to Party policies and deeply embedded in politics (Biddulph 2015; Liebman 2007; Lubman 1999; Minzner 2011; O'Brien and Li 2004; Potter 1999; Stern 2014; Su and He 2010); the failure of law to deliver on its promise can direct legal actions to more extreme activities and undermine the legitimacy and stability of authoritarian rule (Blecher 2010; Gallagher 2017). Likewise, the petition system is considered "deeply flawed and severely inefficient in channeling interest articulation" (X. Chen 2012: 205), is unable to meet aggrieved population's demands, instead inducing local officials to use coercion (Wong and Peng 2015), and tends to intensify the resentment of petitioners (O'Brien and Li 2006). Finally, the media still falls far

---

[14] Andrew Nathan has changed his position more recently. In a 2013 piece, he expressed his expectation of dramatic political change to come in China.

short of being an effective means for citizens – especially disenfranchised social groups – to express discontent, since the conventional media remains under the control of the CCP and the Internet is heavily censored by the government (Zhao and Sun 2007). Because of these deficiencies, the formal institutions as such still play limited roles in maintaining disputes within the authorized channels and may lead to an escalation of social conflicts, which can compromise the authority of institutions and sometimes even the central government (Cai 2008; L. Li 2008; Thaxton 2016; Yu 2004 and 2005).

Hence, while not discounting the role of formal institutions, I argue that focusing exclusively on the institutionalization of contention cannot fully explain regime resilience in China. We should instead devote more attention to *informal* norms.

INFORMAL NORMS AND REGIME RESILIENCE

Scholars such as Douglass C. North (1990: 3) have stressed that informal institutions or socially sanctioned norms of behavior are often as important as their formal counterparts in structuring the "rules of the game." Even in Western democratic countries, where formal political institutions are well established, informal rules are not unusual. Take policing as an example. In the 1980s and 1990s, police in established democracies often adopted informal procedures and strategies to cope with challenges, resulting in *underenforcement* of the law or a growing tendency to tolerate certain violations of the law (Della Porta and Reiter 1998; Waddington 1998). According to the French law, protesters are obligated to notify police of their intentions to march three days in advance, yet prior notification is the exception rather than the rule in many places in France (Fillieule and Jobard 1998). Instead of using the whole set of legal means available to maintain order, the basis of police actions is essentially informal negotiation. In this way, authorities treat illegal protest activities in a relatively soft manner, leaving a gap between written laws and actual rules. On the flip side, law enforcement officers may overstep the law and use excessive force in policing. For instance, patterns of police misconduct – such as beatings and unjustified shootings – are found in many places in the United States; in particular, racial and ethnic minorities are consistently profiled, harassed, and subjected to verbal and physical abuse, disproportionately falling victim to police mistreatment (Amnesty International 1999; Bierma 1994; Legewie 2016; United Nations 2014). The pattern of *overenforcing* the law then suggests a second condition of the existence of inconsistency between operative rules and formal rules.

Likewise, informal institutions that deal with contention are important in contemporary China as well: indeed, they are the focus of this book. I define the concept of "informal norms of contention" as the unwritten rules that shape and constrain the actions of the state *and* protesters, in which actors ignore, bypass, or violate formal rules and procedures. In other words, these informal norms serve to guide, control, and regulate actions *outside legally sanctioned channels*.[15] Different from the common definitions, informal norms, as used herein, exclude conventions, cultural practices, and codes of behavior that exist *before* the formation of written rules; here, I only consider informal norms that emerge *in reaction to* constraints and opportunities within the formal institutional environment (K. Tsai 2007 and 2013). Additionally, the book emphasizes that these informal norms influence the decisions and behaviors of both authorities *and* challengers.

Patterns of interactions between the state and protesters in China reveal two sides of informal norms of contention: *accommodating* – featured by informal tolerance and self-censored resistance[16] – and *antagonistic* – characterized by unlawful repression and unruly protest. In the former, while authorities at times use force to cope with protests, they frequently tolerate illegal or extralegal protest activities. For instance, when disgruntled citizens skip the application for a "demonstration permit," which is required by law, authorities usually do not press charges. Instead, they often do "mass work" geared towards resisters, which includes law and policy education, persuasion, and sometimes negotiation. At the same time, while pushing the limits of tolerance, protesters are also aware of "red lines" drawn by the government and typically practice self-censorship, e.g., steering clear of questioning state authority.

When it comes to antagonistic informal norms of contention, the government can resort to whatever means it has at its disposal and can go beyond the law to stifle resistance. Examples include making unlawful arrests, using torture, and holding dissidents in extrajudicial detention. In the meanwhile, protesters hardly discipline themselves and routinely turn toward transgression. They may raise radical political agendas such as fighting for democracy or may resort to armed attacks.

How Informal Norms Affect Regime Resilience

This book will demonstrate that accommodating informal norms rather than antagonistic ones are at the fore of Chinese contentious politics. This perspective assists in explaining the paradoxical coexistence of mounting protests and regime durability in China. I argue that accommodating informal norms help

---

[15] For similar definitions, see North (1990) and Helmke and Levitsky (2004 and 2006a).

[16] "Accommodating informal norms of contention" as defined in this book differs from "accommodating informal institutions" as used by Helmke and Levitsky (2004 and 2006a). According to their definition, these informal institutions create incentives to behave in ways that "alter the substantive effects of formal rules but without directly violating them" (Helmke and Levitsky 2004: 729); these informal institutions are "accommodating" in that they often aid in *reconciling* actors' interests with the existing formal institutions and may enhance the stability of the formal institutions by reducing demands for change. By contrast, "accommodating" by my definition refers to the dynamic interactions between dissenters and authorities that assist in *conflict attenuation*.

create a larger space for protest than that permitted by formal rules. Confined within this space, citizens are able to articulate their interests and lodge complaints while, at the same time, the state is able to manage and contain conflicts. Within this political space, neither officials nor protesters regard the contention as a zero-sum game; instead, they make efforts towards reconciliation. In this sense, accommodating informal norms aid in containing and controlling protest. Studying accommodating informal norms is crucial to understanding politics and contention in China. In democratic states, the institutionalization of contention helps produce *contained contention*, which contributes to regime resilience. In China where the formal institutionalization of contention is less developed than in democracies, I argue that accommodating informal norms of contention play an essential part in preventing resistance from turning transgressive and thus help shore up regime stability.

To be specific, the stabilizing effect of accommodating informal norms is achieved through functioning as a social safety valve, facilitating institutionalization, and promoting self-censorship among resisters. First of all, the moment when aggrieved citizens begin to take to the streets is often the moment that marks the height of their discontent. At moments like this, a harsh response can easily intensify conflict. To the contrary, adopting accommodating informal norms that allow dissenters to air grievances, voice interests, and vent frustration can act as a safety valve, permitting the letting off of steam and facilitating the mitigation of conflict before everything turns unmanageable and spirals out of control.

Additionally, accommodating informal norms assist in steering claim-making into institutional channels. When disgruntled citizens are shouting on the streets, officials, following the informal norms, often channel street protests into conversation in government offices and then require protesters to resolve their conflicts through legal or bureaucratic institutions. Put differently, these informal norms are vital to the functioning of formal institutions (such as the petition system and the court system). Adopting institutionalized forms to structure conflicts, in turn, can gain the advantage of institutionalization of contention as seen in liberal democracies, including containing contention and reducing uncertainty and unexpected activities by dissenters.

Last but not least, a protest space afforded by accommodating informal norms gives protesters hope of winning their claims through cooperation with officials rather than radical action. On the other hand, since these norms are unwritten and equivocal, it is difficult to predict for sure whether state officials will always tolerate the protest. In fact, the authorities always have the last word in deciding whether or not to impose punishment. Except for some well-marked no-go zones, the central government allows local governments leeway in determining whether a boundary has been transgressed, instead of implementing consistent standards (Stern and O'Brien 2011). Hence, the unpredictability of official response entailed in these informal norms makes repression a veritable Sword of Damocles and compels resisters to discipline themselves to avoid penalties.

By contrast, when accommodating informal norms are absent and antagonistic informal norms come to the fore, the contentious interactions of authorities and protesters typically fall into a vicious cycle of suppression and transgression – with both parties contributing to the exacerbation of conflict – and thereby affect social and political stability.

Informal practices like accommodating informal norms of contention are seen in many aspects of Chinese governance, including the expansion of non-governmental organizations (NGOs) (Fu 2017; Saich 2000; Spires 2011; Teets 2013; Weller 2012), rural public goods provision (L. Tsai 2007), the development of private sectors (K. Tsai 2007), media reporting and criticism (D. Chen 2017; Hassid 2008; Lei 2016; Repnikova 2017; Stern and Hassid 2012), the survival of underground churches (Reny 2018), and, more generally, the process of policy experimentation (Heilmann 2008 and 2011; Heilmann and Perry 2011). These informal politics and procedures are considered as reflections of the flexibility and adaptability of governance and are given credit for assisting in building regime resilience.

With regard to contentious politics, it is found that informal practices such as *bargaining* between government officials and aggrieved citizens, which allows flexible improvisation, have become patterned and routinized in China (X. Chen 2012; Lee and Zhang 2013; Tomba 2014). Informal politics is also seen in *inconsistent* attitudes toward protesters between the central and local governments (Cai 2008; Tong and Lei 2013; Zhao 2012); this inconsistency prevents both excessive repression and unconditional concessions and is instrumental in protecting the legitimacy of the central government. This strand of literature has yielded deep insights into how conflict is depoliticized and absorbed. Nonetheless, as these works center on the conditions under which informal politics functions to maintain authoritarian resilience, we know little about the other side of the coin–the circumstances under which such a role is absent. What is also unclear is whether such informal procedures are equally applicable to *all* social groups or regions across the nation. Yet comparing situations in which informal practices work with situations in which they do not and examining the application of informal politics across social groups and regions is essential for a deeper and more comprehensive understanding of contentious politics. As Dingxin Zhao (2010: 461) remarks, "Without formulating analytical puzzles based on comparative perspectives, we cannot possibly have a sense of the importance of a conceptualized phenomenon…in a larger social process."

Taking a comparative perspective, this book provides a theoretical framework to examine circumstances where accommodating informal norms perform well *and* situations in which they fail to work and instead antagonistic informal norms are at play. I explore the contrasting mechanisms and dynamics of contentious interactions between authorities and protesters in these different circumstances. Furthermore, through analysis of nationwide event data, I show to what extent accommodating informal norms play out in Chinese contentious politics. This work also demonstrates variations in accommodating informal norms across places, social groups, and time.

Why Accommodating Informal Norms

Why can accommodating informal norms exist in China in the first place? Why does the Chinese regime allow the underenforcement of laws? In some democratic states, politicians may turn to "forbearance," or the intentional and revocable nonenforcement of law, in order to mobilize voters to win office (Holland 2015 and 2016). Yet this is clearly not the case in China, where government officials are generally not subject to election pressure and therefore have little incentives to seek voter support. In many cases, the weak enforcement of the law has to do with inadequate state capacity to monitor and sanction (Levitsky and Murillo 2009). The Chinese state, however, has high capacity to enforce laws and mete out punishment, as seen in cases of clamping down on armed insurgency and pro-democracy movements (Millward 2004; Wright 2004).

The answer, in my view, lies in the fact that the regime is caught in structural dilemmas in the face of rampant social unrest. As part of its authoritarian character, the Chinese regime has imposed severe legal sanctions on protests. Even when protesters self-limit their claim-making, they often fail to comply completely with the harsh legal requirements. On the other hand, the political elite have deep concerns about maintaining power and control. The politicians' concern about regime legitimacy and stability combined with the enormous numbers of protests renders punishing *all* challenges by law unfavorable. Faced with this predicament, the central government places significant limits on the use of force by local officials. The local government, in turn, sandwiched between the leadership's legitimacy concerns and self-censored protesters, and facilitated by the ambiguities in formal institutions, sometimes chooses to bend the law for resisters – thereby leading to the establishment of accommodating informal norms (see Figure 1.1).

The Central Leadership
Repression is costly and risky for political elites (Acemoglu and Robinson 2006). While it sometimes deters dissent and decreases rates of protest (e.g., Davenport 2015; Olzak, Beasley, and Olivier 2003; Ritter and Conrad 2016), repression can also backfire – increasing dissent, sparking revolutionary action, facilitating the formation of alliances between challengers, or producing more persistent challenges (e.g., Almeida 2003; Chang 2015; Francisco 1995 and 2005; Franklin 2015; Jumet 2017; Trejo 2012). Even though the great loss of legitimacy does not inevitably lead to the demise of a state (Skocpol 1979), it may not be a feasible option in the long term (Oberschall 1996). To sustain power and control, it is in the interests of rulers to use less violence and adopt pre-emptive, selective, and targeted forms of repression (Boudreau 2005;

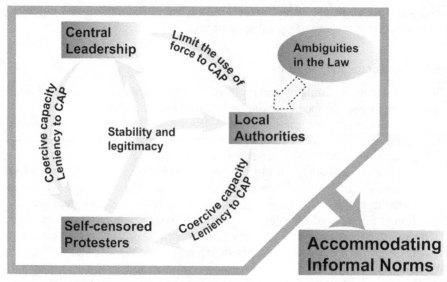

FIGURE 1.1 Why accommodating informal norms?

Dobson 2013; Greitens 2016; Pei 2012; Tilly 1978). Even in South Korea's highly repressive period in the 1970s, the state responded discriminatively to protests with varied characters (Chang and Vitale 2013).

With respect to China, the bloody crackdown on the 1989 Tiananmen incident led to a great loss of regime legitimacy and intense international backlash. In the post-Tiananmen period, to overcome the limits of repression and consolidate its rule in the long run, Chinese leaders have been working on diversifying the strategies in dealing with dissent, especially emphasizing *tacit tolerance*. In this regard, they have revisited Mao Zedong's 1957 theory about distinguishing between types of contradictions. Following Mao, today's leaders stress that coercion should be avoided to handle contention that is regarded as non-hostile to the state, i.e., "contradictions among the people" (CAPs, *renmin neibu maodun*); whereas officials should not hesitate to employ force to deal with resistance that is perceived to be antagonistic to the state, or "contradictions between ourselves and the enemy" (CBOEs, *diwo maodun*). Recognizing the vast majority of mass incidents as CAP events, the central leadership has issued frequent calls for officials to be lenient in their approach.

The distinction between CAPs and CBOEs, however, is not compatible with the rule of law. Chinese laws impose strict restrictions on public protest, rendering nearly all collective contentious activities illegal. In this regard, the leaders' directives for treating CAP events with leniency enable an underenforcement of laws at times of unrest.

On the other hand, the incumbents have learned a second lesson from the Tiananmen crackdown, namely the necessity to enhance the state's coercive capacity for protest control. The ultimate need to dispatch the army to quell the Tiananmen movement illustrates the internal security forces' *failure* to contain demonstrators with minimal bloodshed at earlier stages (Tanner 2002a). To address the issue, in the post-Tiananmen era, the state has dramatically expanded its domestic security apparatus (Fisher 2010; Guo 2012; Tanner 2002a; Xie 2013), raised the bureaucratic rank of police chiefs (Y. Wang 2014; Wang and Minzner 2015), heightened the sensitivity of local authorities to social protest through the cadre evaluation system (Cai 2002 and 2004; X. Chen 2012; Edin 2003; Y. Li 2013), increased funding and personnel for operations related to managing social protest (Wang and Minzner 2015; Xie 2012), and censored discussions of collective action on the Internet (King, Pan, and Roberts 2013). By and large, these efforts are aimed at keeping a lid on popular unrest.

Self-Censored Protesters

Owing to the state's high coercive capacity, staging collective action still entails substantial risks for Chinese citizens today. While the central authorities call for leniency, the standards and conditions to exercise leniency are ambiguous and officials have leeway to extend or retract forbearance. Additionally, apart from harsh penalties, officials can employ "soft" forms of repression and "dirty tricks" to curb resistance. Dissidents may receive police visits at their homes or workplaces, their online forum may be monitored or hacked, or they may be taken to the police station for interrogation. When local officials feel constrained to deploy police force to curtail dissent, they may instead hire thugs. These suppressive measures cast a shadow over protesters, constantly reminding them that the state can show an iron fist anytime it wants. And Chinese citizens have no doubt about the state's ability to come down hard. This quote from a protest sympathizer is typical. "We should face China's reality: the government is very oppressive. It doesn't treat you seriously and would like to do whatever it wants."[17] After all, the Tiananmen suppression is still a vivid memory among many Chinese.

The uncertainty over tacit tolerance combined with the state's high capacity to monitor and check on grassroots activism has a deterrent effect on dissent. It impels many aggrieved citizens to exercise self-control in protest or to abstain from dissident behavior altogether. To these citizens, anti-government activity involves too much risk, which means only the most die-hard activists will persist in a fight against the regime (Franklin 2015; Levitsky and Way 2010). Over the past two decades or so, the majority of Chinese have distanced themselves from calls for democracy. The failed Chinese Jasmine Revolution, introduced earlier, is a clear example.

---

[17] Interviewee 47.

Yet self-limiting resistance does not only occur in the shadow of coercion, it is also encouraged by the regime's more conciliatory position on CAP events. Akin to social movement activists in the Western world, resisters tend to abstain from activities that invite repression when meaningful alternatives seem available (Meyer and Tarrow 1998). To pressure authorities to take their grievances into consideration, disgruntled Chinese normally endeavor to present their case in ways that conform with the CAP category.

Dissidents' self-censorship, to some extent, reflects a long tradition of what Elizabeth J. Perry (2008 and 2010) calls "rules consciousness." Traceable back to imperial China, rules consciousness mirrors a practice of framing one's demands in terms that are acceptable to the state in order to receive a sympathetic hearing and negotiate a better bargain with the government (Perry 2010 and 2012). Refraining from questioning the legitimacy of the state is not peculiar to contemporary resisters: it was also recognized by their counterparts in the Qing dynasty and the Republican era. Yet, in a departure from the concept of rules consciousness, rules in this book are specifically examined in comparison with formal regulations, i.e., through the lens of legality. What's more, while recognizing that the state still shapes the scope of protest and ultimately sets the boundaries of the forbidden zones, this research stresses that the "rules" are not determined solely by the government: they are also affected by aggrieved citizens who keep pushing the boundaries of state tolerance.

Local Authorities

As a third game player, local authorities are pivotal in the generation and function of accommodating informal norms as well. The central leaders' directives for leniency at CAP events and the restriction on the use of force combined with self-disciplined protests leave local officials less justification for harsh punishment. In reality, officials who disobey the political elite's dictums and use excessive force in dealing with mass incidents can suffer a variety of political and material penalties; at worst, they can be removed from office (Edin 2003; Y. Li 2013). What's more, local officials in many cases tolerate illegal but self-restrained resistance in order to contain rather than exacerbate conflict. Local politicians, like their central government counterparts, have legitimacy concerns as well and may not take a hard line on all protests in order to preserve stability and reinforce governance in their own jurisdiction.

Furthermore, local authorities may *voluntarily* resort to informal tolerance when they feel empathy for resisters or when they want to capitalize on protests for their own interests. First, when bureaucrats are *embedded* in the social networks of the local communities (e.g., demonstrators are their relatives, neighbors, or friends), authorities are less willing to impose strict sanctions. If officials live in the same community as resisters, they may share many of the challengers' concerns, such as environmental protection. As will be shown in Chapter 4, police officers literally confessed to protesters their own opposition to a garbage incineration project, putting them ironically on the same side as the people whose protest they had been deployed to control. What's more, authorities may relax law enforcement actions when they see grassroots resistance as an opportunity to advocate their own agenda. This happens when local bureaucrats disapprove higher-level government's decision. For example, residents' objection to an environmentally risky project, which is endorsed by higher-level authorities, is in accord with the interests of local politicians who are concerned that the pollutants from the project would limit their localities' future economic development.[18] In another scenario, if grassroots protests are instrumental in winning funding from above to overcome the local fiscal problems (created by the central policy and reforms), local authorities are more likely to acquiesce or even ally themselves with the protesters (Hurst 2004; J. Wang 2012).

In addition, underenforcement of the law often has to do with ambiguities in formal rules. In practice, local authorities find themselves faced with vague regulations, contradictory institutions, and gaps in formal rules. As an example, while the *Law on Assemblies, Processions, and Demonstrations* (LAPD) and the *Criminal Law* specify how to constrain collective actions and to punish actions that *severely* disturb the social order, the definition of "severely" remains vague. Situations like this allow some leeway in law enforcement.

Taken together, the central leadership's diversified strategies for handling dissent, resisters' self-discipline, ambiguities in formal institutions, and the embeddedness of officials drive local authorities to relax law enforcement in protest control. It is worth stressing that the generation of accommodating informal norms should not be treated as a sign of state weakness but rather as a result and indication of state capacity.

Why Antagonistic Informal Norms

The government bends the rules *for* challengers out of a concern for regime legitimacy; protesters exercise self-censorship out of a fear of repression. If neither of these two conditions is present, accommodating informal norms will fail to function. Instead, when the state bending the rules *against* challengers goes hand-in-hand with unruly protest, what I call "antagonistic informal norms of contention" will prevail.

Under antagonistic informal norms, authorities' goal is to eliminate dissent, which is often regarded as contradiction between ourselves and the enemy (CBOE). Here, the central state, instead of restraining the use of force by local officials, is not hesitant to show its true colors and demands a resolute crackdown on resistance. In this case, eradicating resistance is treated as a critical *political task*, and the rule of law can be sacrificed. This is frequently seen during political campaigns, in which state leaders sit at the top of the chain of

---

[18] Interviewee 100.

command and bureaucrats at all levels and from all departments – including the judiciary system – are urged to serve the needs of the campaigns. In campaigns against violent ethnic unrest, local officials, who are anxious to show their superiors that they are paying considerable attention to the campaigns, put the pressure on local police to solve cases hastily, resulting in a spike in incidents of torture cases in police interrogations (Tanner 2002b).

In addition, law enforcement may resort to unlawful coercion simply for convenience and effectiveness. Compared to legal sanctions, unlawful punishments are less visible and permit more flexibility in police actions. Take illegal detention as an example. Holding political dissidents without formal criminal charges not only forestalls their potential participation in pro-democracy demonstrations in a timely way but also allows the regime to get through politically sensitive moments with minimal popular agitation (Truex 2018),[19] as seen in the foiled Jasmine Revolution in China.

The other side of antagonistic informal norms is composed of fearless protesters who are bold enough to cross the "legitimate" boundaries set by the state and to step into clearly forbidden zones. In many cases, ethnic sentiments, religious beliefs, and pro-democracy ideologies help overcome the fear of oppression. In a bitter struggle between the Chinese state and the Falun Gong, a quasi-religious group, encouraged by their guru's call for fighting against the regime, faithful adherents even saw state suppression as a kind of martyrdom and a means of self-cultivation (Junker 2014a).

REGIME-ENGAGING VS. REGIME-THREATENING PROTESTS

The examination of informal norms of contention suggests that contentious politics in authoritarian settings can be more complicated than is popularly perceived. As discussed, the rise of unrest in non-democratic countries does not necessarily signal regime instability. This points to the necessity of distinguishing between *types* of protests that have different indications for regime durability. In this regard, I classify social contention into two groups: *regime-engaging* and *regime-threatening* protests.[20] In regime-engaging protests, both the state

---

[19] Politically sensitive moments include the convening of important national conferences and the celebration of major national festivals and events, such as the National People's Congress, the National Day, and the 2008 Beijing Olympic Games.

[20] This categorization differs from the typology of "contained" and "transgressive" contention (McAdam, Tarrow, and Tilly 2001: 7–8), which centers on the bounds of the permissible *set by the regime*; contained contention takes place "within a regime's prescribed and tolerated forms of claim making," whereas transgressive contention "crosses institutional boundaries into forbidden or unknown territory" (Tilly and Tarrow 2007: 60). In fact, I argue that such bounds are a product of *dynamic interactions between protesters and authorities*. Moreover, boundary-spanning contention (O'Brien 2003) provides a useful perspective for examining the evolution from transgressive to contained contention over the course of time, but its major focus is *protesters'* framing strategies and how they exploit the divisions within the state to justify their

and protesters are open to negotiation and accept or acquiesce to the legitimacy of the other side. By contrast, in regime-threatening protests, both protesters and authorities treat each other as enemies, reject the legitimacy of the other side, and close the door to negotiation.

In *regime-engaging* protests, disgruntled citizens seek state intervention, support, or concessions; thus, they acknowledge regime legitimacy and endeavor to engage the state in negotiation. Authorities, in order to maintain order and control, are open to negotiation and do not deny the legitimacy of these protests. To legitimize their contention, citizens frame their claims according to official rhetoric, formalized rights, established norms, and conventions. Protests in this category include both fully contained contention that takes place within legal channels (such as filing petitions) and more confrontational activities (such as traffic-blocking). In response, authorities typically show leniency and tolerate these contentious activities. In this process, accommodating informal norms of contention frequently play a role in regulating the action and interaction of both the state and the resisters.

By definition, regime-engaging protests is a term that encompasses most of the current major concepts to describe resistance in China, such as "moral economy,"[21] "rightful resistance," and "protest opportunism." *Moral economy* describes a framing strategy through which protests are expressed by moral claims regarding subsistence and justice (Perry 2001 and 2008), e.g., highlighting a social contract between the government and workers of state-owned enterprises (SOEs) – the right to life-long employment and various welfare benefits (F. Chen 2000 and 2003; Hurst and O'Brien 2002; Lee 2002 and 2007; X. Tong 2006).[22] *Rightful resistance* is seen when resisters "employ the rhetoric and comments of the powerful" (laws, regulations, etc.) and

---

challenges. It devotes little attention to the *state's* strategies and its common practices in handling contention, nor does it elaborate on the process of how authorities and protesters interact with each other. My classification of protests, by contrast, considers both the state *and* resisters along with their interactions, which develops an interactive analysis of contention. In addition, the classification of regime-engaging and regime-threatening protests is different from "state-engaging" protests (aimed to request new rights or the extension of existing rights) and "state-resisting" protests (aimed to stop the state from infringing on protesters' rights) put forward by Ho-fung Hung (2011: 58–59). Hung's classification centers mainly on distinguishing protest *claims* – that is, whether to expand new rights or protect existing rights – while my classification focuses not only on claims, but also on protest actions and organization. Finally, regime-engaging and regime-threatening protests differ from "loyalist" and "revolutionary" protests (Lorentzen 2013), which focus on the side of protesters and not much about the government.

[21] First elaborated by E. P. Thompson (1971 and 1974), moral economy was used to explain direct popular action by the poor in eighteenth century England. Later, James C. Scott (1976 and 1985) employed the notion in his discussion of the peasant rebellion in twentieth century Southeast Asia.

[22] The "social contract" between the state and SOE workers was established in the Mao era but was largely terminated in the post-Mao period when most SOEs went bankrupt or became privatized, resulting in millions of lay-offs (China Labor Statistical Yearbook 2005).

"operates near the boundary of authorized channels" – stopping short of violence yet sometimes involving direct action to confront their target (O'Brien 1996; O'Brien and Li 2006: 2–3). *Protest opportunism* underscores the orientation of collective petitioners who "do not take a principled or consistent position toward being either obedient or defiant" and who are ready to employ any tactics they think might be useful including confrontational and disruptive ones (X. Chen 2012: 136). While these concepts aptly capture some salient features of resistance in present-day China, they do not explore conditions in which these notions may *not* apply. One example is a lack of explanation as to why "rightful resistance" occurs in some cases, but not in others. Furthermore, the framing strategies and action tactics characterized by the previous concepts reveal *protesters'* diverse efforts to *engage* with authorities, and thus all of them can be categorized as regime-engaging protests; in addition to dissidents' tactics and actions, the notion of regime-engaging protests also entails *state* reactions to and interactions with resisters. In this way, it is a more wide-ranging characterization of contentious politics. In a departure from the existing approaches and terms, this book studies not only circumstances when the government and citizens engage with each other but also situations when they fail to, situations characterized as regime-threatening protests.

In *regime-threatening* protests, aggrieved citizens deny regime legitimacy and condemn the prevailing social order as a whole, from its institutional arrangement to its dominant ideologies. In some cases, protesters may use force or operate in a clandestine fashion or, acting in a peaceful, open manner, they may press for ending the current political system. Protests of this type include separatist movements in frontier regions and pro-democracy movements that call for the elimination of one-party rule. They can be underground activities or planned violence by formal independent organizations. More often than not, the state responds with force. Accommodating informal norms *hardly* play a part in these sorts of contentious interactions, whereas antagonistic informal norms are typically at play here.

Rather than a dichotomy, these two kinds of protests are ideal types and represent two ends of a continuum (see Figure 1.2). In practice, a protest may move from one side to the other. It can begin as regime-engaging but shift to regime-threatening. This takes place, for example, in the "agenda shift" in which "what starts out as a protest against a particular policy escalates rapidly into a challenge to the political order as a whole" (Beetham 1991: 216), as seen

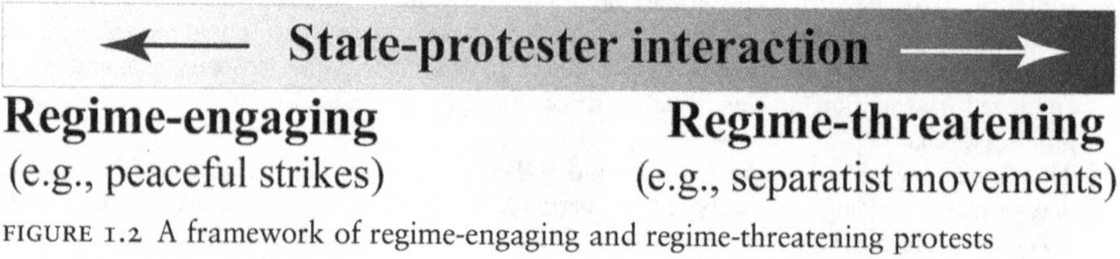

← State-protester interaction →

Regime-engaging   **Regime-threatening**
(e.g., peaceful strikes)   (e.g., separatist movements)

FIGURE 1.2 A framework of regime-engaging and regime-threatening protests

in the transformation of peaceful mobilization into armed rebellion in some Mexican regions in the agrarian reforms of the 1990s (Trejo 2012). The escalation may be sparked by mishandling of protest. Since officials always have the upper hand and can always determine whether to engage with or use an iron fist against protesters, it is possible that even when protesters conform to accommodating informal norms, authorities will still inflict severe punishment. At the same time, protesters are always pushing the envelope; it is this force that has opened up a space for protest in the first place and that keeps it open and expanding. In the process, protesters may lose self-control at times. Thus, a regime-engaging protest can move towards transgression. As James C. Scott (1985) maintains, peasant petitions to the feudal baron in Tokugawa Japan were frequently a prelude to riots and insurrection. Petitions were "invariably cast in deferential terms, appealing for the 'mercy of the lord'. . . (Yet) Everyone involved knows, certainly, that the petition carries a threat, as virtually all such petitions do" (Scott 1985: 95). On the flip side, a regime-threatening protest can move towards regime-engaging. A possible scenario is that, given state commitment to amnesty, anti-government rebel groups will decide to desist from armed resistance and enter into peace negotiations with authorities, as observed in the Colombian peace process in the 2010s. This fluidity depends upon the interaction between protesters and authorities, and especially hinges on how the state deals with resistance.

Fluidity notwithstanding, the distinction matters because the two types of protest provide contrasting indications about regime resilience. Regime-engaging protests are akin to (although not the same as) social movements in liberal democracies; since they are generally "contained" by the state, a proliferation of such protests does not necessarily stand for regime instability. By contrast, regime-threatening protests reflect the lack of legitimacy of the regime; the rise of this kind of protest often signals that regime stability is waning. A regime is in a precarious situation when such protests are prevalent. Here, it is important to acknowledge that even when the *frequency* of regime-threatening protests is relatively small, it does not mean that state stability is guaranteed. For one thing, even only a few of such protests – if they are massive and influential – may pose a severe threat to regime durability. For another, the shift from regime-engaging to regime-threatening protests can be fast and all-encompassing – things quickly spinning out of control – and can ultimately pave the way to regime breakdown. In this sense, it is necessary to monitor closely the interactions between authorities and dissidents. It is also worth mentioning that *state capacities* – both to repress protest and accommodate resisters' demands – are vital factors in ultimately explaining regime stability/instability. The distinction between regime-engaging and regime-threatening protests as drawn in this book comes from the observation of empirical reality. Neither is an ultimate cause of regime stability/instability but rather a critical *indicator*.

Current literature on popular contention in authoritarian regimes other than China has largely focused on contention that falls into the category of regime-threatening protests and how it contributes to regime crisis or demise (e.g., Beissinger 2002; Boudreau 2004; Chang 2015; Francisco 2005; Jumet 2017; Kurzman 2004; Oberschall 1996). Scholarship on contention in China has *either* centered solely on resistance that is regime-engaging (e.g., Cai 2010; X. Chen 2012; Lee 2007; O'Brien and Li 2006) *or* on dissent that is regime-threatening (e.g., Bovingdon 2010; Hillman 2016; J. Tong 2009; Wright 2004), with little systematic research on *both* types together. The former line of scholarship observes the opening of political opportunities for dissent in China, savvy strategies of resisters, and the responsiveness of the government (e.g., Elfstrom and Kuruvilla 2014; Heurlin 2016; Y. Li 2013; Lorentzen 2017; Mertha 2008; Perry 2012); the latter line of research spotlights the brutal side of the regime and its human rights violations with respect to social control (e.g., Becquelin 2004; Dillon 2004; Millward 2007). To reconcile the contrasting versions of contentious politics in the same country, *Playing by the Informal Rules* makes a systematic examination of both types of contention, views them through the lens of a continuum rather than a dichotomy, and thus formulates a more comprehensive and dynamic framework of dissent and its political implications.

METHODOLOGY AND OVERVIEW OF THE BOOK

To explicate the resilience of the Chinese state amidst surging protests, I have conducted two levels of analysis – large dataset analysis (Chapter 2) and in-depth case studies (Chapters 3–5). Quantitative research in Chapter 2 provides a bird's-eye view of contentious politics in China. Studies on popular resistance in the country have been constrained by a lack of available data due to state censorship:[23] Most works have been case studies (e.g., Deng and Yang 2013; Y. Li 2013; Mertha 2008). While a handful of works have taken valuable steps in creating protest datasets (Cai 2010; X. Chen 2012; Tong and Lei 2013), they do not include vital types of contention in one way or another and thus are not suitable for a systematic measure of state tolerance and repression.

To overcome the data limitation, I have generated a dataset of 1,418 protest events that occurred across China between 2001 and 2012, presenting a broad picture of popular protests and state reactions. While the dataset is likely skewed towards protests that are repressed,[24] statistical analysis demonstrates that the state tolerated the majority of protest events in my dataset and most protest events did not take transgressive forms – they stayed away from violence, radical political claims (e.g., opposing communist rule), and linking

[23] News reports and discussions on "mass incidents" or specific protest incidents are highly sensitive and tend to be censored in China.
[24] The construction of the dataset relied on reports on protests collected by Boxun.com, an overseas Chinese community website. Highly critical of the Chinese regime, Boxun inclines to collect repressive events in China. For more detailed discussions of the dataset, see Chapter 2.

organizationally with other protests. These findings challenge the common view that repression and transgression should prevail in an authoritarian regime like China's. Tolerance and non-transgression suggests that neither the state nor resisters close the door to negotiation or deny the legitimacy of the other side. In this sense, I conclude that regime-engaging rather than regime-threatening protests are the predominant form of contention in China at present.

Quantitative research provides important insights into underenforcement of the law in protest control. *By law* protest activities are strictly prohibited, leaving little tolerated space for protest in China. *In practice*, however, some activities that go beyond the limits of laws – peaceful disruptive actions (e.g., demonstrations, marches, and sit-ins) – are *de facto* countenanced. This gap between formal laws and informal practices suggests an *informal protest space* – that is, a gray zone in which authorities show leniency to some illegal or extralegal protests. This protest space is defined by regularized patterns of contentious interaction (rather than laws), with protesters constantly pushing the envelope and the state's daily practice of dealing with protests. I should emphasize here a fundamental distinction between the space for protest "claims" and the space for protest "actions" and "organization." The Chinese state basically sets the boundaries for *claims*, and there is no give and take. The public simply has to accept that; efforts to test the boundaries of protest claims – such as calling for toppling the communist regime, no matter how peaceful – are expected to be suppressed. Informal *organization* is condoned, but authorities inhibit formal organization and links by arresting open organizers. Protests have to be presented as spontaneous, especially when they take actions that approach or cross the borders of the protest space. The space for *actions*, in contrast, is more flexible and there is a constant tug of war between protesters and authorities over the boundaries. It is in this situation that accommodating informal norms can come into play.

Previous research has made astute observations that disgruntled citizens in China are able to create some room for maneuver (e.g., Ho 2007; Mertha 2008; O'Brien and Li 2006; Yang and Calhoun 2007).[25] Yet almost all these works rely on case studies or unsystematic data, and they say little about how common the discussed phenomenon is. In confirming findings of these studies, this book, measures the *extent* of the space for protest using systematically acquired and coded quantitative data.

To look closely at the informal protest space, I conducted seven case studies of regime-engaging protests (Chapters 3 and 4) along with three case studies of regime-threatening protests (Chapter 5). Here, my approach is fundamentally comparative. As noted, seeking a more comprehensive analysis of contentious politics in China, this book explores circumstances in which accommodating

---

[25] For instance, divisions between different levels of government – e.g., the gap between policy-making by the *central* government and policy implementation by the *local* government – may empower protesters in their struggle (O'Brien and Li 2006).

informal norms are in play *as well as* situations in which they are unavailable; I also compare the application of accommodating informal norms across social groups, regions, and time.

To have first-hand experience of popular protests and government reactions, for more than nineteen months from 2007 to 2016, I conducted fieldwork in four locations in China, from the north to south, from urban to rural areas. I joined demonstrators in front of the city hall, sat in a conference room listening to debates between resisters and officials, and interviewed 114 protesters, officials, and informed others (lawyers, scholars, journalists, environmental experts, NGO staff, and so forth). In addition, I also collected government documents,[26] court rulings, internal-circulation journals (including *People's Petition* and *Hebei Petition*),[27] laws, and regulations regarding contention management, petition letters, video recordings and photographs of protests, news reports, and social media posts, all of which helped me to detect informal norms, cross-check my interview data, and reconstruct more comprehensive and detailed stories with respect to protesters' strategies and government reactions.

Based on the in-depth field research, Chapter 3 elaborates *what* accommodating informal norms are in place, *how* and *why* they are created, situations when they are *ineffective*, and the *impact* of these norms on regime stability. I delve into the interactive role that various actors, from top-down to bottom-up, play in determining the emergence and functioning of the unwritten rules. The discussion here is based on case studies of three regime-engaging economic protests, all taking place in the same city. In these struggles, the government frequently acquiesces to actions such as illicit petitions and demonstrations, leading to an extralegal space for protest; meanwhile, aggrieved citizens endeavor to discipline themselves while pushing the envelope. Sometimes authorities resort to lawful or unlawful means of imposing penalties, and protesters may occasionally lose self-control. That said, as long as dialogue between both sides is still possible, the protest can still be considered regime-engaging. Overall, the existence of accommodating informal norms and protest space has a beneficial effect on alleviating conflict, managing contention, and ultimately enhancing regime resilience.

In Chapter 4, I elucidate the *unequal application* of accommodating informal norms. Unlike Chapter 3, this chapter takes *region* as an explanatory variable and looks at regional inequality in the protest space. Holding the contentious issue – environmental protection – in all cases constant, I illustrate how accommodating informal norms differ across places (e.g., urban vs. rural)

---

[26] The collected government documents include minutes of local government meetings on handling particular cases of mass incidents and government reports on petition work.

[27] *People's Petition* (*Renmin Xinfang*) and *Hebei Petition* (*Hebei Xinfang*) are two official magazines sponsored respectively by the National Petition Bureau and the Petition Bureau of Hebei Province. They are circulated exclusively within the government.

and social groups (e.g., middle-class professionals vs. peasants) due to identity politics,[28] distinctions in the resources that protesters have (such as media access and social connections), and local political climates. For a single protest, the protest space can expand or contract over time, depending on the dynamic engagement between the state and protesters.

Chapter 5 investigates three high-profile cases of regime-threatening protests – ethnic unrest in Xinjiang (China's far west), protest by the Falun Gong (a quasi-religious group), and the Charter 08 campaign (pro-democracy resistance) – and reveals the distinct mechanisms and dynamics of contention that separate them from previous cases. Each of these protests here involved one type of political grievance or another that transgressed the official limits, although the type of action and organization varied; in each case, officials responded with resolute repression, through lawful and unlawful means. By reviewing the interactions of challengers and the state over the course of history, this chapter explores how and why antagonistic informal norms come to the fore and, in tandem, how and why these cases moved to the regime-threatening end. We will see when accommodating informal norms fail to work, how contentious politics becomes a zero-sum game, and how it jeopardizes regime legitimacy and stability.

The concluding chapter (Chapter 6) summarizes the main findings of this research and discusses how this book contributes to a deeper understanding of contentious politics and authoritarian resilience in and beyond China. It looks at informal norms of contention and regime resilience in other illiberal states and details how to apply the conceptual model of regime-engaging and regime-threatening protests constructed for this book to the observation and analysis of the trajectory of political contention in other authoritarian states.

BROADER IMPLICATIONS

This book is a timely contribution to understanding the resilience of the Chinese state in the face of surging resistance. More broadly, it brings the case of China to a larger audience interested in the consequences and the configuration of political mobilization. Social scientists have long been concerned with the role of popular protests in regime change, producing studies on a variety of cases from the rise of democracy in Europe centuries ago to the wave of democratization in the post-Cold War world to the more recent Arab uprisings (e.g., Acemoglu and Robinson 2006; Beissinger 2002; Brancati 2014; Bratton and van de Walle 1997; Bunce and Wolchik 2006; Haggard and Kaufman 2016; Howard and Hussain 2013; Lynch 2012; McAdam, Tarrow, and Tilly 2001; Tilly 2003).[29] The bulk of the studies of democratic

---

[28] For instance, police officers tend to identify more with urbanites than villagers.

[29] To be sure, regime change in authoritarian states does not necessarily lead to democratization but may well galvanize a move toward another form of authoritarianism or prolonged instability.

transitions have, in particular, emphasized the important role of political resistance in destabilizing authoritarian regimes and promoting democratization.[30] In this regard, what makes the Chinese case particularly intriguing is not simply the duration of the authoritarian rule but the perplexing *coexistence* of authoritarian resilience and rising unrest. In addition, by explicating the Chinese regime's coping strategies and analyzing how social structural factors affect the mode of contention, this research echoes McAdam and Boudet's (2012) call for putting social movements in broader political and social contexts and Andrew G. Walder's (2009b) call for reviving theories about the impact of social structure on various forms of political behavior in research on social movements.

Further, *Playing by the Informal Rules* has implications for the study of authoritarian resilience. Most existing scholarship in this arena has focused on how formal institutions aid in channeling contention and building regime durability, whereas the role informal norms play has received much less attention. A burgeoning literature has shown that autocrats can adopt quasi-democratic institutions – e.g., legislatures, courts, parties, elections, and constituency service institutions – in an attempt to incorporate potential opposition forces and manage societal discontent (Blaydes 2011; Brancati 2014; Brownlee 2007; Distelhorst and Hou 2017; Gandhi 2008; Gandhi and Przeworski 2006; Geddes 1999; Levitsky and Murillo 2009; Lust-Okar 2006; Magaloni 2006; Manion 2015; Miller 2015; Moustafa 2007; Svolik 2012; Truex 2018). Adopting these nominally democratic institutions in turn contributes to the persistence of these undemocratic regimes rather than indicating the "death of dictatorship" (Huntington 1991: 174). For instance, legislatures and parties have given voice to many contentious elements in society and have served as the institutional means of co-opting would-be opposition into the policy process and of allowing social groups to convey their demands to authorities without having these demands appear as acts of public resistance (Albrecht 2013; Gandhi and Przeworski 2007; He and Thøgersen 2010; He and Warren 2011; Khatib and Lust 2014; Magaloni and Kricheli 2010; Malesky and Schuler 2010; Nathan 2003). While these studies have substantially enriched our understanding of authoritarian governance, since their focus is the role of institutions in *co-opting* potential opponents and *heading off* street protests, they are inadequate for understanding authoritarian stability when social unrest has already been on the rise. Making this largely unanswered question the central focus of this work, I seek to further develop this strand of scholarship by highlighting the importance of *informal* institutions in absorbing contention, facilitating social and political control, and strengthening authoritarian resilience.

---

[30] For reviews, see Ulfelder (2005).

While not questioning the importance of formal institutions, this book brings informal norms more centrally into the picture, presenting a detailed empirical case study of China to throw light on the origins, dynamics, and effects of informal institutions. Indeed, the importance of informal institutions in affecting political behavior and process has gained emergent recognition. Helmke and Levitsky (2004: 726), for instance, have warned that focusing primarily on formal rules risks "missing much of what drives political behavior and can hinder efforts to explain important political phenomena." Scott Radnitz (2011: 362) contends that the persistence of informal politics challenges basic assumptions about the evolution and organization of society and must be dealt with on its own terms. Similarly, Kellee S. Tsai (2016) holds that informal institutions are an essential part of human societies, irrespective of regime type and level of development. This volume joins this body of work and calls for giving greater weight to the significance of informal institutions in shaping political activity, procedure, and outcome. It stresses that the boundaries of permissible protest in a country should not be defined solely by formal institutions but also by informal norms. Highlighting the role of the unwritten rules can facilitate more sophisticated comparisons of contentious politics between authoritarian regimes and democratic regimes as well as between different types of authoritarianism.

In addition, *Playing by the Informal Rules* calls for more attention to be given to the diverse ways of exercising power in illiberal states. For a long time, scholars have tended to focus on harsh repression in reaction to protests in authoritarian contexts. It is of course true that strong authoritarian states place huge constraints on contentious actions and that coercive apparatuses are omnipresent. Nevertheless, to enrich our knowledge of authoritarian politics, repression and radicalization should not be the only lens through which we observe these countries. Rather, I stress the need to pay more attention to how such states diversify their skillset in controlling dissent and employ toleration, negotiation, concessions, and more subtle forms of coercion to stay in power. A growing body of studies points out that today's autocrats understand the advantages of resorting to subtler, selective repression compared to indiscriminate, naked violence (e.g., Boudreau 2005; Cai 2010; X. Chen 2012; Dobson 2013; Francisco 2005; Greitens 2016; Levitsky and Way 2010).

In this regard, it is of importance to distinguish between a regime's coercive *capacity* and its *application* of such capacity in dealing with unrest. The robust capacity for repression does not inevitably translate into high-level repressive reaction at every challenge. A strong regime, possessing an effective and loyal internal security sector that has a demonstrated capacity to penetrate society, monitor opposition activity, and put down protest across the nation, can usually prevent the occurrence of transgressive protests in the first place and thus can avoid shooting protesters on the streets (Greitens 2016; Levitsky and Way 2010) – as happened in the Tiananmen suppression. Indeed, the fear of repression, stemming from the high coercive capacity, can pre-empt resistance or lead to self-controlled dissent. This partly explains why strong authoritarian regimes are often featured by *medium* levels of violence in contentious inter-actions, whereas weak illiberal states more often resort to *high* levels of vio-lence, as Tilly (2006) contends.

Finally, the book presents an original theoretical model for understanding the dynamics of protest and regime resilience, distinguishing between regime-engaging and regime-threatening protests. Offering critical indicators of regime stability/instability, this model is applicable to the investigation of the nature of protests and allows for the monitoring of the trajectory of political contention, not only in China but in other regimes as well. I propose that a state is in relatively stable condition even when it abounds with regime-engaging protests, whereas a regime is in crisis when regime-threatening protests prevail. In China today, we see the former situation; in Eastern Europe during the 1980s and in some Arab countries in 2011, the latter situation was prevalent. The mounting unrest in China is in step with rising contention in the world today, especially in the Middle East, Latin America, and South and Southeast Asia. I hope this theoretically informed study of political contention in China will provide an original cross-national comparison of protests among non-democratic states and, more broadly, will contribute to a nuanced, on-the-ground view of power, resistance, and domination.

2

Mapping the Space for Protest

In the remote Tibetan-dominated reaches of Sichuan province, in China's far west, the crackles erupting on the afternoon of Jan. 23, the first day of the New Year of the Dragon, were not just a symbolic cacophony. They were deadly. At least one (and up to six) Tibetans were shot dead by Chinese security forces, according to Tibetan exile groups, after residents had gathered at a police station in Kardze prefecture (or Ganzi in Mandarin) to protest Chinese rule. It was the biggest outbreak of violence since widespread protests in Tibetan areas triggered a fierce crackdown in 2008.[1]

This dispatch, published in a 2012 issue of *Time* magazine, is a typical journalistic account of contentious politics in China: citizens' resistance to the authoritarian rule met with ruthless suppression. Indeed, such contentious interaction is not rare in non-democratic settings, and we see similar patterns in Stalin's Soviet Union, Franco's Spain, and Kim's North Korea. As scholars argue, resistance in authoritarian contexts takes mainly *transgressive* forms (such as pro-democracy movements and armed struggles), which imposes an outright challenge to the regime's monopoly on power (Tilly 2006 and 2008; Tilly and Tarrow 2007). In this sense, a constricted environment of political contention characterized by violent repression and transgressive protest is often present in such regimes (Davenport 1995; Goldstone and Tilly 2001; Gurr 1986). Hence, popular resistance tends to be a *zero-sum* game: either the authoritarian regime breaks down, or the protests are stifled (Koopmans 2004: 39). This is the theme of the bulk of scholarship on contentious politics in non-democratic states (e.g., Almeida 2003; Beissinger 2002; Chang and Vitale 2013; Goodwin 2001;

---

[1] "An Unhappy Chinese New Year: Chinese Forces Shoot Tibetan Protesters, with At Least One Dead." Hannah Beech. *Time*. January 24, 2012. http://world.time.com/2012/01/24/an-unhappy-chinese-new-year-chinese-forces-shoot-tibetan-protestors-with-at-least-one-dead/.

Kurzman 2004; McAdam, Tarrow, and Tilly 2001; Pfaff and Yang 2001; Rasler 1996; Shock 2005).

Nonetheless, repression and transgression are not the whole story of contentious politics in the authoritarian world today. Less brutal forms of authoritarian states – those using violence more carefully than most previous autocrats – have emerged in recent decades (Dobson 2013; Guriev and Treisman 2015; Levitsky and Way 2010). Some incumbents have granted a significant measure of political participation and shown an increasing tolerance for public expression of discontent (Albrecht 2007; Blaydes 2011; Brancati 2014; Diamond 2002; Lust-Okar 2008). Meanwhile, contentious actors, by limiting their challenges, have avoided direct confrontation with incumbents (Beinin and Vairel 2011: 14–15). For instance, between the late 1970s and the 2000s, the Egyptian government widened the space for the civil society, although the political opening did not follow a linear path; correspondingly, prior to the Arab Spring, collective actions in Egypt were largely transformed into "regime-loyal" and "tolerated" forms, not seeking to overthrow the regime (Albrecht 2013; Vairel 2011). These studies have complicated our understanding of authoritarian politics, yet they typically focus on measures taken by incumbents to *co-opt* dissent and *forestall* street protests rather than on regime responses when protests have already taken place.

In fact, the repressiveness of a government, no matter its regime type, is always *selective* by types of collective action and actors (Tilly 1978: 106). When the Indonesian military was slaughtering members of East Timorese and Acehnese resistance movements in the 1980s, student protesters often went unpunished (Boudreau 2005). Likewise, authorities in Arab states like Morocco came down hard on protest activities by committed Islamists but gave students and secular human-rights activists some space to demonstrate during the 2000s (Tilly 2006: 192).

When it comes to China, the state responses to challenges vary considerably and citizens are keen to adopt shrewd tactics to express discontent (as shown in numerous case studies). Nevertheless, despite flourishing research in this arena, we still lack a broad picture of contentious politics in China; neither do we know much about the major forms of social protests across the nation, nor are there concrete findings regarding the main patterns of government reactions to dissent.[2] To address these limitations, this chapter sets out to map the boundaries of state toleration and repression and to discern the dominant forms of popular contention in the country. Based on an original dataset, I find that most protests are *non-transgressive* and *tolerated* by the government, which is at

---

[2] In my research, a *social protest* refers to a collective action by citizens who express criticism or dissent and raise claims bearing on someone else's interests in the public sphere. Examples of social protests include collective petitions, demonstrations, collecting signatures for protest letters, and armed attacks.

odds with the zero-sum thesis of contentious politics in authoritarian settings.[3] This finding suggests that stories of regime-engaging protests are more common than those of regime-threatening in this one-party state. Yet my analysis also reveals that the space for protest is not equally open to all social groups or all regions. In what follows in this chapter, I will first document the state's diverse strategies for social control, explore factors leading to repression, and then present statistical findings of the limits of tolerance and the dominant forms of collective resistance in China.

TOLERANCE AND REPRESSION IN CHINA: WHAT WE KNOW AND WHAT WE DON'T KNOW

> [T]he central government—like its predecessors in imperial and Republican China—has demonstrated a certain degree of tolerance and even sympathy toward economically driven protests, provided that they remain clearly bounded in both scale and aspirations.
>
> Elizabeth J. Perry (2002a: xiv)

At present, the Chinese state's reactions to contention reveal a mixed picture. Indeed, the state has taken various measures to strengthen its control of protest. It has deliberately increased its coercive capacity by dramatically expanding its domestic security apparatus (Guo 2012; Wang and Minzner 2015), emphasized government officials' responsibility in reducing the occurrence of collective action (X. Chen 2012; Edin 2003; Y. Li 2013), censored discussions that have the potential to generate collective action (King, Pan, and Roberts 2013), and cracked down on dissent such as pro-democracy movements (Wright 2004).

On the flip side, many protests are tolerated, induce government concessions, or end with a combination of repression and concession (Biddulph 2015; Cai 2010; Chan and Hui 2014; X. Chen 2012; Heurlin 2016; Hurst 2008; Johnson 2013; Y. Li 2013; Meng, Pan, and Yang 2017; O'Brien and Li 2006; Perry 2012; Reilly 2012; Su and He 2010). In particular, as Perry (2002a and 2008) contends, making claims to a *basic subsistence* that stay within local confines has seldom been deemed especially threatening by authorities, owing to the political thought entrenched in China's history, namely, that a state's legitimacy depends on satisfying its people's claim to a decent livelihood. Indeed, the Communist regime has often tolerated or even encouraged narrowly targeted protests to identify social grievances, monitor lower levels of governments, and remedy the weakness of its political system (Cai 2004; X. Chen 2012; Dimitrov 2008 and 2015; Lorentzen 2013 and 2017; Luehrmann 2003; O'Brien and Li 2005; Tang 2016). Moreover, grassroots officials may capitalize on social protests to augment their departmental and personal

---

[3] Parts of this chapter draw from a paper published in *Government and Opposition* (Y. Li 2017).

career interests (Lee and Zhang 2013) and to stimulate funding allocation to their jurisdictions (Hurst 2004; J. Wang 2012). In many cases, officials manage conflicts through "protest bargaining," that is, a market-like exchange of compliance for benefits (Lee and Zhang 2013). Additionally, law enforcement seems to shift from a strategy focused on deterrence and quick suppression to a more permissive strategy of containment and management (Tanner 2004; Zhou and Yan 2014).

In the meanwhile, protesters typically employ strategies such as resorting to moral economy claims and rightful resistance to legitimate their demands. Take land disputes as an example. Although they are related to property rights, they tend to be framed by a moral claim regarding subsistence (Perry 2008). It is also common for resisters to carefully take advantage of laws, regulations, and official rhetoric to justify their activism, a tactic known as "rightful resistance" (O'Brien 1996; O'Brien and Li 2006). Furthermore, while the aggrieved Chinese frequently take to the streets and create public disruption, at the same time, they strive to keep a balance between defiance and obedience (X. Chen 2012) and to limit their actions (Perry 2010). Usually, they prefer to keep their confrontation and violence strictly between themselves and specific local officials, while affirming their recognition of the legitimacy of central authorities and the larger political system (Hung 2011; O'Brien and Li 2006). Many protest actions are "boundary-spanning" (neither clearly transgressive nor clearly contained), combining lawful tactics with disruptive but *not quite unlawful* actions (O'Brien 2003), or conjoining legal challenges to injustice with extralegal forms of civil disobedience and collective protest (Zweig 2010). In this sense, the boundaries of acceptable political actions appear fuzzy, and local officials are granted the discretion to judge if a boundary has been crossed or not (O'Brien 2003; Stern and Hassid 2012; Stern and O'Brien 2011).

Despite the preceding informative depiction of contentious politics in China, thus far we still do not know *to what extent* the aforementioned characters of protest are typical in China, nor do we have a clear answer as to the boundaries between state repression and tolerance. Most research has been case studies and its biggest concern has been why some protests succeed while others fail (e.g., Y. Li 2013; Mertha 2008; Shi 2008; Shi and Cai 2006). A handful of studies have *proposed* what kinds of protest are repressed and what kinds are tolerated (Reny and Hurst 2013; Selden and Perry 2010; Zhao 2010), but they have not followed up with quantitative testing. Presenting a systematic analysis of patterns of repression and types of protests is critical because it not only helps predict state reactions to resistance but aids in exploring the diverse political effects that distinct types of protests may have on regime endurance.

WHAT LEADS TO REPRESSION

To investigate state repression, this chapter focuses on protest policing, or the police handling of protest events (Della Porta and Reiter 1998). Authorities may employ a variety of repressive strategies, including arrests, violence, surveillance, channeling (e.g., tax restrictions on targeted groups), stigmatization, and blocking communication; some are overt, others covert (Aldrich 2008; Boykoff 2007; Brancati 2014; Earl 2003 and 2011; Levitsky and Way 2002 and 2010). Policing, of course, is merely one of a wide array of repressive strategies, but it represents the most public and one of the most common forms of repression (Earl, Soule, and McCarthy 2003). Studying protest policing is critical for enhancing understanding of the relationship between protests and the state, since police embody the objectives of the broader political–economic elite (Davenport, Soule, and Armstrong 2011) and can be "conceived as 'street-level bureaucrats' who 'represent' government to people" (Lipsky 1970:1). In Chapters 3 and 4, I will analyze subtler, softer, and less visible forms of repression.

Factors influencing repression are multifaceted and complex, but two of them stand out – the character of protest and the power of social groups.

What Are They Shouting About?

In liberal democracies, authorities have a tendency to quell challenges that wish to displace current political leaders, dismantle the political–economic system, or pursue other revolutionary or radical goals (Gamson 1990; Gartner and Regan 1996; McAdam 1982). Likewise, in China, protests that advance *radical political claims* also tend to be the target of repression. Nonetheless, what is considered "radical" in China differs critically from what is regarded as "radical" in democratic regimes. Claims for democracy and any effort to contest the Communist Party's monopoly on political power are prohibited or strictly constrained. On the other hand, since the reform era began in 1978, the Chinese state seems to have become more willing to tolerate protests addressing *economic, environmental, and even anti-corruption* issues (Selden and Perry 2010).[4]

Additionally, confrontational and violent actions are often subject to repression in democratic regimes (Earl, Soule, and McCarthy 2003; Franklin 2009; McAdam 1982; Soule and Davenport 2009; Tarrow 2011). In China, *violent actions* in many cases lead to penalties. *Peaceful disruptive actions*, such as road blockades and strikes, are at times tolerated while other times are repressed or end with a combination of repression and concession (Cai 2010; X. Chen 2012; Su and He 2010).[5]

---

[4] Here, I come up with Hypothesis 1: Economic, environmental, and moderate political claims are less likely to draw police response, whereas radical political claims are much more likely to suffer repression.

[5] Hence, we have Hypothesis 2: Peaceful actions (disruptive or non-disruptive) are less likely to suffer police coercion, whereas violence generally prompts repressive policing.

In democratic states, protests with more social movement organization (SMO) involvement are considered stronger than the ones with less or no SMO involvement because they have access to more organization vehicles for pursuing grievances (Earl, Soule, and McCarthy 2003). In China, however, the presence of autonomous *formal organizations* does not seem advantageous to protesters because the regime remains intolerant of organized activity not controlled by some branch of the Party (Bovingdon 2002). This comes as no surprise, since a common feature of authoritarianism is the lack of toleration of independent organizations (Przeworski 1991: 54). One case in point is the crackdown on efforts in forming independent labor organizations (Estlund 2017; Friedman 2014; Gallagher 2017; Lee 2007; Lorentzen 2017; Saich 2000). Moreover, since the state is well aware of the dangers inherent in *cross-class, cross-regional, or cross-nationality associations*, it has usually acted swiftly and severely to crush attempts to forge such bonds (Estlund 2017; Selden and Perry 2010; Tanner 2004) but has shown considerable leniency toward conflicts that were more homogeneous in composition and locale (Perry 2001 and 2007).[6]

Scale matters as well. According to previous studies, large protests are more threatening and more likely to lead to repression than small ones (Davenport, Soule, and Armstrong 2011; Earl, Soule, and McCarthy 2003; Soule and Davenport 2009).[7]

Who Is Shouting?

Governments also respond selectively to different kinds of groups. Authorities can be seen as opportunists that will repress when they believe they can win (Gamson 1990). As a result, subordinate groups – such as racial and ethnic minorities – are subjected to harsher repression. Recent quantitative research, for instance, has shown that African-American protesters have been more likely to suffer repression in the United States during certain time periods (Davenport, Soule, and Armstrong 2011). By contrast, the persecution of mainstream, entrenched groups is likely to meet powerful resistance from elites and fail to succeed in stifling dissent (Goldstein 1978). By and large, the more powerful the group, the less repression it receives (Tilly 1978). On the flip side, Tilly (1978) also emphasizes that groups with *a little* power suffer more repression than do the *completely powerless* because the latter pose no threat to the government and their small-scale collective actions are too weak to bother with.

---

[6] Two hypotheses are formulated. Hypothesis 3: Protests linked organizationally to other protests increase the likelihood of protest policing compared with those not linked. Hypothesis 4: Protests organized in an informal way reduce the probability of protest policing compared with those organized in a formal way.

[7] Here is Hypothesis 5: A large protest is more likely to invite police presence and response than a small protest.

In China, peasants and ethnic minorities are conceived of as two important subordinate groups.[8] First, the gap between urban and rural is exceptionally large. The average income of rural residents is far less than that of urban residents.[9] Collective resistance such as land protests staged by peasants tends to lead to state suppression (Cai 2010). Moreover, despite affirmative-action-type policies, minorities are treated as peripheral peoples, marginal to power and politics (Bulag 2010). Within minorities, the state also has disparate attitudes. It is, for instance, more tolerant of Hui protests than Uyghur unrest (Gladney 2004).[10] Uyghur and Tibetan relations with Han Chinese (China's ethnic majority) are considered the worst among the minorities (Mackerras 2004), and the Chinese government has been often criticized for human-rights abuses in Xinjiang and Tibet. In reality, there is no dearth of cases in which protests by peasants or ethnic minorities meet ruthless repression (like the case cited at the start of this chapter). On the other hand, neither peasants nor minorities are completely powerless groups. Instead, the Chinese regime has been deeply concerned with rural unrest and minority protests, especially those deemed to threaten social stability or the unity of the country (Bernstein and Lü 2000; Mackerras 2004).[11]

WHAT THE DATA TELL US

Studies on contentious politics in China have long been constrained by the lack of large dataset. The Ministry of Public Security has statistics about mass incidents, yet they are not open to the public. Although, previously, it occasionally publicized the total number – although not the details – of mass incidents, including the widely cited figures of 8,700 in 1993 and 87,000 in 2005, in recent years, in the face of surging unrest, the government no longer reported these numbers. As in other authoritarian regimes, social protest in China is a sensitive issue connected directly to state legitimacy and social stability. Given this lack of data, several scholars have compiled their own

---

[8] These two groups do not exhaust the list of subordinate groups in China. I selected them as useful examples for analysis.

[9] For instance, the average income per capita of urban residents in 2012 was 24,565 yuan ($3,899), whereas that of rural dwellers was only 7,917 yuan ($1,257). See "Income per Capita of Urban and Rural Households Increased 9.6% in 2012" (Dai Shuang, *CRI Online*, 2013, http://gb.cri.cn/27824/2013/01/18/3365s3995360.htm).

[10] Both the Hui and Uyghurs are largely Muslim minorities. Uyghurs are a Turkic minority, whereas the Hui people are ethnically and linguistically similar to Han Chinese.

[11] Two hypotheses are generated here. Hypothesis 6: Protests by peasants are more likely to be policed aggressively than protests by other groups. Hypothesis 7: Protests by ethnic minorities (especially Uyghurs and Tibetans) are more likely to be harshly repressed than protests by other groups.

datasets, but each has significant limitations that make them unsuitable for identifying the boundaries between repression and tolerance. They only include non-regime-threatening protests (Cai 2010), merely comprise large-scale protests (each with over 500 participants) (Tong and Lei 2013), or only include non-regime-threatening protests taking place in a single city (X. Chen 2012).

To overcome the data limitations, I generated a dataset of 1,418 protest events that occurred across China from 2001 to 2012.[12] This original nationwide dataset consists of both political and non-political, and both large and small protests. Based on this dataset, the study is able to identify the boundaries of a space for protest in this country. In this research, the *protest event* is the unit of analysis.[13]

When constructing my dataset, I relied on data collected by Boxun.com, which is an overseas Chinese community website founded in the United States in 2000.[14] It was blocked in mainland China in 2011 after publishing articles that called for the Chinese Jasmine Revolution. Due to state censorship, a great many protests were not reported by the mainland media. In this sense, foreign media serves as a better source of information. Boxun is critical of the Chinese regime and, as such, is inclined to collect information on the more repressive events in China. Therefore, it is likely that my dataset is skewed towards protests that are suppressed.[15] Yet the potential bias poses no serious problem for this research; on the contrary, they seem to help reinforce my argument. If, using a dataset that is skewed toward the repressed events, I can still find a real protest space, then my argument should be strengthened. Additionally, since it is the more repressive events that define the boundaries between tolerance and repression, the potential bias assists in detecting the limits of government toleration.

---

[12] To create my dataset, I adopted the method of "protest event analysis" (PEA), which is used to "systematically map, analyze, and interpret the occurrence and properties of large numbers of protests by means of content analysis" (Koopmans and Rucht 2002: 231). Being widely employed in studying contentious politics in diverse regions (e.g., Beissinger 2002; Olzak 1992; Tilly 1995), PEA is a useful tool kit for the quantification of many properties of protest.

[13] A social protest can include one event or multiple events. About the definition of an event, I adhere to the guidelines developed in the Dynamics of Collective Action Project (initiated by Doug McAdam, John McCarthy, Susan Olzak, and Sarah Soule, www.dynamicsofcollectiveaction.com). A single event, in order to be considered as part of this study, needs to satisfy all of the following conditions: a. it must include action that is mostly continuous – no gaps of more than 24 hours in time (weekend gaps are acceptable for labor and school protests); b. it must be located within the same city or the same part of the city; c. it must include the same (or a subset of the same) participants whose goals are not different from each other.

[14] Boxun provides reports on nearly 2,000 incidents of resistance across China from January 2001 to December 2012, gathered largely from journalistic sources. Of these, according to my definition of "social protest," I have selected 1,418 protest events, which took place in all of the provincial administrations in mainland China and stemmed from a wide range of grievances.

[15] For more detailed discussion about data reliability and potential biases, see Appendix I.

Protest Policing

My goal is to analyze variations in repression through examining protest policing. I divide my analysis into two steps.[16] First, I focus on police presence or absence. Second, given police presence, I divide policing strategies into four mutually exclusive categories: (1) taking no or limited action (such as erecting barricades and traffic control); (2) using violence only (e.g., grappling, beating, and using tear gas); (3) making arrests only; (4) using violence and making arrests together.[17]

In authoritarian regimes, it is common for local agents to employ thuggery (Johnston 2012; Levitsky and Way 2010; Moss 2014). China is no exception. Some Chinese grassroots officials occasionally hire thugs to harass or attack protesters (Cai 2010; X. Chen 2017; Yu 2004). Thus, this research also takes unlawful means of repression, i.e., hiring thugs, into account. If thugs were employed but *not reportedly deployed by a third party*, they are treated as part of the police violence. Thugs appeared in a total of 33 events in my dataset; in 20 of these events it seems that they were dispatched by the government. This number is small and for some events both thugs and police appeared. In brief, policing became slightly more aggressive when thugs were included.[18] In the following sections, protest policing also includes thugs' activities.

Overall, Figure 2.1 demonstrates that a real space for protest exists in China: 59 percent of protest events were tolerated; that is, police either did not show up at the event or, if they were present, they did either nothing or took only limited action. This is true even though the dataset may have potential biases for exaggerating the proportion of protests that were repressed (as previously explained). The other 41 percent of protest events were met with some kind of coercive measures (see Figure 2.1). This result coincides with Tong and Lei's (2013) statistical findings on large-scale social protests, in which the government tolerated 65.7 percent of protest incidents.[19]

Nonetheless, the seemingly high proportion of state toleration cannot be taken at face value. It does *not* speak for a liberal environment in which protest activities are *not* risky and seldom receive repression. Since if most protesters confine their claims, actions, and organization within the narrow range regulated by the state, even if a majority of protests are countenanced, the space for protest is still quite *limited*. Hence, it is crucial to examine the varieties of protests.

---

[16] For similar analysis strategies, see Earl, Soule, and McCarthy (2003).

[17] For definitions of these categories and statistics of these variables, see the section titled "Police Reactions to Protest Events" and Tables A 2.1 and A 2.2 in Appendix I.

[18] For details, see Tables A 2.3 and A 2.4 in Appendix I.

[19] Tong and Lei's definition of tolerance is wider than mine because their definition also includes detention and arrests.

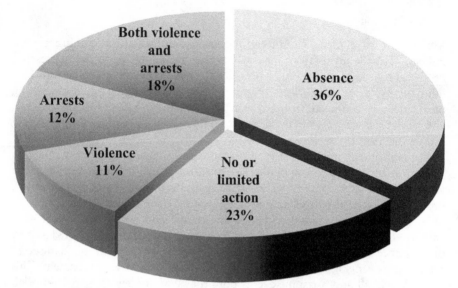

FIGURE 2.1 Police reactions: a meaningful space for protest in China (*N* = 1,418)

The Varieties of Protests

This section disaggregates social protest according to the character of protest (protest claims, actions, organization, and protest size) and the power of social groups.

I divide protest claims into economic claims (e.g., pressing for higher pay), environmental claims (such as a demand to relocate a polluting factory), moderate political claims (e.g., protesting the corruption of a local official), radical political claims (like a demand for an end to one-party rule), and a residual "other" category.[20] In my dataset, 63 percent of events had predominantly

---

[20] Detailed definitions of these concepts can be found in the section titled "Definitions of Key Independent Variables" in Appendix I. In some events, protesters might put forth more than one sort of claim. Environmental claims are sometimes mixed with economic claims. For instance, residents in the vicinity of a factory causing pollution advance both economic and environmental claims when they seek compensations and demand pollution reduction. Moreover, not all protests targeting political authorities raise primarily political claims. As a high-capacity authoritarian regime, the Chinese state controls many resources and exerts great control over people's lives, and thus it often generates state-centered grievances (Zhao 2010). Even if grievances arise from the wrongdoings of third parties, protesters are frequently inclined to invite government intervention. Hence, economic and/or environmental claims are often combined with moderate political claims. In my analysis, any event that expressed at least one radical political claim is coded under the radical political category even if other sorts of claims were also raised. Other than this categorization, I attempt to ascertain the foremost claim by relying on the one mentioned the most in protesters' banners, slogans, and accounts and use it to categorize a protest.

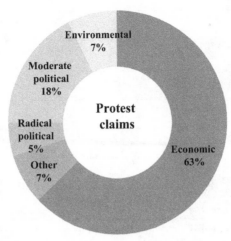

FIGURE 2.2 Protest claims

economic claims, the figures for environmental, moderate political, and radical political claims are 7, 18, and 5 percent, respectively (see Figure 2.2).[21]

Protest actions are classified into peaceful disruptive actions (such as demonstrations and strikes), violent actions (including hitting, shoving, and attacks), and peaceful non-disruptive actions (e.g., publishing protest letters online).[22] Figure 2.3 shows that 77 percent (1,086 events) of my dataset were peaceful disruptive actions, whereas 20 percent (287 events) involved violent actions.[23]

I examine two forms of protest organization: isolated organization (e.g., participants composed of workers from a single factory) and formal organization (e.g., the involvement of an independent formal organization, say, a trade union).[24] Figure 2.4 shows that 60 percent of protests were organized in an isolated way and 96 percent of protests were organized in an informal way.

[21] I create several dummy variables for each kind of claim. The dummy variable for a radical political claim is treated as a reference group in regression analysis.

[22] For detailed definitions of these concepts, see the section titled "Definitions of Key Independent Variables" in Appendix I.

[23] I employ a dummy variable for each sort of action and treat violent protests as the reference group in regression analysis.

[24] As a dummy variable, isolated organization is coded 1 when no linkages across regions, work places, or social groups were established. Formal organization is coded 1 when a protest was organized by an autonomous formal organization with a recognizable name and clear leadership.

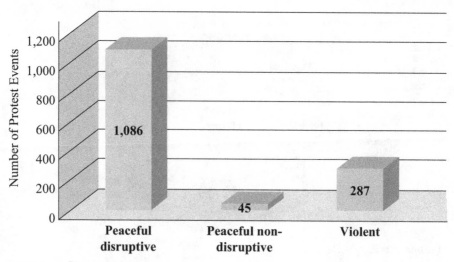

FIGURE 2.3 Protest actions

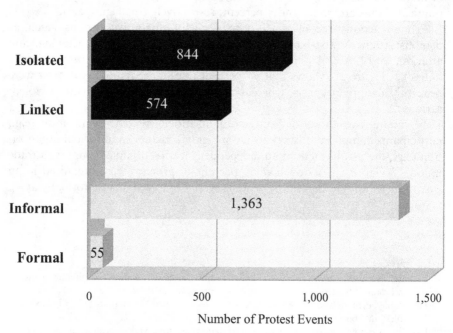

FIGURE 2.4 Protest organization

Another variable is the size of a protest event, measured by the number of protesters reported at the event.[25]

With regard to social groups, a peasant protest refers to a protest exclusively launched by peasants, with no presence of protesters from other social groups. Likewise, I define minority protests as protests staged only by ethnic minorities.[26] A protest by ethnic minority *peasants* is treated as a minority protest. In my dataset, among all minorities, Uyghurs and Tibetans staged the most protests (87 percent out of 98).

Finally, I take two control variables into consideration: location and duration. Location is divided into cities, counties, townships, and villages, respectively.[27] Harsh clampdowns on a protest that occurs in a city are usually more likely to receive public attention and have a more negative effect on regime legitimacy than those that take place in a rural area.[28] Additionally, the duration of a protest might matter, as authorities usually have more time and opportunities to respond to longer events.[29]

Analysis and Findings

Using the dataset I compiled, I set out to test the hypotheses already proposed. My analysis takes two steps to assess how police (or thugs) respond to different kinds of protest. First, I examine under what conditions police are likely to

---

[25] I use a logged count of the number of participants as a measure of protest size, which is a continuous variable. The measure is logged to correct for heteroskedasticity (Davenport, Soule, and Armstrong 2011; Earl, Soule, and McCarthy 2003). For 62 percent of the events ($N = 878$) in my dataset, the numbers of protesters were reported in news articles. As to the events for which there were no news reports, I estimated the number of protesters based on verbal cues in the news articles, numbers specified in similar events, numbers of police officers dispatched at the events, the scale of the community (e.g., a village or a factory), and so forth. As a robustness check, I ran regression analyses on two different sets of events: events for which the number of participants was specified in the news articles, and the full dataset. In both sets, the substantive findings were almost the same (see Table A 2.5 and Table A 2.11 for comparison).

[26] I create dummy variables for each of the groups mentioned above.

[27] I employ dummy variables for protests in cities, counties, townships, and villages, respectively. Protests taking place in townships and villages are not highly correlated with peasant protests: the correlation coefficients between townships and peasants and between villages and peasants are 16 percent and 53 percent, respectively (see Table A 2.8 in Appendix I). This is because peasant protests do not necessarily take place in rural areas but may occur in urban areas (e.g., peasants gathering in front of the city hall); on the other hand, not all protests taking place in rural areas are staged by peasants but may be by groups such as rural factory workers.

[28] When a protest occurred in multiple-level locations, such as in both a city and a village, I select the higher-level location (city in this case) in coding. The dummy variable for protests in cities is treated as a reference group when doing regression analysis.

[29] I put forward two hypotheses here. Hypothesis 8: Protests in cities decrease the odds of police presence and reaction. Hypothesis 9: Extending the duration of protest increases the probability of police presence and reaction. The duration of a protest is measured in hours and is logged to reduce heteroskedasticity (see Earl, Soule, and McCarthy 2003).

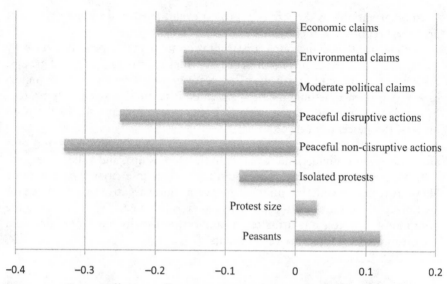

FIGURE 2.5 Factors affecting police presence at protest events ($N = 1,418$)
(*Note*: Only significant factors are included. For full regression results see Table A 2.5 in Appendix I.)

show up at the event, using binary logistic regression (BLR). Next, I scrutinize multiple forms of policing strategies given police presence by analyzing the model of multinomial logistic regression (MLR).

Police Presence

The first regression analysis looks at whether or not police attended an event. Figure 2.5 presents regression results that significantly influence police presence.[30] First, compared with radical political claims, protests advancing economic, environmental, or moderate political claims are indeed less likely to invite police presence. With respect to actions, peaceful protests (disruptive or non-disruptive) are less likely to draw police presence than violent protests. With regard to organization, isolated protests decrease the odds of police presence compared with protests that are linked organizationally with other protests. In addition, peasant protests are more likely to draw police presence than other groups. Protest size also increases the likelihood of police attendance. Other factors, such as formal organization, unexpectedly, have no influence on police presence.

---

[30] Full results of the BLR analysis are available in Table A 2.5 in Appendix I. The results reported here are from the full model, Model 6.

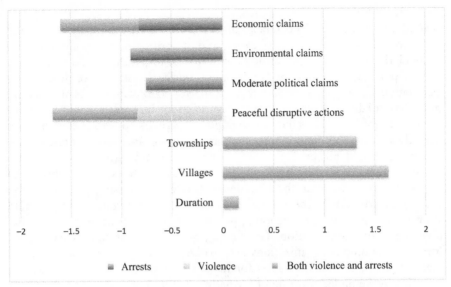

FIGURE 2.6 Factors leading to police actions at protest events ($N = 908$)
(*Note*: Only significant factors are included. For full regression results see Table A 2.6 in Appendix I.)

Police Actions

When police are present at protest events, what do they do? Simply showing up without coercive response is still a relatively tolerant response. Therefore, it is important to distinguish the types of police reactions to protests. I divide protest actions into the aforementioned four mutually exclusive categories and then use MLR models to analyze police actions at protest events.

Figure 2.6 illustrates the key factors that are confirmed to have a significant effect on police actions.[31] In the first place, radical political claims are more likely to suffer police coercion (arrests and/or police violence) than any other claims. Peaceful disruptive actions, in comparison with violent protests, decrease the likelihood of police coercion. Protests taking place in townships and villages, i.e. rural areas, are more likely to be harshly repressed than those taking place in cities. Other variables, such as the form of organization and the presence of ethnic minorities, surprisingly, have no significant effect on police actions. In brief, advancing radical political goals and taking violent actions in protests are triggers for police coercive response; rural protests also predict police coercion.[32]

---

[31] Full results of the MLR analysis are available in Table A 2.6 in Appendix I. The results reported here are from the full model, Model 9.

[32] My BLR and MLR results are in line with C. Chen's (2017) statistical analysis, which also finds that the triggers of police suppression include protests occurring in rural areas, involved with violence, and staged by peasants.

Unexpected Results

Several unexpected results can be gleaned from the statistical analyses. Among them, the effects of formal organization and minority groups on repression are particularly striking.[33] First, protests with *formal* organizations do not predict protest policing. This is at odds with the rigid legal restraints on freedom of association in China. I speculate three scenarios to explain this contradiction: protesters might have had a formal organization, but police might not have been aware of it and thus did not respond; *or* perhaps no formal organization actually existed, but police imagined its existence and used repression; *or* authorities might refrain from using naked force and turn instead to softer means, say, co-opting or penetrating the organization, to establish control. All the scenarios could blur the boundaries between repression and tolerance, thereby contributing to the insignificant result of formal organization. My data shows that only a tiny proportion (4 percent) of protest events were reportedly involved formal organization. This finding provides two insights: first, should formal autonomous organizations get involved in the protests, their involvement might be behind the scenes for fear of repression (Fu 2016 and 2017), resulting in the underreporting of formally organized events; second, the strict constraint and severe clampdown on independent associations might have deterred protesters from establishing formal organizations. Both situations suggest the state's repressiveness of formal organizations, indicating little space for formally organized protests. On the flip side, the statistically insignificant results perhaps suggest that the restriction on organized protest may not be as severe as often thought; a few studies, in fact, show this (Deng and O'Brien 2014; Lu and Tao 2017). In any case, at this stage, it is difficult to draw any definitive conclusions. I will examine the actual limits imposed by the state on protest organization in great detail through case studies in the next three chapters.

Why do regression results find no support for the hypothesis that ethnic minorities are targeted for harsher punishment?[34] This, perhaps, is because minorities (Uyghurs and Tibetans, in particular) engage in protests that have an exceedingly high proportion of radical political claims. In my dataset, among protests by minorities (a total of 98 events), only those staged by Uyghurs and Tibetans put forth radical political claims (58 events; see Figure 2.7). When controlling for protest claims, the effect of minority protests becomes *in*significant.[35] Taken together, these results reveal that minorities, especially Uyghurs

---

[33] For more discussions of the unexpected results, see the section titled "Unexpected Regression Results" in Appendix I.

[34] This is true even when the BLR and MLR analyses were re-run replacing protests by "minorities" with protests by "Uyghurs and Tibetans." See Table A 2.5 (Model 7) and Table A 2.6 (Model 10) in Appendix I.

[35] See Table A 2.12 in Appendix I in which I ran a regression analysis that only included measures of protest claims and minorities. I also ran regression analyses by adding forms of actions alone and forms of organization alone respectively into the model of social groups. In both models the impact of minorities remains significant.

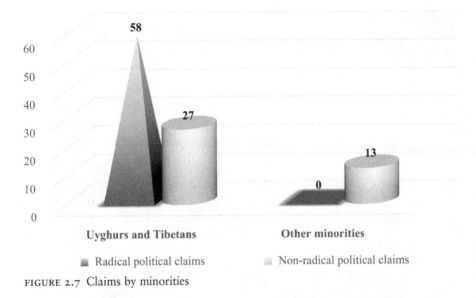

FIGURE 2.7 Claims by minorities

and Tibetans, are indeed singled out for repression. Because it is the state that defines what claims are radical politics and off limits, Uyghurs and Tibetans' protests are usually interpreted by authorities and protesters through an ethnicity lens. Even if a protest arises from economic or environmental grievances, it can easily switch to and be tagged as separatism (Hastings 2005) and thus can result in a crackdown. In contrast, ethnicity and separatism are not an issue among Han Chinese. In this sense, when separatism is regarded as off limits, the protest space for Uyghurs and Tibetans is much *narrower* than it is for the Han. In Chapter 5, I will elaborate on the dynamics of Uyghur unrest and state reaction.

MAPPING THE SPACE FOR PROTEST IN CHINA

Regression results confirm that protest claims, actions, and (to a lesser extent) forms of organization are key in predicting state repression. The results can be illustrated on a continuum of tolerance and repression. This helps map the boundaries of protest space in China. As shown in Figure 2.8, on the left end of the continuum, protests raising economic, environmental, and moderate political claims, and taking peaceful disruptive actions increase the odds of tolerance; on the right end, protests advancing radical political claims, taking violent actions, and linked organizationally with other protests predict repression.

This continuum assists in locating transgressive protests, namely, protests that violate the boundaries of tolerance. Transgressive protests should have the features listed on the right end of the continuum in Figure 2.8. Scholars have expected that protests in authoritarian regimes take largely transgressive forms,

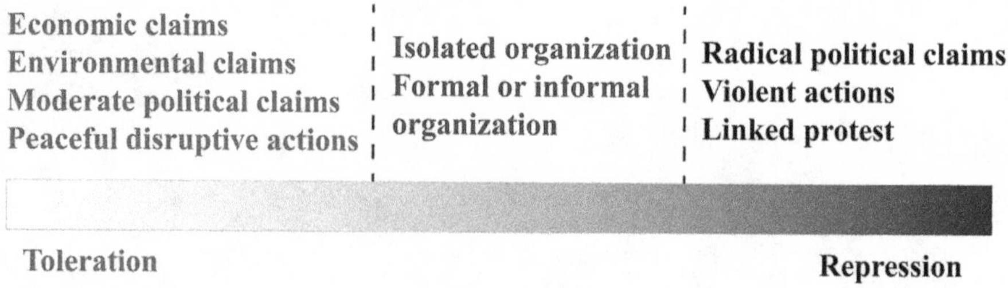

| Economic claims
Environmental claims
Moderate political claims
Peaceful disruptive actions | Isolated organization
Formal or informal
organization | Radical political claims
Violent actions
Linked protest |

Toleration   **Repression**

FIGURE 2.8 Mapping the space for protest in China

which challenge "the regime, its institutions, and its laws all at once" (Tilly and Tarrow 2007: 61). This, however, is not the case in China. In my dataset, only 5 percent of protest events put forth radical political claims, 20 percent used violence, and 40 percent had linkages with other protests as discussed earlier. In this way, non-transgressive protests are prevalent in China at present. It is noteworthy that my dataset may disproportionately comprise protests with radical political claims. Since Boxun disapproves of the Communist regime, it is inclined to collect protests with radical political claims, and the Western media and human-rights groups – the major sources of Boxun data – are also keen to report such protests. Even so, only 5 percent of events fall into this category. This result is consistent with the analysis by Yu Jianrong (2007), who estimates that 90 percent of mass incidents in China are rights protection actions and do not challenge the political power.

All in all, my findings indicate that non-transgressive protests are the predominant form of contention in China today.

CONCLUSION

This chapter explores the main forms of protest and major patterns of state reaction in China. Based on an original dataset, the statistical analysis reveals a real space for protest within this one-party state; nearly two thirds of protest events were condoned by authorities. On the other hand, most protests in my dataset did not transgress the bounds of this space. State tolerance and non-transgressive protest suggest that both sides do not deny the legitimacy of the other and do not close the door to negotiation, which are the essences of regime-engaging protests. Therefore, quantitative research provides evidence that *regime-engaging* protests are the dominant form of contention in China.

While this book discusses the existence of protest space in contemporary China, it is critical to remember that this space is limited in important ways. In terms of protest "actions," the space is fairly broad; even disruptive actions – as long as they are peaceful – tend to be tolerated. However, in terms of "claims," it is narrow. A whole range of political claims that are permitted in many democratic regimes (rights to establish an independent party, to democratic elections, etc.) are all described as "radical" and are off limits. The low percentage (5 percent) of protests raising radical claims suggests that the great majority of people confine their protest activities to this narrow space. Since among all social groups, only Uyghurs and Tibetans explicitly demand regional independence or autonomy in mainland China, which is regarded as transgressive by the regime, the protest space for Uyghurs and Tibetans is even *narrower* than it is for other ethnic groups. With regard to "organization," the low percentage (4 percent) of protests having the involvement of open formal organization suggests that most protests seem to follow the laws that seriously limit the rights to freedom of association.

Therefore, the seemingly high proportion of state tolerance does *not* represent a liberal environment for activism in China. Because if most protesters confine their claims, actions, and organization within the narrow range regulated by the state, even if a majority of protests are not punished, the space for protest is still quite restricted, not to mention that some disgruntled citizens may refrain from initiating protest altogether in the anticipation of state repression (Ritter and Conard 2016). Put differently, the lack or limited use of state violence could actually indicate the effectiveness of state coercion in shaping dissenters' options and capacities for mobilization (Slater and Fenner 2011: 20–21). It should also be noted that the findings of this chapter do not include subtler and more covert means of coercion;[36] if we take those into consideration, the space for dissent shrinks even further.

That said, the existence of a protest space offers important insights into the discrepancy between formal institutions and informal practices of contentious politics. *By law* the boundaries that cannot be transgressed for protest are narrower in China than in many other countries. As a typical strong authoritarian regime, China has made a series of institutional arrangements that restrict or forbid contentious actions. If we simply focus on the formal institutions, we would have to believe that almost all contentious actions taking place through forbidden activities would be repressed (Tilly and Tarrow 2007). *In practice*, however, the boundaries of protest space are not as narrow as they appear to be by law. My data have shown that while disruptive actions commonly violate laws or regulations,[37] they tend to be tolerated as long as they do not go too far (e.g., remain peaceful and put forth moderate claims). Thus, the protest space cannot only be defined by formal rules but also by contentious interactions, with the interactions between the protesters' constant pushing of the envelope and the state's efforts to regulate and control dissent.

---

[36] For instance, the state can employ weak or strong social ties in protest control (Deng 2017; Deng and O'Brien 2013; Luo, Andres, and Li 2017; O'Brien and Deng 2015a).

[37] According to the *Law on Assemblies, Processions, and Demonstrations* (LAPD), passed in 1989, these contentious actions are required to apply for a permit from a local public security bureau, which, however, rarely authorizes such a permit. In this sense, it is reasonable to argue that the majority of disruptive actions in China are illegal. Chapter 3 will flesh out this point.

Since protest space appears to be determined in practice by a back-and-forth dynamic between protesters and authorities, the space is fluid and ambiguous, with boundaries fuzzier in some fields and regions than in others. Moreover, it is likely that there is a *periodic change* in official attitudes. For instance, while the state has enlarged the scope of official tolerance for academia and civic organizing in practice, official guarantees are periodically circumscribed (Howell 2011; Selden and Perry 2010; Teets 2013). The regime also frequently exerts tighter control over civic engagement during the occurrence of significant events within or outside China, such as the 2008 Beijing Olympic Games and the 2011 Arab Spring (C. Li 2012; Truex 2018). Therefore, countries are not merely structurally either open or closed but are *contingently* open or closed to particular issues and movements at different times (Rootes 2004). In the Soviet Union, for example, periods of permissiveness appeared during the 1960s and 1970s when self-limiting dissent was allowed (Karklins 1987; Wintrobe 1998). This is true of all states, and it is certainly true of China. Despite variation over space and time, this chapter shows that we can detect distinct patterns of state responses to various kinds of social protest in China. This is not to say that my analysis encompasses a complete list of factors that lead to diverse state reactions to protests, nor does this kind of statistical analysis definitively predict how a particular protest will be handled. Rather, it maps state reactions to protest in a way that gives us a bird's-eye view of how protests are currently policed in China.

The findings of this chapter call for a deeper exploration of contentious politics and state–society relationships in authoritarian settings. Most of the scholarship suggests that contentious politics in such states is characterized by transgression and repression. Instead, by revealing that the dominant feature of protests in China is regime engaging, findings of the chapter lend support to studies highlighting state tolerance for public expression of discontent in non-democratic settings (e.g., Albrecht 2013; Lust-Okar 2005; Variel 2011). Furthermore, much of the literature on authoritarian politics centers on state strategies in preventing contention but pays less attention to state reactions when protests have been actualized. My quantitative research helps develop this line of scholarship by demonstrating a major pattern of state responses to protest in illiberal states.

This quantitative study poses more questions: Why is a protest space allowed to exist in this strong authoritarian state? How do protesters perceive the protest space and react accordingly? Why do most protests avoid transgression? What leads to transgressive claims and violence? Are there local variations in the protest space? What political impact do protests have? The following chapters will seek to answer these questions through in-depth case studies.

3

Accommodating Informal Norms in Regime-Engaging Protests

> Preventing people from voicing opinions is more devastating than stopping a river from flowing.
>
> *Discourses of the States* (*Guoyu*, fourth century BC)

> In the modern Western world, we think of life and the economy as being ordered by formal laws and property rights. Yet formal rules, in even the most developed economy, make up a small (although very important) part of the sum of constraints that shape choices; a moment's reflection should suggest to us the pervasiveness of informal constraints.
>
> Douglass C. North (1990: 36)

A discrepancy between the law on paper and the law in practice is not unusual in modern Western societies. An example is underage drinking, illegal but widespread in the United States – a strong democracy characterized by well-established, elaborate formal institutions.[1] Failing to strictly enforce the law in an authoritarian context is even less surprising, as it is not unusual that autocrats break the law to persecute political dissidents and to stymie opposition.

What is unexpected here is that Chinese authorities bend the rules *in favor of* resisters. While the ineffective enforcement of the law often results from limited state capacity to monitor and sanction (Levitsky and Murillo 2009), the Chinese authorities maintain a strong grip on power and clamp down harshly on such protests as those that adopt radical positions and use violence. In some strong democracies, officials may deliberately allow a breach of the law in order to win elections (Holland 2015 and 2016). Yet this logic is not applicable to

---

[1] In 2013, about 8.7 million Americans aged 12–20 years (22.7 percent of this age group) reported drinking alcohol in the past month (U.S. Department of Health and Human Services 2014: 44), and the minimum drinking age in the United States is 21 years.

China, which is still a "closed" authoritarian regime (Diamond 2002; Levitsky and Way 2010). The question then is why this illiberal state sometimes shows leniency to claim makers.

This chapter illustrates that, due to both top-down and bottom-up forces, lax law enforcement when it occurs can be seen as a manifestation of "accommodating informal norms" in dealing with contention. For example, authorities frequently tolerate peaceful demonstrations without official permits, even though it is against the law. Indeed, it is these informal norms that determine the actual space for protest, which is wider than that regulated by formal institutions. In democratic regimes, forbearance or the non-enforcement of law can come as an exchange for votes and electoral support (Holland 2015 and 2016). I argue that, in China, leniency toward resisters is incentivized for an exchange of obedience and loyalty on the part of citizens; put differently, forbearance is aimed at keeping protests in check and sustaining authoritarian rule.

As already stressed, the accommodating informal norms are not available to all types of contention. In order for them to work, the *claims* raised by the resisters should not be off limits, which is the key element of regime-engaging protests. Chapter 2 revealed that the protest space tends to open up to citizens whose claims are economic or environmental. Seven protests with these demands have been included in my case studies as examples of regime-engaging protests. Based on three economic protests, this chapter illustrates what accommodating informal norms are at play, how they are learned, why they emerge, conditions when they break down, and their political effects. Chapter 4, focusing on four environmental protests, scrutinizes the uneven enactment of accommodating informal norms, especially in terms of regions and social groups.

Based upon participant observations, detailed interviews, and document collection, this chapter not only invites us to think like aggrieved citizens and local officials whose daily work is to cope with citizens' grievances and contention, but also permits us to think like the Chinese rulers whose primary concern is to preserve power and control. Throughout the chapter, I will present a framework that shows the interactions between authorities and citizens matter in the creation, the function, and the influence of accommodating informal norms.

INTRODUCING THREE CASES

The three regime-engaging cases described in this chapter include a factory struggle for higher severance pay, a strike for raising taxi fares, and opposition against privatizing a hospital. All three protests erupted in the 2000s in D City,[2] a northern municipality adjacent to Beijing. With a population of nearly three

---

[2] D City is the fictitious name for an actual city. In order to protect the identities of the interviewed protesters and government officials who shared their experiences and thoughts with me, I use pseudonyms for the places and the people involved. A descriptive overview of these individuals is provided in Appendix II.

million, D City is a typical middle-sized municipality in China, not only in terms of size but also in terms of economic performance and industrial structure. It is worth mentioning that the three cases should be considered illustrative rather than necessarily representative of all regime-engaging protests in China.

Winning Higher Factory Severance Pay

"Kneel down! Kneel down!" The deafening shout rose from the throats of the nearly 3,000 people gathered in an indoor stadium one spring afternoon in 2005. The shouts were directed at Fan, the head of a super large state-owned enterprise (SOE) called Giant Corporation, who sat at the center of the stadium, his head bowed. In front of him stood a teenage boy, in tears, holding a portrait of his mother, who had been killed several hours before. Officials from a variety of government departments, including the head of the D City Public Security Bureau (PSB), sat beside Fan. Security was tight at the site, but no officials dared to speak for Fan when people were shouting for him to kneel. The whole scene looked like the denunciation of cadres during the Cultural Revolution period, four decades before. However, this was, in fact, a negotiation meeting between workers and authorities. What happened?

The story started in 2004 when, after years of zero production, Hill Factory in D City, filed for bankruptcy. Left behind were 3,000 angry workers. Feeling betrayed, workers argued that the standard severance payment of $200 per year was unfair considering their many years of sacrifice and contribution to the factory. So they stood up to fight for higher severance pay; they also accused the factory cadres of corruption, which they believed was the root cause of the bankruptcy. They petitioned the local and national governments as well as the Beijing-based Giant Corporation, Hill Factory's parent corporation. In an attempt to draw more attention to their plight, workers blocked roads in D City and in Beijing.

Although their aim, at the outset, was not to cause big trouble, their efforts failed to bring about the changes they wanted. Then, in May 2005, thousands of workers gathered near a key railway route between Northeast China and Beijing. There, they announced their plan to "walk" to Beijing along the tracks. The local government dispatched armed police to stand between the tracks and the crowd. The Mayor of D City also showed up. Using a loudspeaker, he warned the crowd to stay away from the railroad. His request went unheeded; under the watchful eyes of officials, law enforcement, journalists, and curious bystanders, workers went around the armed police and surged onto the railway tracks. Heady with the euphoria of defying the authorities, they failed to notice the oncoming train and, unable to react in time, one worker – the mother of the teenage boy – died and another got his arm broken. Workers blamed the tragic incident to Fan's long-term disregard for their grievances.

After the tragedy, the government gathered the workers in the stadium to open negotiations. And it was here that they demanded that Fan kneel before the picture of the boy's mother. Feelings ran high and, despite the presence of police, some workers threatened to beat Fan. At last, one protest leader was able to calm her fellows and persuade them to allow a peaceful dialogue with the authorities. After four hours of negotiations that day, workers secured compensation fees to families of the railway incident victims, although an agreement on the issue of severance pay was not reached.

To make their grievances known to a wider audience, protest representatives contacted an American journalist but the government got wind of it and the representatives were arrested before they could meet. The arrest sparked a confrontation between law enforcement officers and protesters at a local police station, where protesters demanded the release of their representatives. Authorities, impressed by the workers' solidarity and feeling the pressure to maintain local stability, ultimately approved an increase in severance pay, although it was less than hoped for. The victory was later marred by the fact that protest representatives were imprisoned for a few years.

The Taxi Driver Strike

On the morning of November 18, 2009, when residents of W District (a district of D City)[3] woke up, they were shocked to find that taxis had vanished off the streets overnight. In the wake of this disappearance, urbanites had to scramble to find alternate transportation to work, to school, to the train station. It wasn't until later that the reason for the missing taxis became clear; driven by soaring gas prices and shrinking incomes, taxi drivers of W District, which had a total of nearly 3,000 cabs, had decided to go on a strike. To minimize the disruptive effect of the strike, the government offered a bonus of $16 a day to taxi drivers who agreed to resume to work. Although many drivers took the money, they did not, in fact, come to work for fear of being marked as a "traitor" and suffering retaliation from other cab drivers. Authorities also dispatched plain-clothed policemen to drive cabs around town to create an impression that cabs were still running on the street; not surprisingly, these "police cabs" refused to take any passengers.

Anxious to restore the social order, the city government held a public hearing, just two days after the strike began, to discuss about raising taxi fares. Representatives from all involved parties – taxi drivers, passengers, and the government (including D City Traffic Bureau (DCTB) and D City Commodity Price Bureau) – attended the hearing. Immediately after the meeting, the government announced that it would impose a "gas surcharge" (one yuan) to increase the taxi fares. A local factory worked overnight to print notification of this surcharge for passengers and ensure that each cab got one. After the strike ostensibly came to a satisfactory end on November 21, police arrested

---

[3] "District" is an administrative level lower than the "city."

several taxi drivers on suspicion of having organized the strike. Although insufficient evidence led to their release two weeks later, the arrests and their disappointment that no other drivers fought for their release made most of them quit the taxi job afterwards.

Stopping the Privatization of a Hospital

With more than 10,000 employees, Shining Factory was one of the largest SOEs in D City. Like other large SOEs in China, Shining Factory had a social service component – Shining Hospital, which had 350 employees and retirees. In the wave of SOE reform in the early 2000s, Shining Hospital was told it had to be separated from its factory (Y. Li 2013). The hospital was faced with two paths, one of privatization and the other of government takeover. Hospital employees and retirees favored government takeover because that would stabilize and increase their incomes as well as benefit the hospital's future development.[4] The local government, however, leaned towards privatization so as to avoid the burden of funding the hospital. And thus, the struggle began. In December 2004, Shining Hospital protesters petitioned the D City Petition Bureau (DCPB) and Shining Factory, demanding a government takeover.

Things got off to a hostile start. The leaders of both Shining Factory and Shining Hospital forbade hospital employees from engaging in the struggle. In response, the employees temporarily grew silent, but a group of retirees took up the torch. Half a year later, the protest took a favorable turn when, in June 2005, protesters' threat of a demonstration in front of D City Hall won them a meeting with Jian – the head of Shining Factory. At the meeting, Jian expressed his full support of their cause. This 180-degree change in attitude can be traced directly back to the tragedy of the Hill Factory railway blockade, which took place one month earlier. Considering his responsibility for maintaining stability in his jurisdiction, Jian preferred to pass the hot potato to the local government and therefore endorsed municipalizing the hospital (Y. Li 2013).

Jian's endorsement, however, did not immediately change the city government's position. Half a year later, protesters threated to take their case to the central government. Throwing his weight behind them, Jian took them to the DCPB and said bluntly to two deputy directors of the DCPB: "Today I came here not only as board chairman and party secretary of Shining Factory, but

---

[4] Hospital employees and retirees treat municipalization as an opportunity to increase their income in light of the big gap between themselves and their counterparts in city hospitals, which belong to state-run institutions (SRIs, *shiye danwei*). Salaries and pensions from SRIs on average grew substantially more than those from SOEs, owing to the national income-redistribution policies (See "Income Growth Rate of Government and State-run Institutions Is about 3% Higher than the Rate of Companies," *National Business Daily*, August 7, 2009, http://finance.ifeng.com/news/hgjj/20090807/1053412.shtml). Moreover, Shining Hospital had been performing poorly for years due to lack of funding, and government subsidies were considered critical for its survival.

also as a petitioner. If you still take no action [in taking over Shining Hospital], I will remove myself from this issue." (Zhi 2014)[5] The directors, ranked administratively lower than Jian,[6] understood that, if Jian stepped away, it would be even harder for the DCPB to control the protest. Stunned by Jian's stance, they promptly reported the situation to D City leaders and, the next day, the municipal government agreed to take over Shining Hospital.

However, agreement is one thing, action another. Objection from the D City Health Bureau, which hoped to avoid the financial burden a takeover would entail, coupled with buck passing and procrastination in other government departments meant that there was still a long way to go before things actually changed.[7] But the protesters did not give up. In June 2007, around 200 hospital employees and retirees gathered in front of the city hall to press their case. Although the demonstration did motivate the government to take more action, progress ground to a halt again two months later. Then, on October 15, 2007, the opening day of the 17th National Congress of the Communist Party of China, the primary protest leader, Zhi, a figure who had a strong personality, was highly articulate in making his case, and often won debates with authorities, went to Beijing. Days earlier, two other protest leaders had also left for Beijing. Their action then unnerved local officials because it created an impression that they would collectively petition the central government, although all three insisted that their trip was simply for personal issues. Worrying about the possible petition (Zhi 2014), the heads of D City Health Bureau, Personnel Bureau, and Labor Bureau and other officials stayed overnight in the Health Bureau on the eve of Zhi's departure to Beijing, discussing about how to prevent Zhi's petition there to avoid its negative impact on their official positions.[8] Although it turned out that no petition was filed in the capital, Zhi's trip accelerated the municipalization of the hospital. It was taken over right away by the Health Bureau, with increased salaries and pensions for employees and retirees. The struggle stopped temporarily in March 2008.

A year and a half later, however, the protest resumed. This time the demand was the payment of several allowances incurred after the takeover. After numerous ineffective meetings and petitions to authorities, resisters held a second demonstration in front of the city hall in 2011. In response, the government paid most of the claimed allowances. Eventually, the struggle concluded in late 2011, with government concessions without coercion.

---

[5] Zhi is the primary leader of the Shining Hospital protest, a male retiree of the hospital. He wrote down the major protest events in *Record of the Shining Hospital Takeover* (1st edition 2009; 2nd edition 2014).

[6] Jian was then a high-ranking official at the same level as a vice mayor.

[7] For detailed discussion about the takeover process, see Y. Li (2013).

[8] Interviewees 8, 9, and 91. In the past decade, the central government has exerted great pressure on the local governments to prevent petitioning in Beijing – in particular at sensitive moments (such as the convening of major national conferences) – by relating local officials' performance in handling petitions to their promotions and penalties (Y. Li 2013).

ACCOMMODATING INFORMAL FORMS OF CONTENTION

OFFICIAL A: "It's fine that you come here [to the city hall] as long as you don't do anything off-limits."

PROTESTER A: "Don't worry. All of us are people who know how to behave."

OFFICIAL B: "Haven't you gone too far already?!"

OFFICIAL A: "Chanting slogans, displaying banners, and singing all go beyond the limits and disturb the public order; they are not allowed and are illegal."

PROTESTER A: "We are not out-of-bounds. We have informed the municipal public security bureau."

OFFICIAL B: "Yet you were not approved."

PROTESTER A: "Even so, the event was put on the PSB's record."

. . .

PROTESTER B: "We will be offered a dialogue, right?"

OFFICIAL A: "That's right. I have contacted relevant government departments to come to the [D City] Petition Bureau [for the dialogue]."

. . .

OFFICIALS A & B: "You have achieved your purpose [as officials have agreed to a dialogue]. That should be enough. Don't go too far!"

PROTESTER C: "We will talk to our people, all right? We will ask everyone to [leave the city hall and] move to the [D City] Petition Bureau."

These are some conversations I heard in a demonstration in front of the D City Hall on July 27, 2011. On this cloudy morning, I joined the demonstration with approximately 100 Shining Hospital retirees. At the scene, the retired doctors, nurses, and pharmacists – holding small national flags in hand – shouted slogans such as "We want to see the Mayor" and chanted the *Internationale*, an anthem of the international socialist movement (see Figure 3.1). Dozens of police officers were present, watching and videotaping protesters' actions. Officials from the DCPB – including Officials A and B in the above dialogue – also showed up. At the officials' request, demonstrators moved to the DCPB for negotiation. At the DCPB, most protesters waited in the hall while their five elected representatives bargained with officials in the conference room upstairs. After the meeting, protesters dispersed peacefully, and nobody was penalized for participation.

Although this collective action was not repressed, it violated formal rules in several ways. First, as Official B pointed out, the demonstration had not been authorized by the PSB and thus was illegal by law.[9] Second, shouting slogans in collective actions should be subject to punishment according to the Ministry of Public Security's regulations.[10] Last, officials framed the demonstration as a "collective petition" (*qunfang*) and managed to direct the demonstrators to

---

[9] According to the *Law on Assemblies, Processions, and Demonstrations*, a demonstration is required to have a permit granted by law enforcement.

[10] The Ministry of Public Security's *Instructions on Dealing with Illegal Criminal Actions in Petitions*, issued in 2008.

FIGURE 3.1 Shining Hospital demonstration in front of the D City Hall in 2011
(To protect privacy, faces have been blurred. Courtesy of a protest activist.)

the petition bureau. Yet, they should not have qualified as lawful collective petitions, given that the location of the demonstration and the number of participants did not conform to government regulations.[11] In analyzing these violations, we can see how a series of accommodating informal norms of contention were applied here.

It is worth noting that although protesters broke the prescribed rules, they were cooperative with authorities at the demonstration site and were eager for negotiation. Both the authorities and protesters were aware of the legal limits of collective action. At the outset of the demonstration, police repeatedly played a three-minute recording, which gave a precise definition of "illegal petitions" and announced corresponding legal penalties. That said, the formal rules were bypassed, and the hospital's "illegal petition" was tolerated.

Informal Norm No. 1: Unauthorized Protest Can Be Acceptable

China's Constitution grants citizens freedom of assembly, procession, and demonstration.[12] However, ordinary laws infringe upon these rights. The

---

[11] According to the 2005 *Regulations on Letters and Visits*, petitioners should not congregate around state institutions or offices (such as the city hall), and collective petitions should send no more than five people as representatives to visit the designated petition agencies. Both of these regulations were contravened by this hospital's "collective petition," for the petitioners assembled in front of the city hall and the number of the petitioners was far above the five-people limit.

[12] The current constitution was adopted at the Fifth National People's Congress in 1982, with revisions in 1988, 1993, 1999, and 2004.

Law on Assemblies, Processions, and Demonstrations (LAPD) requires citizens to apply for an official permit from the PSB to conduct these collective actions. Without the permit, organizers or activists are expected to receive police warnings or face detention of up to 15 days.[13] In reality, such a permit is rarely granted by the PSB (Qi and Wang 2013; Zhang 2006). As a government official frankly stated, "It is required that citizens should submit applications for demonstrations and parades, but will the PSB approve them? Never!"[14] A PSB captain even asserted that, "It is forbidden to take to the streets and demonstrate."[15] This should come as no surprise because contentious collective actions are usually perceived to create disorder and threaten social stability and are therefore seldom authorized by an authoritarian state.

Nonetheless, an inability to obtain a permit does not prevent the occurrence of contentious collective actions. In fact, it is common to see disgruntled citizens taking to the streets in China on a daily basis, as exemplified by the enormous number of "mass incidents" that take place in China (see Chapter 1). Since authorities seldom authorize these contentious actions, they can be said to be *de jure* illegal.

To circumvent the legal restrictions and avoid punishment, protesters are innovative in describing their actions. A popular practice is to select words such as "taking a stroll" (*sanbu*) or "taking a tour" (*lüyou*) to avoid being identified as an illegal demonstration or march.[16] An activist explained the difference in this way: "Taking a stroll is not a march. A march is organized, with slogans, banners, and purpose. By contrast, a stroll is not organized, nor can you identify any organization. This is a tactic created by people in order to bypass the law. By law, a march is allowed but needs to be registered by application, yet applications usually are not approved."[17] A second activist confirmed the distinction saying, "Taking a stroll is not an open confrontation: I just stand on the road, without unified slogans, organization, or leadership. You have no idea who the leader is. [The walk] is mobilized via the Internet, and then people just appear on the street."[18] Another common practice is to interpret a collective action as a way to "express opinions" to counter the official discourse of "disturbing public order." As one protester put it: "It is OK to stand *by* the gate [of a government building] as long as you aren't *blocking* it. Don't interrupt their [officials'] work. It is *illegal* to storm the government buildings, but you can stand outside just to *express your opinions*." "Your goal is simply a kind

---

[13] Item 28 of LAPD.   [14] Interviewee 22.   [15] Interviewee 19.

[16] "*Sanbu*" or "*lüyou*" are popular words used by protesters to describe their protests and have even been adopted by news reporters. See, for example, "Two Thousand Workers of Galanz Smashed the Factory, Strolling around (*Sanbu*) with Their Upper Body Naked" (*Xinhuanet*, April 16, 2014, http://news.hsw.cn/system/2014/04/16/051906010_01.shtml).

[17] Interviewee 38.   [18] Interviewee 39.

of claim-making," he further emphasized. "If you go beyond and disturb the public order, then it is you who is *crossing the red line*" (emphasis added).[19]

Such strategies seem to work, and non-violent collective actions are often tolerated (see Figure 2.8 in Chapter 2). In other words, tolerating unauthorized peaceful protests has become a widely accepted unwritten code in China. This is seen in the Shining Hospital demonstration and also the Hill Factory struggle. Over the course of their struggle, factory workers took to the streets several times. Even without permits, their peaceful road blockades ended with no punishment.

Informal Norm No. 2: Diplomacy First, Force as Backup

If breaking the law does not necessarily lead to sanctions, what factors really matter? My field research reveals that the interaction between authorities and protesters is key in determining state reactions. When a contentious collective action occurs, authorities normally try peaceful means of controlling it first and only resort to coercion if diplomacy fails, thus, "diplomacy first, force as backup." According to this informal norm, a demonstration's illegality notwithstanding, if protesters conform to authorities' orders and impose self-discipline upon their actions, they can probably get away with it. Protesters, on the other hand, often prefer to enter into negotiation with officials rather than fighting with the police.

At a protest scene, the police's primary responsibility is to maintain order, not to enrage resisters. As one police officer put it, "When a collective petition incident occurs, we arrive at the spot as soon as possible, contact the local government, and prevent any extreme action." In his opinion, "The target of collective petition is the government [not the police]. We are only responsible for containing the petitioners ... In the past, our system was unsound, and basically police were used as weapons and shields (*dang qiang shi, dang dunpai shi*) ... Nowadays, it has all changed ... Instead of producing conflict [between the petitioners and ourselves], we shift the conflict to others [other government departments]."[20] According to this policeman, intensifying conflict indicates a local government's "failure" to cope with protests, rather than a norm. My interviews thus confirm Murray Scot Tanner's (2004: 148) finding about the change of policing style in China: "The new goal of security forces today is to minimize popular anger through more *moderate*, professional policing of protests and to limit police use of violent coercive tactics" (emphasis added).

Yet, whether "moderate" policing is enforced hinges on authorities' interaction with dissenters. Although the aforementioned PSB captain said that it is forbidden to take to the streets and demonstrate, he also mentioned: "If they [protesters] do so, we will not arrest them as long as they *listen to us*. Only

---

[19] Interviewee 35.   [20] Interviewee 18.

when they do not listen, will we take forceful measures" (emphasis added).[21] This view was echoed by an official from a petition office of the D City Political and Legal Affairs Commission (*zhengfawei*). He told me, "When taking disruptive actions, such as besieging the Party and government offices, protesters are not punished if they *follow police instructions* and disperse; those who refuse to follow are detained or even imprisoned according to *Public Security Administration Punishment Law* [PSAPL]" (emphasis added).[22] Eight months after the 2011 Shining Hospital demonstration, I interviewed Official B who appears in the previously quoted conversation, and he elaborated on government responses to contention: "Petitions in front of government offices that block the gate will be tolerated if petitioners are *persuaded to leave* the municipal government area. After all, *they are petitioners*" (emphasis added).[23] Here, Official B acknowledged the legitimacy of the collective action and did not treat the protesters as enemies or anti-government forces. "However," he continued, "if our persuasion is ineffective and protesters continue waving banners and chanting slogans, I am afraid that the police will take measures."[24] Put differently, forceful measures will ensue.

As noted, chanting slogans and displaying banners when gathering around government offices or in other public spaces are punishable offenses according to PSAPL.[25] Shining Hospital demonstrators shouted slogans and chanted the *Internationale* while rallying in front of the city hall. But they were neither stopped by law enforcement nor did they get into trouble for doing so. Nonetheless, when they attempted to unfurl a banner, a round-faced policeman interfered and required them to put it away. Protest activists initially argued with the officer, but he seemed quite determined so they stopped. The policeman informed the retirees that although it was okay for them to stand along the road not blocking the traffic, they were not allowed to display banners. He made these directives clear by saying, "I cannot afford to lose my job and be unable to feed my wife and kid just because of your staff." Protesters conceded and kept the banner folded throughout the demonstration. Obeying the policeman's order thus helped prevent authorities from resorting to coercion.

Behind diplomacy and persuasion, force is always lurking. Police presence and their videotaping at the hospital demonstration is a case in point (see Figure 3.2). The filming was not only a means of deterring unacceptable actions but also a means of collecting evidence that could be used against demonstrators at any time. According to Yan, the captain of a district PSB, when a mass incident breaks out, a subgroup of policemen is responsible for obtaining

[21] Interviewee 19.   [22] Interviewee 21.   [23] Interviewee 7.   [24] Ibid.
[25] This was also written in the *Recommendations on Public Security Organs' Using Applicable Laws to Deal with Illegal and Criminal Activities in Petitioning*, issued in 2008 by the Ministry of Public Security and revised in 2013 (July 19, 2013, http://bhxfy.chinacourt.org/article/detail/2014/05/id/1298034.shtml). Following the regulations, local governments across the country enacted corresponding local regulations that strengthen punishment for illegal petitions.

FIGURE 3.2 A policeman videotapes the 2011 Shining Hospital demonstration
(To protect privacy, faces have been blurred. Courtesy of a protest activist.)

evidence to identify the leader(s) of the incident or anything else that can be used to press charges afterwards.[26] Recently, the state has passed new laws and regulations to enhance the role of security forces in handling mass incidents and maintaining social safety,[27] providing the local authorities greater power to enforce regulations and punish violations.

Informal Norm No. 3: Converting Contentious Actions into Institutional Actions

When authorities adhere to the norm of "diplomacy first," they often avoid using "pejorative" terms such as "gatherings" and "demonstrations" as labels for contentious actions.[28] Rather, they classify them as "collective petitions"

---

[26] Interviewees 19.

[27] For instance, China's first law of armed police force, passed in 2009, detailed the responsibility of the armed police in handling mass incidents (*China.com.cn*, August 28, 2009, www.china .com.cn/military/txt/2009-08/28/content_18419525.htm). Moreover, in 2006, the Central Military Commission issued a mandate that allows mobilizing the military forces in support of local governments when mass incidents threaten local social or political stability (Cai 2008).

[28] A document issued by the National Petition Bureau regarded it as inappropriate to call collective action such as "petition through *gathering*" prior to a thorough investigation of the event; instead, "collective petitions" should be the correct term because it does not contain the *negative* meaning implied in the former vocabularies (see "Issues to Standardize Words Relevant to Petitions," *People's Petition*, 2009, No. 10: 17). In the hospital case, the deputy secretary-general of the municipal government and the deputy director of the DCPB used terms such as "actions" and "event" to refer to the hospital demonstration.

and then shepherd the *de facto* demonstrators to a petition office for dialogue.[29] Through dialogue, officials may further advise or require dissenters to resolve their conflicts through legal and bureaucratic institutions such as mediation, arbitration, litigation, and petition rather than to take to the streets. Protesters, on the other hand, are eager to be considered "petitioners" so as to meet with officials, lodge their complaints, and avoid punishment of their collective action. This was the case in the Shining Hospital demonstrations. For both authorities and protesters, playing the name game as a way of institutionalizing contention reflects another accommodating informal norm of contention.

The boundaries between public protests and collective petitions are therefore usually blurred. Existing studies have pointed out the fluidity between "contentious actions" and "petitions," but their focus is largely on the way aggrieved citizens escalate petitioning to street protests in order to press for their goals (Cai 2004 and 2008; X. Chen 2008 and 2012; Lee 2007; Y. Li 2013). The move in the opposite direction – converting street protests to institutionalized action – is less discussed. Yet this practice of conversion is important because it leaves room for civil disobedience, helps de-escalate tension, and facilitates the operation of formal institutions.

Framing *de jure* illegal gatherings as "collective petitions" helps legitimize the informal tolerance but does not make the events legal. The official regulations state that no more than five petitioners may visit petition agencies at any one time.[30] Despite this rule on the books, the five-person limit has been frequently violated across China and large collective petitions have been routinely tolerated (Cai 2004 and 2008; X. Chen 2008 and 2012). Official B in the above dialogue recognized the "five-petitioners limit" regulation, while, at the same time, remarking that nobody could do anything about the violation. As he put it, "Generally speaking, we tolerate collective petitions comprised of more than five people."[31] His accounts are confirmed in my case studies. In the hospital case, according to one protester leader's estimate, at least seven collective petitions of more than 50 people were organized over six years (Zhi 2014). Similarly, the Hill Factory workers also visited the DCPB and D City Federation of Trade Unions (DCFTU) in groups that numbered well over five, and none of them suffered punishment for this. In fact, when a group of more than five people visits the petition agencies, officials usually ask them to choose five representatives to file their petition.[32]

Recently, in addition to petitions, officials have become increasingly willing to provide a platform for negotiation between labor and management, and many local authorities generally take a neutral stance – rather than on the side of capital – in mediating labor disputes (China Labor Bulletin 2013 and 2015). A telling case is the Nanhai Honda strike of 2010, in which officials and trade

---

[29] See also X. Chen (2012).   [30] The 2005 *Regulations on Letters and Visits.*
[31] Interviewee 7.   [32] See also X. Chen (2012) and Lee and Zhang (2013).

union cadres played an active role in presiding over and guiding negotiations between workers and management (Friedman 2013).[33] As we have seen, when the taxi strike in D City broke out in 2009, the municipal government acted promptly to open a space for dialogue through the public hearing. Even though several interviewed cab drivers complained that the driver representatives who attended the hearing were pro-government (they were selected by taxi management companies, not elected by workers), the government's compromise of raising the surcharge fee, one of the biggest grievances of drivers, suggested that at least some of the workers' concerns were both expressed and heeded in the hearing.

LEARNING CURVE OF ACCOMMODATING INFORMAL NORMS

After exemplifying some accommodating informal norms of contention, a question arises: how do these informal forms of contention emerge? In the absence of written rules, time is necessary for the emergence, awareness, and functioning of the informal norms. This section argues that the way that informal institutionalization appears to be a "process of learning by example" (Helmke and Levitsky 2004: 731). What follows will illustrate actors' learning curve through scrutinizing Shining Hospital's two demonstrations in front of the city hall: one in 2007 and the other in 2011. A comparison of the two demonstrations will show how officials changed from anxious "firefighters" to mediators who became so blasé that some of them could doze off at the meeting; it will also illustrate how protesters turned their second demonstration into a quasi-reunion party.

On the morning of June 28, 2007, when hospital demonstrators started to gather in front of the city hall, the head of the DCPB rushed to the scene, acted like a "firefighter," and began tirelessly exhorting demonstrators to withdraw in exchange for negotiation (Zhi 2014). A deputy secretary-general of the municipal government, who represented a vice mayor, presided over the subsequent negotiation as the highest-ranking official. Four years later, however, when the same protesters stood at the same place, the highest-level official who showed up was a vice head of the DCPB (Official A in the recorded conversation). In other words, only much lower-ranking officials were present in dealing with the demonstration than the last time. What's more, the vice head, presiding the subsequent negotiation meeting with protesters, fell asleep near the end of the two-hour meeting![34] This would never have happened before. In our conversation, a protest leader criticized the DCPB officials for "grinning cheekily" (*xipi xiaolian*) and suggested that the officials were not as anxious about the demonstration as they had been the first time around.

---

[33] See also "The Whole Story of Wage Collective Bargaining in Nanhai Honda" (*Xiaokang Magazine*, August 8, 2011, http://news.sina.com.cn/c/sd/2011-08-08/101422953422.shtml).
[34] Audio recording of this negotiation meeting, provided by a protest leader, Interviewee 9.

Not only were the authorities more anxious in 2007, but so were the demonstrators themselves. That time, the white-coated doctors, nurses, and pharmacists, lined up and marched toward the city hall following a big banner, like a dramatic scene in a movie. A quarrel erupted when a protest leader was elbowed by a policeman who sought to rip the banner. Just before the quarrel developed into a fight, Guang – a hospital retiree and the wife of a retired police officer – stood up and smoothed over the situation. After this confrontation, both sides took a step back: the protesters retreated to the sidewalk to the city hall, and the police, albeit reluctantly, allowed protesters to continue to display their banners. Barring this confrontation, the 2007 demonstration was, by and large, peaceful and orderly (Y. Li 2013). The atmosphere at the 2011 demonstration, by contrast, was much less tense and confrontational; while protest leaders passionately defended their claims, others were engaged in small talks, smiling and laughing as at a party. Their chatting topics ranged from health to their children's jobs to the market price of golden jewels. Many of these retirees had not seen their former colleagues for a while so treated the gathering as a reunion and a time for catching up. Having grown up in the hospital community, I knew many of the retirees personally and was able to join the conversations as well.[35] Even a policeman joined the group and conversed gaily with Guang, the aforementioned hospital retiree.

Through the 2007 contentious interaction, the police learned not to touch any protesters, the protesters found that a street demonstration worked as well as a march in getting government attention, and officials learned that offering to dialogue with demonstrators could lead to their peaceful withdrawal. Unwritten codes that would guide actors to interact with each other were formed in the process. Back in 2007, authorities were uncertain what level of disruption the demonstrators would create, and protesters were uneasy about the official response. By contrast, in 2011, each side was more familiar with the other and behaved according to the established unwritten rules, lending predictability to each side's actions. This is evident in Officials A and B's words to demonstrators (as shown in the cited 2011 dialogue): "You have achieved your purpose [for a dialogue]. That should be enough. Don't go too far!" This was, in fact, a veiled threat and meant that, since the government has already agreed to talk, it is your turn to comply and you know the consequences of crossing the line. These words were quite effective; perceiving the menace, demonstrators recognized that it was time to take a step back, and so withdrew.

Informal norms thus played a part in stabilizing mutual expectations and rendering both sides more relaxed in the second demonstration. The demonstrations actually resembled a kind of "theatrical performance" (Esherick and Wasserstrom 1990; Wasserstrom 1991). In the second performance (the 2011

---

[35] My mother worked in Shining Hospital for nearly 30 years and participated in the hospital struggle.

demonstration), following "scripts" of accommodating informal norms helped reassure both sets of actors – officials and demonstrators – that the collective action would lead to a negation not confrontation. Unlike in the first one, the scripts as to how to act out a demonstration and when to return to negotiation were unclear. Back then, while resisters might have prepared their part of the performance based on observations of other cases (contemporary or historical ones), whether it would work for their own case and how authorities would perform remained unknown.

As a side note, the change between the two demonstrations seems to be consistent with a national trend in conflict handling. As the National Petition Bureau (NPB) claimed in an internal document of 2009, "Nowadays, although various sorts of conflicts arise and the number of petitions remains high, they are handled actively and effectively [in the country], unlike in the 'hurry-scurry' fashion of a couple years before."[36] Put differently, the past several years have witnessed the growing routinization in dealing with contention, implying the development of accommodating informal norms.

WHY ACCOMMODATING INFORMAL NORMS

The preceding discussion demonstrates how officials and protesters play by the informal rules, permitting a space for extralegal or illicit protests, but a question remains: *why* do accommodating informal norms of contention come into being in the first place, especially in such a strong authoritarian state?

This section argues that the generation and function of accommodating informal norms are the result of a combination of both top-down and bottom-up forces. To stay in power, the central government has been calling for government officials at all levels to diversify approaches to resolving social conflicts. In particular, officials are required to handle with care – rather than simply crush – "contradictions among the people" (CAPs, *renmin neibu maodun*), which are regarded as *non*-antagonistic to the state. At other times, officials are encouraged to suppress contention that is considered antagonistic to the state, namely "contradictions between ourselves and the enemy" (CBOEs, *diwo maodun*). The Chinese leaders' directives combined with protesters' efforts at self-discipline in addition to the ambiguities and discrepancies in formal laws frequently drive local officials to bend the rules for challengers (see Figure 1.1).

Leaders' Directives

The Mao Era (1949–1976)
The leaders' strategies of differentiating contradictions date back to the early Mao era when social unrest arose both outside and within China. In 1956,

---

[36] "Deeply Understand and Effectively Implement the 'Two Documents.'" *People's Petition.* 2009, No. 12: 17.

massive uprisings broke out in socialist Poland and Hungary. Workers' demonstrations in Poznan (Poland) and students' marches in Budapest (Hungary) developed into large-scale protests involving tens of thousands of people and calling for reforms in their own countries. In parallel with this tense international context, popular contention occurred in China from September 1956 to March 1957 (Bo 2008).[37] Dozens of worker strikes and petitions took place, with the number of participants reaching a total of 10,000; college and high school students boycotted classes and presented petitions in dozens of cities; rural areas witnessed a wave of disturbances in which peasants demanded to withdraw from their agricultural cooperatives.[38] The social disturbances at home and abroad unnerved leaders of the Chinese Communist Party (CCP) who worked around the clock during that period. The Politburo of the CCP and Politburo Standing Committee organized 14 meetings in just 20 days in late 1956. The Third Plenary Session of the Eighth CCP Central Committee also treated the Polish and Hungarian revolts as one of the central topics (Bo 2008).

To preserve regime stability and legitimacy, the Party leadership reached a consensus: correctly handling CBOEs and CAPs can determine the life or death of the regime (Bo 2008: 407). This was shown in Chairman Mao Zedong's keynote speech at the 1957 Supreme State Council Meeting: Mao stressed that members of any social class, status, or group who supported, embraced, and participated in socialist undertakings fell into the category of the "people," whereas those who resisted the socialist revolution, were hostile to the socialist construction, and attempted to undermine it were classified as "enemies" of the people. Mao pointed out that CAPs – labor strikes, student boycotts, peasant unrest, and so forth – originating from *bureaucratism*, should be allowed and treated through democratic and peaceful means, such as education, criticism, and persuasion; forceful methods should be avoided. By contrast, the state should exercise dictatorship (repression) over CBOEs.[39] By permitting a space for protests considered as CAPs, Mao, who was anxious to defuse domestic contradictions, hoped to release social tensions in China and to forestall a larger and more serious insurgency like the one then sweeping Eastern Europe

---

[37] Bo Yibo (1908–2007) was a Chinese leader, holding a series of top-ranking posts, including being a member of the Communist Party's Politburo and a Vice-Premier.

[38] "On the Correct Handling of Contradictions among the People and the Rectification and Anti-Rightist Movements (I)A." *News of the Communist Party of China.*
http://cpc.people.com.cn/GB/69112/70190/70192/70271/4765778.html.

[39] "On the Correct Handling of Contradictions among the People." Mao Zedong. February 27, 1957. www.marxists.org/chinese/maozedong/marxist.org-chinese-mao-19570227AA.htm.
"On the Correct Handling of Contradictions among the People and the Rectification and Anti-Rightist Movements (I)B" *News of the Communist Party of China.*
http://cpc.people.com.cn/GB/69112/70190/70192/70271/4765790.html.
"The Publication of Mao Zedong's 'On the Correct Handling of Contradictions among the People' and Its Implications." *News of the Communist Party of China.*
http://cpc.people.com.cn/GB/64107/65708/65722/4444778.html.

(Perry 2002b: 211). Mao's CAP theory is considered one of the most important thoughts in the history of the CCP since it took power in 1949 (Bo 2008).

Nonetheless, the CAP theory was barely put into practice after being proposed. The rest of the Mao era witnessed waves of political campaigns – from the 1957 anti-rightist campaign to the Cultural Revolution (1966–1976); in those campaigns, a massive number of citizens – arbitrarily labeled as "enemies" of the people – were persecuted or executed. These practices were clearly at odds with the spirit of the CAP theory inasmuch as the theory acknowledged counter-revolutionaries (enemies of the people) as merely a tiny minority of the population and called for a more lenient stance toward critics and protesters.[40]

The Post-Tiananmen Era

Shooting protesters – composed of students, workers, and ordinary urban residents – to end the 1989 Tiananmen movement came at a huge cost to the CCP, especially with respect to the damage done to regime legitimacy, both domestically and internationally. To rebuild regime legitimacy and safeguard its rule since Tiananmen, Chinese leaders returned to Mao's CAP theory and continue to value it as a critical guideline for dealing with social conflict. From the 1990s onward, faced with a rapid growth in protest among peasants, SOE workers, and other groups deemed as the "people" in official rhetoric, authorities have recognized that violent mishandling of these protests would risk the loss of regime legitimacy and cause backlash (Tanner 2009). Against this backdrop, President Jiang Zemin underscored that leaders at all levels should study Mao's CAP theory and, in this way, improve their abilities to handle CAPs.[41] Similarly, Jiang's successor, President Hu Jintao, pointed out that Mao's CAP theory remains highly instructive and admitted that most of the mass incidents were caused by CAPs.[42] To be sure, the boundaries between the people and the enemies have been redrawn in the reform era, and the methods of dealing with CAP events have shifted from centering on persuasion and ideological education to encompassing a more diversified skillset that combines economic and lawful means with others.[43] Nonetheless, the principle remains the same – adopting peaceful means to handle CAPs but getting tough on CBOEs.

[40] "On the Correct Handling of Contradictions among the People." Mao Zedong. February 27, 1957. www.marxists.org/chinese/maozedong/marxist.org-chinese-mao-19570227AA.htm.
[41] "Speech at the Second Plenum of the 14th CCP Central Committee." Jiang Zemin. *People.cn*. March 7, 1993. http://cpc.people.com.cn/GB/64184/64186/66685/4494247.html.
[42] "Speech at the 23rd Collective Study of the Politburo of CCP." Hu Jintao. *Xinhuanet*. September 29, 2010. http://cpc.people.com.cn/GB/64093/64094/12859820.html.
[43] "Speech at the 20th Anniversary of the Third Plenum of the 11th CCP Central Committee." Jiang Zemin. *People.cn*. December 18, 1998. *Selections of Important Documents since the 15th National Congress of the CCP*. http://theory.people.com.cn/GB/40557/138172/138173/8302188.html.

"The CCP Central Committee's Resolution about Major Issues on Constructing the Socialist Harmonious Society." *gov.cn*. October 18, 2006. www.gov.cn/gongbao/content/2006/content_453176.

What is the cause of a CAP incident? The central leadership attributes it not only to changes in interest distribution in the economic reform but also to defects in governance, including bureaucratism, power abuse, and corruption, which infringe upon the interests of the masses.[44] As Premier Wen Jiabao pointed out, many mass incidents "have to do with government agencies and their staff who do not conform to laws and policies."[45] Zhou Zhanshun, a director of the NPB, recognized that greater than 80 percent of petitions delivered to the governments throughout China are valid and should and can be resolved by the government.[46]

Correspondingly, the top leaders frequently emphasize that coercive methods, such as those recommended for dealing with CBOEs, should be resolutely avoided in cases of CAPs.[47] Regulations were passed to restrain officials from the use of violence in handling peaceful CAP events. In particular, authorities emphasized the principle of "three cautions" – caution about employing police forces, caution about taking coercive measures, and caution about using weapons (*shenyong jingli, shenyong qiangzhi cuoshi, shenyong wuqi jingxie*).[48] The three-cautions principle was later reiterated in a series of policies and regulations.[49] In 2008, the Minister of Public Security, Meng Jianzhu, highlighted that the main tasks of police at the scene of a mass incident were to maintain order, prevent extreme action, keep the situation under control, and not to escalate the confrontation; he stressed that incidents leading to death and injury should be firmly avoided and prevented (Meng 2008).

No doubt, it was concern for regime stability that made the leadership veer toward toleration in the face of contention. Both Jiang Zemin and Hu Jintao

---

[44] "Speech at the Central Political and Legal Work Conference." Jiang Zemin. *Qstheory.cn*. December 24, 1993. www.qstheory.cn/books/2016-08/31/c_1119486337_10.htm. "Speech at the 20th Central Conference on Public Security." Hu Jintao. *People.cn*. November 2003. http://dangshi.people.com.cn/n/2012/0919/c349398-19052942-2.html. "Speech at the Second Plenary Meeting of the Third Plenum of the 16th CCP Central Committee." Hu Jintao. *People. cn*. October 2003. http://dangshi.people.com.cn/n/2012/0919/c349398-19052942-1.html.

[45] "Speech at the State Council's Fourth Conference on a Clean Government." Wen Jiabao. February 24, 2006. www.gov.cn/ldhd/2006-02/27/content_212769.htm.

[46] In 2003, Zhou argued that more than 80 percent of all petitions reflect problems created during the reform and development process, more than 80 percent of them are reasonable and should be resolved by the government, and more than 80 percent can be resolved by the government if an efforts is made. *China Comment*. November 2003. www.southcn.com/news/china/zgkx/200311200686.htm.

[47] "Speech at the Second Plenum of the 14th CCP Central Committee." Jiang Zemin. *People.cn*. March 7, 1993. http://cpc.people.com.cn/GB/64184/64186/66685/4494247.html.

[48] *Regulations on How Public Security Agencies Should Handle Mass Incidents*, issued by the Ministry of Public Security in 2000 and revised in 2008. "How to Enforce the Principle of Cautions to Use Force in Practice?" *Guangzhou Daily*. November 5, 2008. http://opinion.people.com.cn/GB/8285232.html

[49] See, for example, the *Recommendations about Actively Preempting and Appropriately Handling Mass Incidents*, issued in 2004 by the General Office of the CCP Central Committee and the State Council.

spoke straightforwardly that the inappropriate handling of CAP incidents would undermine social stability, harmony, and the undertakings of the Party and the state.[50]

On the flip side, in the wake of Tiananmen, the state has stepped up efforts to strengthen its capacity for social control. One of the key lessons learned by authorities from the mishandling of the 1989 uprising was the security forces' inability to timely and effectively contain it. In the post-Tiananmen era, People's Armed Police (PAP) – the paramilitary police force and one of China's most important internal security organs – has been upgraded to improve its capacity and effectiveness in responding to social disorder, especially to large-scale political unrest (Fisher 2010; Tanner 2002a).[51] In addition, the regime has increased funding and personnel for other operations related to managing social protest (Wang and Minzner 2015; Xie 2012), exerted more pressure on local authorities to preserve stability through the cadre evaluation system (X. Chen 2012; Edin 2003; Y. Li 2013), and raised the bureaucratic rank of police chiefs (Y. Wang 2014; Wang and Minzner 2015). Furthermore, the government has stressed the imperative of *preventing* public discontent and mass incidents and has endeavored to develop less overt, low-violence means to keep a lid on civil unrest (Guo 2012; Tanner 2004; Yan 2016). One measure in this regard is to advance the state intelligence activities to oversee the population and monitor political dissidents and other anti-government sentiments, both in the physical and virtual world (Guo 2012; Xie 2012). Not only are extensive security bureaucracies established, but hundreds of thousands of ordinary citizens, including taxi drivers, sanitation workers, parking-lot attendants, and street peddlers, are recruited as "security volunteers," or "security inform-ants," to report on "suspicious people or activity" (Youwei 2015). The state's improved capacity for maintaining order and control, in turn, paves the way for the development of informal rules such as "diplomacy first."

Protesters' Self-censorship

The state's dual strategies to stay in power – granting tacit tolerance and enhancing coercive capability – encourage self-discipline among aggrieved citizens in their claims, actions, and in the forms of organization they follow.

---

[50] "Speech at the Second Plenum of the 14th CCP Central Committee." Jiang Zemin. *People.cn.* March 7, 1993. http://cpc.people.com.cn/GB/64184/64186/66685/4494247.html. "Speech at the 23rd Collective Study of the Politburo of CCP." Hu Jintao. *Xinhuanet.* September 29, 2010. http://cpc.people.com.cn/GB/64093/64094/12859820.html.
  "Correctly Handle Contradictions among the People in the New Era." Hu Jintao. *The Publicist.* September 29, 2010. www.71.cn/2013/0815/728034.shtml.
[51] The PAP has received sizable increases in funding from the government, has been equipped with advanced weaponry, and its commander and political commissar have been made members of the Central Committee (Guo 2012).

Claims

In a great many cases, protesters make an effort to reassure officials that they are not foes of the state. Chapter 2 shows that the vast majority of protests eschewed raising a radical political agenda (see Figure 2.2). In all three cases discussed here, protesters focused on economic and localized issues and did not target Party leadership. Both protesters and authorities understood this. To gain authorities' trust, protesters overtly expressed their respect and loyalty to the state. In their petition letters to the Mayor, Shining Hospital protesters paid him compliments; in their demonstrations, each participant held a small national flag in an effort to counter anti-state charges (see Figure 3.1). Hill Factory workers took it even further; their representative knelt down in front of Fan, the head of Hill Factory's parent corporation, in their first meeting.

To legitimize their claims, many protests draw upon official rhetoric, ideology, or policies, acting as rightful resisters or making moral economy claims (O'Brien and Li 2006; Perry 2008). Relying on the provincial government's policy, Shining Hospital protesters framed their objection in a way that their protest would facilitate the city government's implementation of the higher-level government's policies. They displayed banners and chanted slogans such as "Strongly Demanding Implementing the No. 19 Provincial Document"[52] in demonstration (Y. Li 2013). Likewise, Hill Factory workers presented their protest as a means of helping the state reduce the loss of state assets and exposing the corruption of factory cadres.[53]

Nonetheless, expressing loyalty is, in itself, not enough to forestall suppression. This is exemplified in the repression of the China Democracy Party (CDP),[54] an opposition party. CDP claimed to recognize the Communist Party as the ruling party in China's political reform and utilized the regime's language and proclamations to work toward its own goals, yet it was swiftly crushed by the state (Wright 2004). Therefore, in addition to framing strategies, other factors matter as well.

Actions

While at times they may push the envelope, protesters still typically strive to self-control their actions before going too far, especially when it comes to eschewing violence (see Figure 2.3). Take the hospital struggle as an example. At the beginning of the 2007 demonstration, a representative read articles from the *Regulations on Letters and Visits* to emphasize discipline and to pre-empt radical actions, and senior citizens were arranged in the front row so as to be

---

[52] The provincial government's No. 19 document gave guidance to lower-level governments on separating hospitals from SOEs. Interviewees 8, 9, 63, and 64. See also Zhi (2014).

[53] Interviewees 1, 2, and 3.

[54] The CDP is an overtly political organization, established in 1998. It aims at creating the first true opposition political party in China and calls for free and fair multi-party elections (Wright 2004).

the first to confront the police,[55] an anti-violence tactic that relied on the tradition of respecting the elderly. Additionally, to play it safe, resisters usually inform authorities of the planned collective actions beforehand. In both the hospital and factory cases, protesters had applied for permits for their public protests in advance, even though they did not anticipate official approval. For protesters, getting approval was less important than the act of informing authorities and, in this way, acting to reduce the possibility of confrontation. For instance, when a police captain rejected an application for demonstration by the hospital resisters but promised to report it to the city government leaders, the resisters approved of this action and urged him to report their case as an emergency (Zhi 2014). Furthermore, dissenters often claim that their decision to engage in boundary-pushing activities such as demonstrations was the only choice they felt they had. As a female protester grumbled at the 2011 hospital demonstration: "We have made so many visits [to the government], but you rejected [our demands]. Last time when we visited the Health Bureau, nobody received us. We have no other options. Who would like to stand here?!"[56]

Nonetheless, while dissenters are able to practice self-censorship most of the time, at any moment they may turn transgressive, which can become a nightmare for both officials and protesters.

Organization

Disgruntled citizens also self-limit the way in which they organize a struggle. The statistical analysis in Chapter 2 reveals that only a tiny portion of protest events involved formal organization (see Figure 2.4). None of the three cases recounted here had autonomous formal organization, although some informal organization was used to mobilize and coordinate collective actions. The extent of such informal organization differs among protests. The hospital and factory cases had identifiable leaders and activists who were active in both routine petitions and boundary-pushing actions. In the hospital demonstrations, Zhi's role as a leader was quite conspicuous. In 2011, it was Zhi who stood in the center and led the demonstrators in chanting the *Internationale*. He also directed the group to move from the city hall to the petition bureau and acted as the primary representative in bargaining with officials. As for the factory struggle, Luo, the primary protest leader, guided workers walking along the railway line in full view of the public. In the aftermath of the railway accident, she also played a leading role in calming the restive workers and negotiating with authorities.

The situation in the taxi case, however, differed sharply. Apart from the 2009 strike, taxi strikes also broke out in 2000 and in 2006 in D City, both stimulated by economic grievances. In 2000, strikers parked their cabs in front of the city hall and, upon official request, sent representatives to negotiate with

---

[55] Interviewees 11, 12, and 13.   [56] Interviewee 67.

officials. On the heels of the incident, the representatives were arrested. The strategy of punishing protest representatives while letting ordinary participants go strongly discourages activism and gives pause to those who might want to take the lead in collective action. Learning from previous experience, the 2009 strikers kept their vehicles at home, and no one showed up at the government office. Gao, a male driver in his early thirties, remarked on this in detail:

Honestly speaking, no one organized the [2009] strike ... If it was known that you or I incited the protest, things would get screwed up ... In the 2000 strike, six people, including cab drivers and the so-called "layabouts," were jailed for as long as half a year. After the 2006 strike, a driver was detained for three months. I actually know this guy ... He was not even an organizer but might have played a relatively active role in the strike and thus was treated as a fall guy. The government's purpose was to kill a chicken to scare the monkeys (*shaji gei hou kan*). Nobody will bother you if you just park your car at home during the strike. But it's prohibited to lead a demonstration in front of the city hall ... No one has the guts to admit to being an organizer ... because everyone is aware that this is illegal. For gatherings, you have to report to the government [to get its approval].[57]

Once the 2009 strike began, traffic management officials came down to ask drivers about their grievances, but nobody explained their position or lodged complaints to avoid "getting into trouble."[58] This further shows the drivers' wariness toward standing out and setting themselves up for being picked on by the government. Their concern was not unwarranted. Several strikers, who performed more actively than others, in fact, were arrested; Xu was singled out because he made a phone call to a local radio talk show that has a large audience of taxi drivers. During the call, Xu complained about the gas price hike and warned that if the government was not going to do anything about it, the drivers would take action. His threat came true – the strike started a few days later. Xu, accused of instigating and organizing the strike, was arrested under the allegation of "having disturbed social order" and was put into *criminal* detention. Under the same charge, Yong, a second driver, was also arrested but he was placed in *administrative* detention (a punishment less severe than criminal detention). Yong was charged with attempting to dissuade other drivers from working. Both drivers were released within 15 days, with a fine of 10,000 yuan ($1,600).

Xu thought it unfair that he was arrested and found it humiliating to have his head shaved when he was in jail, but he still felt fortunate to have survived police interrogations without conceding that he was an organizer. The police had threatened to use an electric prod on him and to confiscate his valuable taxi-operating permit if Xu persisted in denying his role in organizing the strike; the police never carried out the threat, though. "If I had admitted anything under pressure," Xu said mercifully, "there would have been no way that

---

[57] Interviewee 16. [58] Interviewee 28.

I would have been released in just a few days. Instead, I would have had to face a court trial. Who knows how many years I would be in prison then?!"[59] Here, Xu was vigilant about the harsh punishment to be meted out to a strike organizer.

If nobody dared take the lead, then how could a district-wide strike actually erupt? Gao reviewed the process of mobilization prior to the strike: "When drivers chatted with each other during their break, A asked B, 'Somebody said there will be a strike tomorrow. Have you heard about it?' B answered: 'No.' Later on, B asked C the same question; C then asked others. In this way, the idea spread. On the rumored strike day, when drivers found no taxis on the road, the strike was confirmed and other drivers would not go out to work."[60] A female driver in her late forties also acknowledged that there was no organizer in the 2009 strike, yet in her account, she suggested that there was coercion in the call for strike: "During our break, it was stated that on which date we *should* not come out to work. In 2009, half a month ahead of the strike, somebody came and *required* me to stop working [on a particular date]" (emphasis added).[61] This coercive call for a strike is clearly reflected in this account from another female driver: "There was no strict organization for the strike. It was rumored that there would be a strike the next day, but no one was certain about this. As a result, on the first morning of the strike, my husband [also a taxi driver] found no cabs running on the street. Then he did not dare to work either." What was he afraid of? The female driver explained: "In previous strikes, if you continued working while others were on strike, somebody would follow you on the road and then smash your car, or they would remember your license plate number and get you into trouble afterwards. It has happened in the past."[62] In this sense, despite the absence of clear leadership, the fear of being treated as a "traitor" and suffering retaliation by striking drivers compelled drivers district-wide to join the strike.

To sum up, despite differences, case studies confirm that the form of organization is an important factor that affects punishment. This helps explain why the vast majority of protests in China do not involve – or admit to involve – formal organization (see Figure 2.4).

Flexibility, Ambivalence, and Gaps in Formal Rules

A third factor that plays into the formation of accommodating informal norms lies in the flexibility, discrepancies, and fissures within official institutions. Since formal rules set general parameters for behavior and cannot cover all contingencies, this encourages actors to develop informal norms to address problems that are not anticipated by formal institutions (Helmke and Levitsky 2004). Thus, the flexibility inherent in laws and policies allows leeway in enacting

[59] Interviewee 24.   [60] Ibid.   [61] Interviewee 28.   [62] Interviewee 33.

them. For instance, although the LAPD and the *Criminal Law* specify a series of articles to constrain collective actions and regulate ways to punish actions that *severely* disturb the social order,[63] the definition of "severely" remains nebulous. In addition, for a country in the midst of rapid change, local officials are often hazy about precisely which claims are politically acceptable; what is institutionalized and what is not is often hotly contested among authorities (O'Brien 2003; O'Brien and Li 2006: 52–62). In this sense, it is exactly the ambiguities in laws and regulations that permit the existence of the informal norms.

Formal institutions sometimes contradict each other, which facilitates the emergence of informal rules. The LAPD, which prescribes penalties on illegal collective action, is at odds with a vital official document on handling mass incidents, which requires that mass incidents be dealt with by using education, negotiation, and conciliation in order to prevent them from expanding and intensifying; force, according to this official document, should be used with caution.[64] Thus, authorities, instead of punishing these illicit actions according to LAPD, sometimes bypass the law and bend the rules for resisters. Interestingly enough, the central government's directives regarding protest policing are also internally contradictory. As previously mentioned, police are instructed to follow the principle of "three cautions" when it comes to using force. On the other hand, police are ordered to overcome their "three fears": fear that they will be held responsible for botched operations, fear that the masses will surround and attack them, and fear that the police will suffer either official punishment or popular revenge (Tanner 2004: 148), all of which seem to encourage the use of force in a between-the-lines kind of way. Hence, officials' ambivalent approaches to coping with protests lead to confusion among local authorities, providing opportunities for accommodating informal norms of contention to grow.

Vacuums in laws also matter in the generation of these informal norms. Legal regulations governing strikes are a prime example. Currently, Chinese laws do not acknowledge the right to strike,[65] although neither do they forbid strikes. The 2001 *Trade Union Law* states that, in the event of work stoppage or slow-down, trade unions should, on behalf of the workers, consult with the employers.[66] There is, however, no definitive remark on the legality of labor

---

[63] For instance, according to Item 296 of LAPD, if protest organizers or activists refuse to follow a dispersal order or *severely* disrupt social order, they can suffer more serious punishment in terms of the *Criminal Law*.

[64] *Recommendations about Actively Preempting and Appropriately Handling Mass Incidents.*

[65] China's Constitution of 1975 and 1978 granted workers a right to strike, but the right was removed in the 1982 Constitution.

[66] Article 27 of the *Trade Union Law*, enacted in 1992 and revised in 2001 (Legislative Affairs Commission of the Standing Committee of the National People's Congress, www.china.org.cn/english/DAT/214784.htm).

strikes, so it is not entirely clear to citizens *or* officials whether strikes are legal in China.[67] The vague legal constraint thus provides local officials and workers with some space to maneuver in time of strikes.

Local Practices

Sandwiched between the top leaders' directives and self-censored protesters, promoted by the ambiguities in formal institutions, local officials sometimes choose to bend the law, which, in turn, can lead to the establishment of accommodating informal norms (see Figure 1.1). Local leaders who disobey the political elite's directives, misuse weaponry in handling mass incidents, or neglect disputes and lead to conflict exacerbation would suffer penalties from demerits to demotion to dismissal.[68] In a series of large-scale mass incidents in 2008 and 2009,[69] the abuse of power by local officials in response to protest events was found to have intensified tension and fueled popular indignation. As a result, leading officials of the involved jurisdictions were dismissed.[70] In 2010, due to land disputes, approximately 1,000 villagers knelt for half an hour in front of the City Hall of Zhuanghe (northeastern China), demanding to see the Mayor, who never showed up throughout the event; the story went viral on the Internet and provoked extensive criticism of the government. The higher-level government then stepped in and ordered the Mayor of Zhuanghe City to resign.[71] Learning lessons from incidents like these and to preserve social stability in their jurisdiction, local bureaucrats are wary of taking a hard line on or turning a cold shoulder to social protests.

---

[67] In this context, some government officials and labor experts advocate legislating the rights for economic strikes (Chang 2010; Friedman 2013).

[68] *Provisional Regulations about Disciplining Petition Handling.* National Petition Bureau. July 24, 2008. www.gjxfj.gov.cn/2008-07/03/c_133457359.htm.
    Provisional Regulations about Punishment for the Breach of Discipline in Petition Work. National Petition Bureau. July 24, 2008. www.gjxfj.gov.cn/xxgk/2010-02/24/c_13186207.htm.
    Provisional Regulations about Enhancing Accountability of Party and Administrative Leaders and Cadres. People's Daily. July 13, 2009. http://politics.people.com.cn/GB/101380/9640147.html.

[69] In each of these incidents, thousands of people stormed into government buildings, clashed with law enforcement, and smashed police vehicles. These high-profile riots took place in different parts of China, including Weng'an in Guizhou Province (Southwest China), Menglian in Yunnan Province (Southwest China), and Shishou in Hubei Province (Central China).

[70] "The Party Secretary and the Head of Weng'an County Removed from Office." *People's Daily.* July 5, 2008. http://cpc.people.com.cn/GB/64093/64096/7473464.html.
    "Officials 'Firefighting' Major Incidents Got Promotions, and Their Experiences of Safeguarding Stability Were Appreciated." *Chongqing Morning Post.* October 13, 2012. http://news.qq.com/a/20121013/000340.htm.

[71] "One-Thousand People Kneel Down; Mayor of Zhuanghe City Forced to Resign." April 25, 2010. *Xinhuanet.* http://news.qq.com/a/20100425/000119.htm.

In particular, when officials are embedded in local communities, they tend to identify protesters as the "people" – not the foes of the government – and to show leniency. If bureaucrats personally know protesters as family members, neighbors, or colleagues, they will be less likely to take a tough stance. As described in the hospital struggle, tension was heightened in its first demonstration when law enforcement attempted to prevent protesters from marching toward the city hall; Guang, whose husband was a retired police officer, helped ameliorate the situation because policemen at the scene were her husband's former colleagues. What's more, if bureaucrats live in the same community with dissidents, they may share many of the latter's complaints. Officials, whose living expenses were increased owing to the skyrocketing gas prices in the district, revealed sympathy toward the taxi strikers and admitted that the cab drivers' profits were dwindling sharply as a result of the surging prices.[72]

In reality, whether officials follow accommodating informal norms in their day-to-day work is often determined by their evaluation of the nature of the protest. This assessment goes beyond the dichotomy of "legal" and "illegal," with "reasonable" or CAPs as a critical third standard. After a protest takes place, more often than not, authorities simply consider it *inappropriate* (*bu heshi*) but do not attempt to quell it at first, a reflection of the informal norm of "diplomacy first."

In D City, officials used terms referring to the issues concerning the common people (*laobaixing*), the masses (*qunzhong*), or petitioners to define a CAP incident.[73] For instance, "Issues regarding the *common people* should not be escalated ... My feeling is that when handling matters about the *people* and the *masses*, our government in general follows this principle: better to be relaxed than to block; better to be lenient than harsh" (emphasis added).[74] In line with the political elite, D City officials blame the large number of petitions on officials' corruption, abuse of power, and negligence toward the people's interests as well as unfair court verdicts.[75] "Channels for the people to express claims are very limited," one D City official boldly complained. "In fact, the state does not at all encourage collective petitions ... [But] if you do not block the gate of the government [to attract attention], how can you get your problems resolved?"[76] Likewise, a PSB captain in D City recognized that most claims by the common people had *rightful* reasons and only very few were unreasonable.[77] In his mind, CBOEs, including attacking people, damaging property, and violent riots, were much more common in Xinjiang or Tibet than D City.

In terms of dealing with CAPs, officials of D City tend to take a softer tone. "Very few people receive sentences or are detained," a DCPB official told me,

---

[72] Interviewees 4 and 5.　　[73] Interviewees 17, 29, and 30.　　[74] Interviewee 17.
[75] Interviewees 17 and 22.　　[76] Interviewee 22.　　[77] Interviewee 19.

"Normally, we just do mass work (*zuo qunzhong gongzuo*)."[78] "Doing mass work," a principal advocated by Mao since the 1930s and reemphasized by Hu Jintao in the 2000s, has various meanings, the most common practice being to use laws, regulations, and policies to deny protesters' demands. In some circumstances, officials are also willing to make concessions and bargain with protesters, particularly when it comes to economic interests. A popular saying circulates among officials: "Using people's currency to resolve people's conflicts" (*Renminbi jiejue renmin neibu maodun*).[79] Lately, it has become fashionable for local governments to set up a system called "Petition Relief Fund" or "Stability Maintenance Fund" to pay off veteran petitioners (among others) for conflict resolution, focusing primarily on conflicts labeled as "unlawful but reasonable" (*fadu zhiwai, qingli zhizhong*).[80]

Although resisters in all three cases cited here performed illegal activities in one way or another, local officials did not deny the legitimacy of their collective actions. DCPB officials explained the causes of the Shining Hospital protest in a similar way to protesters: economic disputes resulting from the SOE reform.[81] The deputy secretary-general of the municipal government criticized the hospital demonstration as improper but not unlawful (Zhi 2014), the latter of which would foreshadow harsh treatment. DCFTU officials admitted that it was quite normal and understandable for Hill Factory workers to demand more severance pay, although whether or not the government would agree was another issue.[82] A road blockade by the workers was considered "inappropriate, though not illegal."[83] Similarly, officials held the public hearing to address taxi strikers' grievances and raised the taxi fares afterwards, reflecting that the government recognized the strikers' demands as legitimate. Hence, admitting the legitimacy of these protests and showing mercy to self-censored protesters make accommodating informal norms possible and leave some room for civil disobedience.

LOCAL DISCRETION OVER INFORMAL TOLERANCE

Being unwritten codes, accommodating informal norms are not as clear-cut as formal rules and are subject to the discretion of local officials. To be clear, even

---

[78] Interviewee 7.

[79] This view is reflected in my fieldwork (e.g., in an interview with a petition office official – Interviewee 7), Lee and Zhang (2013), and news reports, see "Zhu Minguo: Some Leaders Believe in 'Using People's Currency to Resolve People's Conflicts'" (*Legal Daily*, September 12, 2009, http://news.ifeng.com/mainland/detail_2012_09/12/17541353_0.shtml) and "Overcoming Laziness in Governance by Using People's Currency to Resolve People's Conflicts" (*Xinhuanet*, June 19, 2006, http://news.sina.com.cn/o/2006-10-19/000010267838s.shtml).

[80] This new coping mechanism has been reported in multiple issues of *People's Petition* and remarked on by Benney (2016), Lee and Zhang (2013), Ma (2014), and Tsinghua University (2010).

[81] Interviewee 7.   [82] Interviewees 6 and 31.   [83] Interviewee 6.

though protesters and officials can have negotiation meetings, their relationship remains unequal. In effect, the authorities always have the last word in deciding whether or not to employ coercion. Aside from some well-marked no-go zones, the central government grants local officials discretion to judge if a boundary has been crossed, instead of enforcing consistent standards (Stern and O'Brien 2011). As a result, the same type of collective action may receive different treatments. For instance, several protesters had been jailed after blocking a road during a housing protest in D City. To justify the repression, a DCPB official explained, "Blocking the traffic is a *severe disruptive action*, whereas sit-ins in the petition office are generally not handled by law enforcement but dealt with through mass work" (emphasis added).[84] Although this official considered the road blockade to be blatant law violation, the Hill Factory workers were not punished for that.

"Skip-level" petitions – appeals to a higher-level authority than that specified by the state – are another example of local discretion. To some officials, even if petitioners bypass the city government and lodge complaints directly with the central government, the petitioners do not suffer punishment as long as they do not take extreme action.[85] Other officials, however, do not let things pass that easily. Two police officers specified penalties for petitioners who went over their heads: first, a warning; second, an administrative detention; finally, reeducation through labor.[86] Another interviewed official candidly admitted that, at politically sensitive moments, petitioners who went to Beijing would be taken back and detained in so-called "study classes" (*xuexi ban*), that is, an illegal detention facility, because "they violated security regulations."[87] When asked what petitioners would do in the study classes, the official answered ambiguously, "Study." He then introduced me to an old petitioner, who had the experience of being detained in the study classes. The petitioner told me that they did nothing but sit idly there.[88] His experience differed from those in other provinces who suffered torture in study classes.[89]

Officials' different attitudes in handling protest are also reflected in the taxi strike case. After the drivers were detained, the D City Traffic Bureau (DCTB) intended to teach them a bitter lesson in order to deter future strikes. As a major department in charge of the taxi industry, DCTB is responsible for forestalling the disruption created by a strike. An inability to do so can get the leaders of DCTB into trouble. For instance, their counterparts in Chongqing, a large southwestern city, received administrative warnings after a citywide taxi strike

---

[84] Interviewee 7.   [85] Interviewee 17.   [86] Interviewees 18 and 19.   [87] Interviewee 21.

[88] Interviewee 20.

[89] For instance, see "Jiangsu Xiangshui: Petitioners Put into Study Classes by Force" (*China Youth Daily*, March 30, 2009, http://fanfu.people.com.cn/GB/140194/9047275.html) and "Shanxi Chenggu: 'Law Training Classes' Jailing Petitioners, One Starved to Death" (*Jinan Daily*, July 15, 2011, http://news.sohu.com/20110715/n313466094.shtml).

in 2008.[90] With this in mind, DCTB officials paid a visit to the PSB, proposing to revoke the detained drivers' taxi-operating permits.[91] Such a permit at that time went for more than 500,000 yuan (around $80,000). Thus, confiscating it would deprive the drivers of a tremendous chunk of their property. Nonetheless, the PSB, with no intention of pushing the drivers up against the wall, declined the revocation proposal. Should the permit be rescinded, the drivers might take extreme action and cause an even bigger threat to social stability. As Xu, a detained driver, put it: "If I were deprived of hundreds of thousands of yuan, what would be the meaning of life? I would definitely risk my life to fight against them!"[92] Yong, a second detained driver, added, "Then [we would] have to steal and rob!"[93]

The inconsistency in officials' reactions to protests reflects the fuzziness of the boundaries of informal tolerance. This kind of uncertainty sometimes leads to self-discipline among protesters as repression hangs like the Sword of Damocles over their heads, whereas at other times it emboldens them to cross the line.

WHEN ACCOMMODATING INFORMAL NORMS BREAK DOWN

My discussion hitherto has depicted a contained picture of contentious politics: officials bypass formal rules, creating an extralegal space for protests, and resisters endeavor to self-control their claim-making activities. In fact, both protesters *and* the government may break the accommodating informal norms and veer towards transgression.

Protesters Deviating from Accommodating Informal Norms

The Hill Factory protest is a perfect example of a struggle in which protesters deviated from the informal norms. After multiple rounds of unsuccessful bargaining with representatives of the parent corporation, workers became frustrated and desperate, and began taking increasingly extreme actions to command authorities' attention. First, they blocked the roads in D City. Then they obstructed the roads in Beijing. And finally, in spring 2005, joined by workers from another state-owned factory, Hill Factory workers blocked the nearby railway, paralyzing a key route between Northeast China and Beijing for a couple of hours. This incident caused more than a billion yuan ($159 million) in damage and caused two casualties, as noted. Soon afterwards, families that had suffered losses received compensation, but no agreement was ever reached on the issue of severance pay. Workers then took further action; they contacted an American journalist to schedule an interview to publicly air their grievances. This action was provocative to the authorities,

---

[90] "Large-Scale Taxi Strike in Chongqing City; Bo Xilai Holds Dialogue with Strikers." *People's Petition*. 2008, Vol. 298, No. 11: 18.
[91] Interviewee 24.   [92] Ibid.   [93] Interviewee 25.

since it would embarrass the Communist Party – a party which claimed to represent the working class – by revealing to the world its indifference to workers' well-being. Workers' plan was foiled when all six protest representatives were arrested on a criminal charge of "endangering public order"[94] right before their meeting with the journalist.

Did protest leaders understand the risk of turning towards transgression? There is no easy answer to this question. In regard to the railway incident, Dai – a Hill Factory doctor who was a friend of Luo, the primary protest leader – recounted that Luo did not explicitly direct workers to block the railway but she probably implied that this was what she was hoping by leading workers in a march alongside the railway under the guise of *walking (sanbu)* to Beijing.[95] At some point, they took a half-an-hour break right beside the tracks while awaiting an official response. Although it is unclear what Luo was thinking at that moment, having the break suggests that she was hesitant about appearing too defiant. However, eventually, in Dai's view, Luo seemed to believe that they could only achieve their goal by causing big disturbances (*ba shiqing naoda*), and she was determined to sacrifice herself for their goal. Dai referred to the traditional insurgent maxim to describe Luo's heroism: "One who does not fear death by one thousand cuts dares to pull the emperor from his horse" (*shede yishengua, ganba huangdi laxiama*).[96] In this way, although Luo was aware of the risk of turning transgressive by blocking the railroad, she was willing to take that risk.[97] On the other hand, Dai and two other interviewees admitted that when the workers were waiting beside the railroad tracks, it was difficult for Luo to control the crowd of thousands. Somebody, but not Luo, yelled "Go ahead and do it!" At this goading, the crowd bypassed the security forces and stormed the tracks.[98] Then, even if Luo was not prepared for escalating the conflict, somebody else could easily incite the huge crowd to transgression.

Why did protesters run the risk of taking extralegal actions? The straight answer is to pressure officials to attend to their grievances. The results of the demonstrations, the road blockades, and the strike in the three cases discussed here provide evidence that pushing the envelope can work, although it at times carries the risk of harmful consequences, as can be seen in the factory and taxi

---

[94] Interviewee 1.   [95] Interviewee 15.   [96] Ibid.

[97] In my fieldwork, I made several attempts to interview Luo, but workers I contacted declined to introduce me to Luo, saying that nobody in their community talked about the protest anymore, especially Luo herself. Dai explained that it was such a heartbreaking experience that after being in jail for three years and enduring all manner of hardships as a prisoner, Luo, once released, no longer mentioned anything related to the struggle. Luo had undertaken the protest at the behest of her fellow workers who trusted her. There was really nothing in it for her: she had already retired by the time of factory bankruptcy, so she did not benefit from the increase in severance pay, which was exclusively for incumbent employees. And her pension was not paid during her three-year imprisonment. Dai speculated that while Luo expressed no regret, she must feel somewhat regretful.

[98] Interviewee 1.

cases. Following the hospital demonstrations in 2007 and 2011, the government acted promptly to take care of demonstrators' demands. In the wake of
the factory workers' road and railway blockades, authorities began to take
workers' claims and opinions seriously. Finally, only after the taxi strike did
workers' complaints about the skyrocketing gas prices no longer fall to deaf
ears. Therefore, it is clear that pushing the limits to capture the authorities'
attention can be a weapon of the challengers, although it entails risks.

Officials Deviating from Accommodating Informal Norms

In the face of dissent, rather than bending the rules in favor of protesters,
authorities can mete out punishment through lawful or unlawful means. They
may accuse protesters of disturbing social order and take legal action against
them, as seen in the Hill Factory struggle and the taxi strike. What follows
shows that the government has also designed a variety of tactics, illegal or
extralegal, to curtail contention.

Faced with proliferating unrest, the central government has increasingly
emphasized that it is the local leaders' responsibility to reduce the occurrence
of collective action (X. Chen 2012; Edin 2003; Y. Li 2013; J. Wang 2015).
Social stability has emerged as a core element of cadre evaluations and is tied to
local leaders' salaries and career promotion prospects (Wang and Minzner
2015; Xie 2012).[99] Local governments have been scored and ranked according
to the numbers of petitions brought from their own jurisdictions to the central
or provincial governments. Localities with the most petitions would be ranked
at the bottom, receive warnings, or be evaluated as "unqualified," which might
impact local leaders' promotions or even lead to demotion.[100] In some cases,
local leaders were removed from office by virtue of their inappropriate way of
dealing with mass incidents (such as neglecting protesters) that tarnished the
Party's image or caused an escalation of conflicts, as previously mentioned. The
imperative to preserve stability (*weiwen*) sometimes pressures local authorities
to cave in to resisters' demands. In the case of Shining Hospital, whenever
protesters threatened to petition Beijing or organize a demonstration, officials
would make some compromise (Y. Li 2013). At other times, officials may resort
to unlawful methods to quash resistance. Under the umbrella of "stability
control," they keep petitioners under surveillance, employ "illegal security
guards" or thugs to intercept petitioners, put petitioners in illegal detention

---

[99] One key official document on this is the *Central Party Committee and State Council Recommendations about Further Strengthening Comprehensive Management of Public Security* (September 5, 2011, State Council, www.gov.cn/gongbao/content/2001/content_61190.htm).

[100] Data from internal documents of W District Petition Bureau in D City (e.g., *W District Party
Committee and Government Recommendations about Strengthening Disctrict-Wide Peititon
Work*) and various issues of *People's Petition* (e.g., No. 1 of 2011) and *Hebei Petition* (e.g.,
No. 11 of 2008). Also, see "Petition Becomes an Important Criterion in China's Cadre Evalua-
tion" (*Xinhuanet*, March 30, 2007, http://cpc.people.com.cn/GB/64093/64100/5545386.html).

facilities, bribe petition officials to eliminate petition records, enforce sanctions through "reeducation through labor,"[101] and justify punishment by resorting to conspiracy theories.

To prevent petitions to the central or provincial governments, local authorities dispatched cadres to keep veteran petitioners under 24/7 watch, especially at politically sensitive moments.[102] Sometimes local officials accompanied petitioners to tour to places that petitioners wanted to see – except petition offices.[103] If petitioners escaped the surveillance and set out to bring their petitions to Beijing or provincial capitals, officials would devote time and effort into taking them back.[104] The demand for intercepting petitions gave rise to private security companies that specialized in this type of action.[105] Paid for by local governments, these security companies would illegally detain petitioners and force them to return from Beijing under armed guard.[106] When petitioners were taken back, they were sometimes put in one of the extralegal detention centers,[107] such as the so-called "black jails,"[108] "study classes," or "training classes of petition regulations." Again, while some detainees might sit idle in a study class,

---

[101] See, for example, "Strategies to Deal with Petitions to Beijing" (Chen Ruhai, *People's Petition*, 2008, No. 6: 32) and "About the Predicament and Solutions on Issues of Abnormal Petitions" (Yuan Zhoubin, *People's Forum*, 2013, Vol. 11, http://star.news.sohu.com/20130424/n37386 0209.shtml).

[102] Data came from Interviewees 22 and 23, internal documents of W District Petition Bureau, and various issues of *People's Petition* and *Hebei Petition*.

[103] Interviewee 23.

[104] Internal documents of W District Petition Bureau; see also a series of articles that appeared in *People's Petition* (2011, Vol. 324, No. 1: 6, 11, 31, and 32), including "Speeches at the National Conference of Petition Bureau Directors (excerpt)" by Ma Kai (the Secretary General of the State Council) and Wang Xuejun (NPB Director), respectively, "Evaluation Prior to Action" by Dong Haitao (Director of Ji'nan City Petition Bureau), and "Using the Three-Color Early Warning System to Resolve Long-Pending Cases" by Shi Zengfu (Director of Hangzhou City Petition Bureau).

[105] "Deputy Director of the National Petition Bureau, Xu Ye'an, Commits Suicide in Office." *Youth.cn.* April 10, 2014. http://news.sohu.com/20140410/n398026407.shtml. "Intercepting Petitioners Produces 'Black Securities.'" *People's Daily.* February 7, 2013. http://opinion .people.com.cn/n/2013/0207/c1003-20455533.html. "Villagers in Anhui Detain Six 'Black Security Guards' Who Intercepted Petitioners." *Caixin.com.* December 6, 2012.
    http://china.caixin.com/2012-12-06/100469526.html. "The Tour of Intercepting Petitioners: Both 'Black Security Guards' and Petitioners Are Victims." *Southern Metropolis Daily.* December 14, 2012.
    http://news.sohu.com/20121214/n360398240.shtml.

[106] "Investigation of Intercepting Petitioners in Beijing by Anyuanding" *Southern Metropolis Daily.* September 24, 2012. http://nd.oeeee.com/comments/focus/201009/t20100925_1150785 .shtml.

[107] "Strengthen Five Mechanisms of Petition Work and Devote Every Effort to Preserve Social Stability." Wei Zengshun (The Secretary of Political and Legal Affairs Commission of Lulong County). *Hebei Petition.* 2008, Vol. 259, No. 11: 17.

[108] A notorious one is located in Majialou in Beijing. "National Petition Bureau: Petitioners Detained in Beijing Majialou 'Black Jail' Belonging to Abnormal Petitioners." *People.cn.* November 28, 2013. http://politics.people.com.cn/n/2013/1128/c1001-23683625.html.

others might suffer torture in black jails. If petitioners successfully made it to the NPB, local officials could bribe NPB officials to eliminate the petition records from their jurisdictions (Li, Liu, and O'Brien 2012). Deleting petition records was pervasive in the NPB, and a number of officials were accused or convicted of doing so. Among them, Xu Jie, a former deputy director of the NPB, who used to take charge of petition data, was found guilty of receiving more than 6,100,000 yuan ($968,254) in bribes.[109] In addition, authorities could sentence dissidents to "reeducation through labor," an arbitrary detention system and a kind of extrajudicial and administrative punishment allowing police to sentence people to as many as four years of forced labor without a trial. For the past decade, this system has served local authorities as a retaliation tool against long-time petitioners.[110] A cumulative total of four instances of "abnormal petitions"[111] could lead to a reeducation-through-labor penalty. Even a former judge suffered this punishment.[112] Thanks to strong opposition from society, the reeducation-through-labor system was abolished in 2013.

Last but not least, officials typically adopt conspiracy theories to mete out punishment: they blame the occurrence of protests on oppositional forces, those with "ulterior motives" (*bieyou yongxin*) or with the evil purpose of undermining the regime. A CAP incident can be utilized by hostile forces or anti-government forces who organize the masses to "make trouble" (*naoshi*), as a PSB captain said.[113] The Hill Factory struggle, for example, was considered

[109] "Deputy Director of the National Petition Bureau, Xu Jie, Takes Bribes of 6,100,000 Yuan and Receives a 13-Year Prison Sentence." *China News/Legal Evening News*. December 7, 2015. www.sd.chinanews.com/2/2015/1207/6847.html. It was reported that the price of record deletion ranged from 2,000 yuan ($317) to 5,000 yuan ($794) per record. For details, see "The Fall of Xu Jie: Uncover Collective Corruptions in the Petition System" (Liu Chengwei, *China Newsweek*, July 27, 2015, http://news.inewsweek.cn/detail-1957.html).
[110] See, for example, "Reeducation through Labor Has Become a Tool for Retaliating against Petitioners; Lawyers Consider It a Violation of the Constitution and Call for Adjustment" (August 20, 2012, www.china.com.cn/news/2012-08/20/content_26279769.htm), "A Couple from Hebei Put into the Reeducation-through-Labor System for 25 years of Petition" (Wang Heyan, *Caixin.com*, July 26, 2011, www.yzhbw.net/news/shownews-2_14621.html), "A Female Petitioner from Heilongjiang Was Kept in a Deserted Mortuary for Three Years after Being Released from Reeducation through Labor" (*China National Radio*, January 24, 2013, http://china.cnr.cn/yaowen/201301/t20130124_511846484.shtml). Nevertheless, none of the protesters in any of my cases were forced to be reeducated through labor.
[111] Abnormal petitions include a wide array of activities that violate the regulations as set down in *Petitions on Visits and Letters*. These range from visiting politically sensitive sites (such as the Tiananmen Square and foreign embassies) to engaging in disruptive actions (such as demonstrations and rallies).
[112] The judge became a petitioner after being removed from his position due to the local government's displeasure with his court decision. See "Fan Zhongxin: What Does a Judge Being Reeducated through Labor Suggest?" (Yang Qiubo, *Caixin.com*, December 6, 2012, http://opinion.caixin.com/2012-12-06/100469193.html).
[113] Interviewee 19.

contaminated by international and domestic oppositional forces – the US journalist and protest representatives. Once the government identifies a protest as a CAP that has been penetrated by hostile forces, it would then move to single-out the "ringleader" for punishment, leaving the majority of participants alone, who were termed as "the masses being unaware of the truth" (*buming zhenxiang de qunzhong*).[114] A police captain described the divide-and-control strategy in handling protests:

"We use division of labor to deal with collective petitions. We, the criminal investigation division, are mainly in charge of taking activists away from the protest spot. But our action should not be detected by the masses [to avoid trouble], for these are contradictions among the people (CAPs) not contradictions between ourselves and the enemy (CBOEs). After taking activists away, we investigate who the mastermind is. Once we have evidence, [the mastermind] could possibly be placed in either criminal detention or administrative detention in light of the law and regulations. At the same time, to prevent a worsening of the situation, other divisions were assigned to take charge of educating the masses and maintaining order at the scene."[115]

This sort of selective repression was aimed at "killing the chicken to scare the monkeys" or, in other words, to deter participants and demobilize activism. Nonetheless, the practice of imposing sanctions by blaming a handful of dissenters with ulterior motives has recently drawn criticism from official media and high-level officials who maintain that local officials are taking advantage of this excuse in order to hide their own mistakes and evade responsibility.[116] With contention rising rapidly in China, many top internal security specialists are now *de*emphasizing conspiracy theories (Tanner 2004).

Unlawful repression tends to escalate contradictions between citizens and the state.[117] If unchecked, it can chip away at regime legitimacy. As Scott (1985: 105) argues, the dirty work of power "if exposed, would contradict the pretensions of legitimate domination." Political elite's efforts to eliminate or limit these sorts of repression reveal their anxiety of the damaging impact of excessive coercion.[118]

---

[114] This principle has a legal basis. For instance, Article 29 of LAPD regulates that if collective action (such as occupying public places and blocking traffic) severely disturbs the public order and traffic, ringleaders should be punished according to the *Criminal Law*.

[115] Interviewee 7.

[116] "Reduce the Use of 'Not Knowing the Truth' in Dealing with Mass Incidents." *Xinhuanet.* July 29, 2009. http://view.qq.com/a/20090729/000028.htm. "Party Secretary of Guizhou Province Talks about Quelling the Weng'an Incident." *Beijing Times.* March 7, 2009. http://news.163.com/09/0307/04/53PBU3PI000136K8.html.

[117] "About the Predicament and Solutions on Issues of Abnormal Petitions." Yuan Zhoubin. *People's Forum.* 2013, Vol. 11. http://paper.people.com.cn/rmlt/html/2013-04/11/content_1234553.htm.

[118] To eliminate "illegal" repression like the interception of petitions, in 2013, the central government abolished the rule that entailed officials' performance of handling petitions in cadre evaluations. Yet to what extent the reform can decrease the dirty tricks used by local officials remains to be seen.

POLITICAL EFFECTS OF ACCOMMODATING INFORMAL NORMS

Thus far, we have seen that accommodating informal norms of contention rather than the inscribed regulations of formal institutions help define the actual space for protest. What influence, then, do these norms have on the regime? I argue that through functioning as a social safety valve, channeling street protests to the negotiation table, and promoting self-discipline among aggrieved citizens, accommodating informal norms have a containing effect on contention and keep the discontented engaged with officials in ways officials can control. And yet, I caution against exaggerating the positive effects of such informal norms on regime durability in the long term.

In the first place, that moment when people actually take to the streets and demonstrate is often the very moment that signals the peak of their discontent. Shining Hospital's two demonstrations were staged when protesters had made numerous petitions to the governments and become extremely frustrated with official unresponsiveness and procrastination. Similarly, in the wake of a negotiation breakdown, around 600 Hill Factory workers blocked a road in front of their parent corporation in Beijing, aimed at pushing Beijing municipal government to put pressure on the parent company to re-engage in dialogue.[119] Tough reactions at moments like this can easily exacerbate tension. Instead, applying accommodating informal norms that allow protesters to air discontent, express opinions, and vent frustration can act as a safety valve, permitting the letting off of steam and aiding in alleviating conflict before it gets out of control.

Furthermore, accommodating informal norms are critical to the functionality of formal institutions that are designed to manage contention and disputes. These informal norms help direct claim making into institutional channels. According to informal norm No. 3, officials often transform street protests into conversation in government offices and then require protesters to resolve their conflicts through legal or bureaucratic institutions. Adopting institutionalized forms to manage conflicts can gain the advantage of institutionalization of contention as seen in Western democracies, including controlling contention and reducing uncertainties in protest control.

Lastly, self-censorship is critical in the generation of accommodating informal norms; once in place, these norms can further reinforce self-discipline among resisters. A permissive space afforded by accommodating informal norms gives protesters hope of winning their claims by cooperating with officials instead of taking extreme action. Similar to activists in mature democracies, resisters tend to eschew activities that invite repression when meaningful alternatives seem available, and with this perception comes the willingness to work on controlling extremist elements within their ranks (Meyer and Tarrow 1998). Furthermore, the fuzzy boundaries of protest space and local officials' discretion in reacting to contention compel resisters to discipline themselves to

---

[119] Interviewee 1.

avoid the accusation of illegal protests. Repression constantly hangs like a shadow over protesters. This is especially true for protest leaders and activists who are usually the target of repression. That is why in the taxi strike nobody owned up to being an organizer. Absence of a clear leadership saved the detained drivers from harsher treatment but also made it easier for the government to break the strike. Once the local government made some concessions, the strike came to an end. The jailing of several strikers did not provoke other drivers to take further collective action. Thus, while the strike was disruptive and massive in scale, the fact that it lacked effective organization and solidarity rendered it frail to break and not quite so challenging to the regime.

By contrast, when protesters deviate from the accommodating informal norms, contention enters into uncharted territory, and it becomes more difficult for state authorities to take control. This is evident in Hill Factory struggle. When hundreds of desperate workers stopped self-disciplining themselves, it led to railway disruption and the loss of life and money. The railway blockade caused the conflict to escalate, and authorities needed to work much harder in order to bring the struggle back into control and restore stability in the local community. These efforts include thwarting workers' attempt to storm a local police station, dispatching officials to the workers' community to re-establish order, and caving in to workers' demands.

As noted previously, the arrest of worker representatives prior to their meeting with the US journalist provoked workers to besiege a local police station where they believed their representatives were being held. Workers were emotional, jostled the police, and even hurled plastic water bottles at the officers, but no more violent clashes broke out. Following the siege, some workers staged a sit-in outside the police station day and night for two weeks. In reaction to this intense situation, the municipal government dispatched scores of officials from multiple departments to Hill Factory,[120] where they stayed for two months. Divided into small working groups, the officials went door-to-door to visit workers' homes, framing their visits as apologies to workers and as listening to workers' opinions, demands, and questions about the factory bankruptcy and severance pay. Some workers denied entrance to the officials, although many others received them. During their visits, officials expressed sympathy toward the workers and openly laid the blame on a few cadres whose dereliction of duty, they said, had contributed to the intensification of conflict. Officials acknowledged that workers' economic demands were understandable, their accusations of cadre corruption not groundless, and all their actions – except blocking the railway tracks and contacting foreign media – acceptable.[121] In this sense, these visits were aimed at appeasing

---

[120] The departments include the municipal State-Owned Assets Supervision and Administrative Commission, Labor Bureau, PSB, and DCFTU. Among them, the DCFTU sent as many as 16 officials to the community.

[121] Interviewee 15.

workers and reiterating the limits of toleration. Meanwhile, authorities made concessions to pacify workers; the allegedly corrupt cadres were arrested and the parent corporation raised workers' severance pay by more than 60 percent (for ordinary workers, increasing from 1,200 yuan or $190 to 1,970 yuan or $313 per year employed). Later on, the six worker representatives were put into prison, with a maximum sentence of three years. Factory cadres were also sentenced to a maximum of five years behind bars. A review of the struggle reveals that when protesters stop conforming to accommodating informal norms, authorities need to devote more effort to regain control of the conflict and re-establish stability.

Finally, even accommodating informal norms have their own limitations when it comes to controlling contention and preserving stability. To date, they have been effective in appeasing protesters and absorbing contention. They allow more time for state procrastination, even though the settling of conflicts ultimately hinges on the state's capacity to distribute resources and to use coercion. In the long run, however, there is some doubt about whether or not these informal norms will contribute to containing protests. Especially within the informal protest space, when bargaining between protesters and officials depends heavily on a market-like exchange of compliance for benefits, the mode of domination can be precarious because it comes at the expense of the rule of law and of state authority and may backfire in times of fiscal crisis (Lee and Zhang 2013). When regimes encounter periods of weakness, dissidents can exploit these periods as opportunities for larger-scale mobilization, as was seen in the East Germany revolution (Francisco 1995). Additionally, state toleration and successful cases can spur and inspire more resistance. A possible scenario is that protest participants who feel empowered by their experience and become more likely to take part in other challenges or onlookers who are heartened by a successful struggle could take part in a future protest with similar claims (O'Brien and Li 2005 and 2006). Furthermore, notwithstanding protesters' self-control, they also continue testing the limits of state tolerance, and if a kind of boundary-pushing resistance is not punished, others will exploit that breach: "A small success is likely to encourage others to venture further, and the process can escalate rapidly" (Scott 1990: 196). In this scenario, the regime must either reassert its dominance through extreme repression or enter negotiations with society over more fundamental issues of political change (Tanner 2004: 151).

CONCLUSION

By examining real-life interactions among actors, this chapter sheds light on the role of accommodating informal norms in contentious politics. As we have seen, sandwiched between rulers' directives from the top and resisters' self-censorship from the bottom, faced with vague and sometimes self-contradictory formal institutions, local officials frequently relax law enforcement, leading to an extralegal space for protest. In particular, the likelihood of tacit tolerance increases when authorities are embedded in the local societies. Accommodating informal norms are common among regime-engaging protests, yet they can break down at times. When protesters continuously push the envelope, they may turn transgressive at some point. On the other hand, officials sometimes utilize legal or unlawful means to impose penalties. Yet, as long as both officials and protesters can return to dialogue, these protests are still regime-engaging. When both the state and protesters play by the informal rules and work on resolving conflict through dialogue not force, such kinds of interaction can prevent the contention from becoming a zero-sum contest and can contribute to regime resilience.

Through examining the dynamic interactions between authorities and protesters, case studies demonstrate a series of accommodating informal norms of contention, reflected in the underenforcement of laws. The informal norms revealed herein are not meant to be comprehensive, merely illustrative. My cases, by no means, represent all regime-engaging protests in China, yet they capture important characteristics of this type of protests in terms of claims, actions, and organization. It should be noted that the struggles in this chapter were allowed a considerable amount of leeway in terms of protest *actions* because their (economic) *claims* fell within the state-set boundaries. Informal *organization* can be tolerated at times, but protests tend to be presented as spontaneous, especially when borderline actions are taken. While the regression analysis in Chapter 2 does not reveal that organization has much of an effect on repression, the qualitative research in this chapter confirms the importance of organization in predicting official reaction. This is particularly evident in the taxi strike, in which strikers carefully avoided being identified as an organizer.

To be clear, in the factory case, both the state and the protesters saw the Hill Factory struggle not in isolation but rather as part of a larger category of labor unrest taking place in the context of SOE reforms. Local variations aside, the norms for such protests had been set in a broader context – neither the Hill Factory workers nor the local government had set the standards. Thus, local transgression and repression did not lead to the "regime-threatening" cycle because both protesters and authorities had the broader norms of engagement to return to. However, for these broader protest categories, even in the economic and environmental terrains, there could be national tipping points that lead authorities and protesters to enter a vicious cycle of transgression and repression.

The unwritten rules and extralegal space illustrated by these cases are not limited to popular resistance but can be observed in other realms of activism in China as well. During the reform era, social organizations, through various strategies, frequently evade government restrictions on the establishment of organizations, and some do not even bother to register at all, making them technically illegal (Saich 2000). That said, authorities normally choose to turn a blind eye, to overlook such extralegal behavior, and often even collaborate with unregistered groups on issues such as the provision of social services as long as the groups keep within certain limits, resulting in an enormous increase in the social gray area that is not legally sanctioned (Teets 2013; Weller 2012). Grassroots organizations, on the other hand, take on a self-limiting character, e.g., keeping their operations small and making no calls for political representation or democratic reform (Ho and Edmonds 2007; Spires 2011). The ambiguous gray zones also exist in areas such as legal advocacy and media reporting. Owing to unclear rules and the mixed signals sent by the central leadership, the boundary between acceptable and unacceptable behavior remains blurry, leaving room to maneuver (Stern and O'Brien 2011). As a result, uncertainty about the limits of the permissible encourages self-censorship among public professionals, including lawyers and journalists (Stern and Hassid 2012).

Scrutinizing accommodating informal norms of contention in no way overlooks the repressive side of authoritarian governance. Rather, it aims at extending our knowledge of the complexity of authoritarian politics by exploring how China is governed at moments of unrest. Local officials, pressured by imperatives to preserve social stability, sometimes tolerate illegal activities or even yield to protesters' demands, whereas at other times they employ dirty tricks or impose legal penalties on dissidents, especially on protest activists and leaders. These strategies reflect the Janus-faced character of the Chinese regime. Additionally, accommodating informal norms alone are not enough for reconciliation. To be effective, they need to be backed up by state capacity to make concessions and use repression. Nonetheless, such informal norms are vital in that they permit a space for airing grievances, for communication between protesters and authorities, and help keep aggrieved populations in line through the encouragement of self-censorship among resisters. Finally, it is important to understand that accommodating informal norms are not equally available or accessible to all citizens across the country, and this is the topic of the following chapter.

4

Unequal Application of Accommodating Informal Norms

Inequality in Protest Space

On June 4, 2007, on the eve of a 1,000-person demonstration, a mobilization meeting was held in an urban residential compound. A police officer showed up and took photos of the meeting. Police behavior agitated the attendants, who were largely composed of middle-class professionals. A few grabbed the policeman's camera and hit him; he then fled the scene. Surprisingly, the assaulted officer did not come back for revenge, and nobody was punished afterwards.

> An episode in the N City protest

On May 27, 2011, two protesters, including an old lady, were arrested. Out of rage, villagers beat up a police captain against whom they harbored a grudge. This incident sparked a bloody clash between law enforcement and aggrieved villagers. Thousands of police forces were at once dispatched to the spot. Riot police used batons to attack villagers. Villagers, unarmed, responded with punches and kicks. Around 100 of them were injured, and two were crippled. At midnight, police forced their way into protesters' houses and made dozens of arrests.

> An episode in the Banana Village protest ("May 27th incident")

The above two episodes illustrate a central theme of this chapter: unequal application of accommodating informal norms of contention. While in both episodes a police officer was attacked, the consequences of this action diverged significantly. The previous chapter has elaborated how accommodating informal norms play out in regime-engaging protests. Unlike Chapter 3, in which all cases took place in a single city, Chapter 4 treats *region* as an independent variable and explores its effect on the performance of accommodating informal norms. Despite the prevalence of accommodating informal norms in China, whether authorities are willing to bend the rules for resisters or to what extent they would like to do so is contingent upon context. In a decentralized system, even the same government policy or legal regulation may be enforced unevenly across regions, not to mention the unwritten codes. Furthermore, authorities may harshly punish lawbreakers in one group but show mercy to those in another. Such discrepancy is not unique to China. In the United States, for example, African Americans are nearly four times more likely to be arrested for marijuana possession than whites (American Civil Liberties Union 2013).

The statistical analysis in Chapter 2 reveals that factors including locations and social groups affect protest policing (Figures 2.5 and 2.6). This chapter will further illustrate how and why these factors matter. By and large, I find that the urban middle class can wring more lenient treatment from the state because, in comparison to rural peasants, they typically have more ready access to the media or more social connections that allow them to gain support of political figures; the media publicity and political elite's backing make local authorities more hesitant to take a hard line with resisters. Moreover, because police officers largely live outside of villages, they are less likely to identify themselves as rural residents and probably feel less empathy toward villagers than toward urbanites. That said, the demonstration of solidarity among villagers can still exert pressure on officials to follow accommodating informal norms. Furthermore, the local political environment affects the extent of the permitted space for dissent. In addition, for the same protest, authorities may abide by accommodating informal norms at one moment but not at another, depending on their interactions with resisters.

To demonstrate these variations and to hold other factors constant, this chapter centers on struggles against garbage incineration. Four of such environmental protests were chosen, including the two listed above. In all four cases, the basic claim was the same – environmental protection – but the protest trajectories diverged. Starting with a brief introduction to the four cases, this chapter will proceed to illustrate similarities and distinctions of accommodating informal norms applied or perceived by actors in different cases. Next, I will explore how the government's attitude toward a single protest can shift throughout the process. The following sections will look at "soft" forms of repression and analyze distinct repercussions on regime legitimacy with respect to the uneven practice of accommodating informal norms.

INTRODUCING FOUR CASES

In 2004, China surpassed the USA as the world's largest generator of municipal solid waste (World Bank 2005). Urban China is estimated to produce more than 190 million tons of waste in 2004, and the amount is projected to reach at least 480 million tons by 2030, according to the World Bank (2005). To cope with the rapidly rising mountains of trash, the government has decided to develop incineration into one of the main methods of waste management. In the early 2000s, less than 1 percent of garbage in China was incinerated

(World Bank 2005). The percentage jumped to 15–20 percent in 2011, and it was projected to rise to 40 percent by 2020.[1]

Incineration as a method of waste disposal is widely debated in the world. Incomplete burning in an incinerator may create highly toxic and persistent environmental pollutants, such as dioxins, which can cause reproductive and developmental problems, damage the immune system, and cause cancer.[2] In recent history, citizens in many places such as the USA and Taiwan have mobilized waves of environmental movements against incineration. By the same token, the construction of incineration plants in China has aroused a growing number of protests by local citizens and environmental activists as well. Since 2006, residents of at least 30 cities (which include rural territories) across the country have launched objections to incineration.[3] Among these protests, I have singled out four cases (see Table 4.1).

The PC Community, N City

The struggle in the PC Community of N City (N City protest hereafter)[4] was the first significant anti-incineration protest in China. N City is an affluent and large city, with a population of more than 10 million.[5] PC Community has 260,000 people and is composed of a number of residential compounds and high-tech industrial parks.[6] The story started in late 2006 when local residents first learned of the planned incineration plant. Concerned about the environmental and health hazard associated with incineration, the community residents initiated a four-year struggle, which ultimately pressured the government into canceling the project. The protest participants were largely comprised of well-educated middle-class professionals with stable incomes. Some were retired cadres from the central government, academic institutions, and state-owned

---

[1] "Report on Garbage Disposal Industry: Waste Incineration Is Facing Opportunities to Develop Rapidly." *Xinhuanet*. November 30, 2011. http://stock.jrj.com.cn/hotstock/2011/11/30041211 680046-4.shtml.

[2] "Dioxins and their Effects on Human Health." World Health Organization. June 2014. www .who.int/mediacentre/factsheets/fs225/en/.

[3] "Residents Oppose Building the Planned Project of Asia's Largest Incineration Plant in Beijing." China Central Television (the state television broadcaster). June 26, 2010. http://news.sohu.com/ 20100626/n273097403.shtml. "Waste Incineration Planned to Be Categorized as Low-Carbon Technology Is Questioned by 46 Environmental Organizations; the National Development and Reform Commission Responds to the Questions." *The Paper*. August 8, 2014. http://m.thepaper .cn/newsDetail_forward_1260648.

[4] Pseudonyms for names of places and people are used throughout.

[5] In 2012, the annual net income per capita of N City (36,469 yuan or $5,789) was much higher than the national average (24,565 yuan or $3,899). "Disposable Incomes per Capita of Residents of Cities and Towns." http://baike.baidu.com/view/2332455.htm.

[6] See "Oppose Building an Incineration Plant in PC Community," a 40,000-word petition letter written by PC Community residents. The letter was submitted to the central and city governments in March 2009.

TABLE 4.1 *Four anti-incineration protests*

Cases	Time	Protesters	Locations			Protest actions	Outcome
			Urban/ Rural	North/ South	Close to		
PC Community, N City	12/2006–7/2007; 10/2008–2/2011	Middle-class professionals	Urban	North	Beijing	Petitions, lawsuits & demonstration	Project canceled
MAC Community, S City	9/2009–7/2012	Middle-class professionals	Urban	South	Hong Kong	Petitions & demonstration	Project canceled
Apple Village	4/2009–present	Peasants	Rural	North	Beijing	Petitions & lawsuits	Project suspended
Banana Village	1/2011–present	Peasants	Rural	South	Shanghai	Petitions, sit-in & violent clash with police	Project suspended

enterprises, while others were lawyers, engineers, and entrepreneurs, among others. Galvanizing support from technical experts, the N City protest was characterized by presenting sound arguments against the incineration project. In the struggle, the PC Community residents filed lawsuits against the local government, organized a demonstration with about 1,000 people, paid visits to government offices, and so forth. Considered a successful model, the N City protest has inspired a series of later anti-incineration protests to follow suit.

The MAC Community, S City

The MAC Community of S City (S City protest hereafter) is another high-profile case. A prosperous city,[7] S City has over 10 million people, and the MAC Community has 300,000 residents.[8] With 200 journalists residing in the community, its incineration project and protest received extensive media coverage. The online forum of MAC Community residents played an essential role in mobilization and was a hub of information flow, witnessing more than 1,900 new posts in just one day at the peak of the struggle.[9] In the physical world, besides collecting signatures and petitioning the government, resisters also orchestrated a demonstration joined by 1,000 residents. By and large, the protesters consisted of middle-class professionals, including entrepreneurs, retired cadres, civil servants, journalists, and other white-collar workers.[10] Villagers belonging to the community were also mobilized, but they comprised only a minority of protesters and were largely followers of the professionals. Unless otherwise noted, protesters from the MAC Community will simply be referred to as middle-class professionals. After three years of resistance, the government revoked the project in the end.

Apple Village

Winning lawsuits against the government is exceedingly difficult in China, yet Apple Villagers accomplished just that. Apple Village is a typical northern village in China, neither rich nor poor.[11] With a population close to 2,000,

---

[7] In 2012, the annual net income per capita of S City (over 38,000 yuan or $6,032) was much higher than the national average (24,565 yuan or $3,899). "Disposable Incomes per Capita of Residents of Cities and Towns." http://baike.baidu.com/view/2332455.htm.

[8] "MAC Community Will Build an Incineration Plant, and 300,000 Homeowners Are Worried about Its Health Risks." *New Express Daily*. September 24, 2009. http://gz.house.163.com/09/0924/08/5JVBCIFH00873C6D.html.

[9] "Homeowners of MAC Community Take Rational Actions to Protect Homes." *Southern People Weekly*. January 1, 2010. http://news.sina.com.cn/c/sd/2010-01-01/214819383652_2.shtml.

[10] "MAC Community Residents: We Don't Want to Be Represented." *Southern Metropolis Weekly*. December 31, 2009. www.wenku1.com/news/FEC378F5CEE4805E.html.

[11] In 2012, the annual net income per capita of the county to which Apple Village belongs (8,691 yuan or $1,380; China County Statistics) was slightly higher than the national rural average

the village is located in D City, the same city mentioned in Chapter 3. Like other Chinese municipalities, D City encompasses both rural and urban areas. The city has seven county-level units: three urban districts and four rural counties, and Apple Village belongs to one of the rural counties. When the construction of an incineration plant initiated in spring 2009, the villagers did not immediately consider litigation, starting instead with petitions. These efforts paid off and, in the fall, officials called a halt to the construction. But the good news did not last long. The project resumed nine months later, and this time it seemed unstoppable. Left with no alternative, with the help of the same lawyer who served the N City case, the peasants filed lawsuits against the government. Villagers found fatal defects in the project's environmental impact assessment report – for instance, the name of a murder suspect who had fled the village eight years before appeared in the survey – [12] so they concluded that the survey attached to the report was forged. As a result, the provincial environmental protection department withdrew its permit for the incineration project. Put differently, the peasants won the lawsuit, which was hailed as one of the first successful environmental lawsuits filed by peasants against the government. Since then, the project has remained suspended (see Figure 4.1).

Banana Village

Based on one lie after another, an incineration plant was built in Banana Village (see Figure 4.2). A prosperous village proximate to Shanghai, Banana Village had a population of over 10,000 people, including migrant workers employed in the village factories.[13] With more than 100 industrial enterprises, the village's income per capita is far higher than the national rural average.[14] In January 2011, the plant gave off a nauseating smell during its trial operation. Until that moment, the villagers found out that the construction in the village was not a power plant but an incineration plant, and they then rose up to fight against the project. Villagers' frequent collective petitions (sometimes comprised of more than 300 people) pressed officials to promise to stop the incineration operation, but the project continued covertly until challengers staged a sit-in, blocking entrance to the plant for two weeks. While the local government allowed a prominent *anti*-incineration expert to give a lecture in the village, it

(7,917 yuan or $1,257). "The National Annual Rural Net Income per Capita in 2012 Is 7,917 yuan, Increasing by 10.7 percent." *Ecns.cn*. January 18, 2013. www.chinanews.com/cj/2013/01-18/4499857.shtml.

[12] Interviewees 49 and 50.

[13] Data is from the fieldwork collection. "An Overview of Banana Village."

[14] In 2007, its annual net income per capita (14,000 yuan or $2,222) was far above the national rural average (4,140 yuan or $657). "The Annual Rural Net Income per Capita in 2007 Is 4,140 yuan, Increased by 9.5 percent." *Ecns.cn*. January 31, 2008.
    www.chinanews.com/cj/hgjj/news/2008/01-31/1151914.shtml.

FIGURE 4.1 The suspended incineration project in Apple Village
(Author's photograph.)

FIGURE 4.2 The incineration plant in Banana Village
(Left: author's photograph; Right: courtesy of a protest activist.)

also invited *pro*-incineration experts to evaluate the incineration project. When
the experts gave it a pass,[15] the municipal government firmly announced that

---

[15] According to the experts, the incineration plant could comply with national standards after
improving its equipment. As far as environmental activists were concerned, because these pro-
incineration experts (some working on developing incineration technology) could often personally benefit from developing garbage incineration, they were not about to provide impartial
evaluations. Environmental activists also suspected that the experts must have received money
from the local government. According to an anti-incineration expert, it was routine for experts to
be paid by those who invited them to give their opinions and, therefore, were likely to present an
evaluation in their sponsors' favor. If they did not react in this way, they risked future invitations, the loss of a source of extra income (Interviewee 40).

the project would resume,[16] foreshadowing the May 27th repression. Distinct from the other three cases in which the incineration project stalled out in the site selection phase or remained under construction, the incinerator in Banana Village was available for operation. Therefore, the cost of removing the plant would be huge.[17] This explains, in part, the state's move toward repression in the face of persistent objection. That being said, after the May 27th incident, the project came to a standstill and stood idle as of fall 2016.

All protests in this chapter achieved varying degrees of success (although some at a high cost), but there have been cases of failed anti-incineration protests in other communities around China. These four cases were selected because they illustrate variations in the trajectories of protests. The chapter does not claim that they are representative of all anti-incineration protests or even of all kinds of regime-engaging protests across China. Neither does it argue that these cases are typical of rural/urban or north/south cases. Rather, they should be considered simply as illustrative of how accommodating informal norms differ across regions, social groups, and time.

CLAIMS

Since protest claims are a critical factor in prompting officials to bend the rules, resisters go to considerable lengths to make their demands acceptable to authorities. This section scrutinizes protesters' efforts to *desensitize* protest claims, that is, to clearly differentiate their specific, localized demands from those that question the authority of the government. Regional difference in this regard can be detected as well.

Desensitizing Resistance

To avoid repression, it is critical for protesters to desensitize their objection. In the anti-incineration cases, some activists emphasized, "Waste disposal is an issue of people's livelihood, not involving state security."[18] Others argued that, "Opposing incineration is not against the government but is a way to help the government improve decision-making that does not conform to public opinion."[19] The desensitizing strategy was also reflected in the careful selection of the date of the collective action. The choice of June 5 (World Environment Day)

---

[16] Interviewees 37 and 52.

[17] It was said that a total of one billion yuan ($1.59 billion) – half from the government and half from the incinerator owner, a large state-owned enterprise – was invested in the project. "Why Was an Incineration Plant, Representing a Hugh Investment, Lying Idle?" *Chinese Environmental News.* July 7, 2014. http://gx.people.com.cn/n/2014/0707/c347804-21597325-4.html.

[18] Interviewee 34.

[19] A petition letter written by N City protesters, "Oppose Building Incineration Plant in PC Community."

instead of June 4 (the anniversary of the crackdown of the 1989 Tiananmen movement) was strategic: an action on June 5 could be interpreted as targeting environmental protection,[20] whereas an action on June 4 would risk being perceived as having political intentions such as memorializing the 1989 movement, which is still taboo in China today. What's more, when words such as "yearning for justice and democracy" appeared in the community online forum, many residents advocated "avoiding the use of the word of 'democracy' to prevent the government from treating us as June 4th members which would distort our anti-incineration demand."[21]

Interestingly enough, the S City protesters even held an online rehearsal for their negotiations with officials, further illustrating their consciousness of the need to depoliticize their resistance. In the rehearsal, a resident, AB, acted as an official, while other residents bombarded her with questions and comments criticizing the incineration project. In the following dialogue, AB's answer reveals her understanding and expectation of authorities' tactics in coping with objections.

A RESIDENT: Please explain the foundation of the government legitimacy.
AB: This kind of question is my [official's] favorite. Once it was raised, I could define all of you [resident representatives] as a handful of people with ulterior motives, deluding the masses who were kept in the dark. The nature of your opposition would be changed, and all of your rational efforts would come to nothing. In this way, your representatives would be repressed, and the game would be over. How eagerly my counterparts in brother cities [officials of other cities] hope to see people like you [the questioner] appear! If you don't show up, they even arrange for people to join your group for the sole purpose of creating chaos and fishing in troubled waters (*hunshui moyu*).[22]

Highlighting the risk of raising the sort of question that contested the legitimacy of authorities, AB warned, "You should be wary, enforce self-discipline, and remain rational!! Be careful not to let this happen again." AB's words not only reveal the government's tricks to produce excuses for suppression but clearly explain the logic of the necessity to self-censor claims.

Regional Disparity

Despite eschewing radical goals, protesters across cases may put forth different levels of demands. When the local political climate is relatively more liberal, challengers may feel relatively freer to press for higher demands. In N City and

---

[20] Interviewee 35.
[21] Homeowners' online forum of MAC Community, posted by "Under yellow skinned fruit tree," November 21, 2009. www.rg-gd.net/forum.php?mod=viewthread&tid=177247.
[22] Homeowners' online forum of MAC Community, posted by "Representative of the opposite side 007," November 12, 2009. www.rg-gd.net/forum.php?mod=viewthread&tid=176042&extra=page%3D170&page=12.

the two villages, the protesters' goal was simply to remove the incineration project from their own communities, a typical "not in my back yard" (NIMBY) demand. A protest leader of N City even got upset when an official assumed they would present more demands as soon as the government compromised. By contrast, enjoying a more liberal environment, S City protesters objected to building incinerators *anywhere*, a kind of "not in anyone's backyard" (NIABY) claim. This type of demand places an even greater challenge to the government than NIMBY because it advocates a fundamental change in the waste disposal policies that favor incineration and instead emphasizes developing waste sorting and recycling to reduce the necessity of incineration. The S City government tolerated the claims and even made a gesture of accepting the protesters' suggestions of promoting waste recycling measures. When this struggle came to an end, the municipal government gave a protest activist the green light to the establishment of an environmental non-governmental organization (NGO), specializing in waste sorting and recycling.

In addition to the environmental demand, S City protesters also added another more controversial request: anti-corruption, which was intentionally avoided in other cases. The S City protesters charged that Ying, a deputy secretary-general of the city government, had a personal interest in promoting incineration because his brother and son both worked in the incineration industry. Although Ying dismissed the accusation as nonsense (*hushuo badao*), criticism and derision of Ying continued to flourish on the homeowners' online forum, and some protesters endeavored to find evidence of Ying's power abuse. In contrast, N City protesters deliberately stayed away from the anti-corruption issue. A leader attributed their success to keeping their attention exclusively on environmental protection. "You should not broaden the scope of a struggle; instead, you must be focused." He emphasized, "Don't hit out in all directions ... You cannot deal with so many things at all."[23] Neither did protesters in the rural cases target official corruption, although in my interviews, protesters in both villages complained about embezzlement and misconduct of local officials.

The more tolerant environment in S City is linked to social, geographical, and historical factors. As a protester explained,

Like in Hong Kong, we [S City citizens] have an awareness of service (*fuwu de yishi*). The quality of the service industry in S City, including in the grassroots government, is relatively higher. If you give kickbacks (*hongbao*), officials do not dare to accept them because if they did somebody would get them into trouble. They would be finished after media exposure. Neither the media nor citizens are afraid to expose the corruption. So the whole environment is fairly tolerant ... The forces of market, society, and the government sometimes parallel, and at other times the market force even exceeds the other forces ... In history, S City subscribed to the saying 'the mountains are high, and

---

[23] Interviewee 35.

the Emperor is far away' (*shangao huangdiyuan*). Additionally, S City was an important spot on the marine Silk Road, influenced by both the Western and traditional Chinese cultures.[24]

In this context, S City residents felt confident enough to put forward demands at a level that protesters in other cases might be wary of for fear of making enemies within the government and thereby hindering the redress of their grievances.

ACTIONS

To motivate authorities to show leniency, protesters also strive to distinguish their activities from clearly transgressive ones. Officials' reactions to the same sort of protest actions may vary in terms of region, social class, and time.

Giving Face to Authorities

In a prolonged struggle, frustration and anxiety can breed discontent, which can accumulate and even develop into hatred for officials. To keep the protest peaceful and boost morale, protest activists often need to go to considerable lengths to maintain patience and calmness among protest participants. A post in PC Community's online forum is revealing: "May I ask everyone to be patient please? We will continue to express our claims; meanwhile, we will have to wait according to government procedure. We should walk step by step and eat one bite after another. Believe in ourselves and in the government. Believe tomorrow is going to be better!!!"[25]

In addition, protesters highlighted the importance of giving face (*gei mianzi*) or showing respect to authorities. Protest leaders in N City frequently stressed that participants should not offend authorities at will, speak groundlessly, make trouble, or break the law.[26] As one leader put it:

Both sides [police and protesters] should give face to each other. I have been advocating that we should be considerate and avoid embarrassing them [the police]. Though we are not afraid of taking responsibility for conflicts, we should do things in a legal and legitimate manner. Otherwise, you would put police who have to handle this [protest] in a difficult position. When a conflict occurs, I think both sides should share the blame. Police brutality is one thing. [On the other hand,] The police have their own dignity. If you offend them, they will respond recklessly. They are the tools of law enforcement.[27]

Even the Banana Villagers were mindful of self-control and avoided transgression several months prior to the May 27th clash with authorities. This is evident

---

[24] Interviewee 42.
[25] PC Community's online forum, posted by "A live fish on Mount Everest." December 3, 2010. http://house.focus.cn/msgview/1396/202724868.html.
[26] Interviewee 47.   [27] Interviewee 35.

in remarks made by a female villager, whose brother-in-law was crippled by a police beating in the May 27th incident: "In fact, we had no intention to *revolt* (*zaofan*). We are mature enough to have some knowledge regarding this.[28] [To express our grievances] We could simply go to the village committee" (emphasis added).[29] By her account, the villagers clearly attempted to differentiate their struggle from a "revolt," a transgressive action.

Regional and Time Variations

The employment and perception of accommodating informal norms differ by region and social group. By and large, in urban areas, officials feel more compelled to play by the informal rules than in rural areas. Urban middle-class protesters often have more resources (such as media access and social capital) to draw on and thus have more space to act, whereas village protesters typically have fewer resources and less space. Law enforcement officers also tend to identify more with urbanites than villagers. Yet if aggrieved villagers are able to mobilize a large number of participants, it can create more space for resistance as well. Additionally, officials may follow accommodating informal norms at some moment but not another.

Spatial Variation

Accommodating informal norms are more common in urban areas, while, in rural areas, police tend to treat protesters more harshly. This pattern, found in the regression analysis in Chapter 2 (see Figure 2.6), can also be observed in my case studies. Law enforcement in S City took an approach similar to the "negotiated management" style of protest policing (McPhail, Schweingruber, and McCarthy 1998: 51–54) or the "soft" policing style in the Western world (Della Porta and Fillieule 2003), in which negotiations and protest rights prevail. When protesters rallied in front of the S City Hall, the police told them: "We are doing our job. You have your rights to make lawful claims; just be rational, and we will enforce laws impartially."[30] In this sense, the police recognized the rights of protesters and suggested that their aim in handling the protest was to maintain order. In N City, police officers even gave tips to protesters. An activist recollected, "When policemen came to our residential compound, we explained to them why we opposed incineration. We told them, 'You are victims as well!' Finally, the police officers [won over by us] told us in private that we should get more people involved [in order to be more effective]."[31]

The urban-rural disparity is most clearly demonstrated in the two episodes described at the outset of the chapter. Incidents of protesters assaulting police took place in both N City and Banana Village, but the outcomes differed

---

[28] Both the female villager and her brother-in-law were in their mid-thirties.   [29] Interviewee 41.
[30] Interviewee 43.   [31] Interviewee 36.

FIGURE 4.3 The N City protesters demonstrate at the SEPA[32]
(To protect privacy, faces and other identifying marks have been blurred.)

sharply: the former was ignored while the latter triggered a ruthless crackdown. Although the N City protest was mostly peaceful, protesters hit a police officer at the mobilization meeting for the next day's demonstration at the State Environmental Protection Administration (SEPA; see Figure 4.3).[33] Not being seriously injured, the officer "ran away with his tail between his legs (*jiazhe weiba paole*)."[34] Ironically, protesters met the same policeman again when they were escorted home on a bus after the SEPA demonstration. Recognizing him, many resisters criticized the residents for hurting the officer the day before. Interestingly, the officer responded "Never mind! Never mind!" In their conversation on the bus, police officers confided that, living and working in the same neighborhood as the demonstrators, they were not happy about the

[32] "Pictures: The Mass Movement against Building an Incineration Plant in the PC Community Reaches New Height." Homeowners' online forum. June 6, 2007.
   http://house.focus.cn/msgview/1396/85473593.html.
[33] In 2008, the SEPA was upgraded to ministry status as the Ministry of Environment Protection.
[34] Interviewee 36.

FIGURE 4.4 An anti-incineration poster made by Banana Villagers
(The poster, titled "XXX Incineration Plant Can Affect Places 15 Kilometers Away," illustrates
a chain of devastating consequences of the incineration plant, from environmental pollution
to local economy recession; the name of the incineration plant has been omitted for privacy.
Courtesy of Meng, a protest activist.)

incineration project either, but, wearing the police uniform as they did, they
dared not express opposition and could not afford to lose their jobs.[35]

By contrast, the police–resident relationship in Banana Village was much
more strained. The large-scale clash on May 27 was foreshadowed by a police–
villager confrontation two months earlier. On an early morning in late March,
three policemen – in plain clothes and driving an unmarked car – came to the
village. According to villagers, the police attempted to "kidnap" Meng, an
activist, for printing and disseminating posters and leaflets about the formid-
able effects of incineration (see Figure 4.4). Meng's cousin had been detained a
couple of days before for the same reason. This time, however, a crowd of
villagers encircled the police, stopped the arrest, and demanded to see an arrest
warrant. Even when the warrant was finally delivered several hours later,
villagers still did not let the police take Meng away, continuing instead to
surround the policemen until the evening. Ultimately, the arrest ended in
failure, which served to heighten tension between the authorities and the

---

[35] Ibid. It is worth mentioning that there was moment of confrontation between the demonstrators
and the police during the demonstration. Law enforcement had attempted to arrest a demon-
strator and had put him into the police vehicle. However, he was soon released at the demonstration site because other demonstrators refused to leave until he was freed.

villagers.[36] The tension came to a head on May 27 when villagers attacked a police captain, which triggered the massive crackdown. The beaten captain was, in fact, the one who had led the failed attempt to arrest Meng. It was said that the officer was taken to the hospital afterwards. Indeed, the hospitalized officer suffered a more serious injury than the assaulted policeman in the N City case. Yet, it was still striking that the law enforcement let the residents off in the urban case.

The application or perception of accommodating informal norms may vary across *cities* as well, depending on the local political contexts. For instance, Chinese laws restrict protesters from developing foreign contacts independently.[37] In the Hill Factory case analyzed in Chapter 3, one of the accusations against the arrested workers was their contact with foreign media. In the N City protest, resisters took this red line seriously. "What I said just now," said its leader in the field interview, "is to gain *outside* support. Note that it is not *foreign* support! You know we [protesters] are particularly clear about this, right? We do not dare to step over this red line even a little bit! We declined all [interview invitations from the] foreign media" (emphasis added).[38] Similarly, another leader of this protest expressed doubt that turning to overseas media would do any good whatsoever. "Some foreigners may have political purposes," he said. "We should not get involved in this."[39] What he meant was that the protesters should depoliticize their resistance and stay away from foreign reporters. By contrast, in a more permissive environment, such as found in S City, dissenters enjoyed greater room for action and felt relatively freer to accept overseas media interviews. Yet, they still understood that constraints existed and accordingly avoided media that "attempted to induce us to express discontent against the government." Moreover, the careful wording of protesters in the interviews done by foreign journalists reflects their self-control even in the more tolerant political environment of S City: "We are not against the government," they are quoted as saying, "but simply oppose garbage incineration."[40]

Reasons for Regional Disparity

Why do authorities tend to show a benevolent face to urban protesters? This is partly explained by the resources that are available to urbanites. S City protesters had considerable professional connections and support – especially among the media. With 200 media professionals literally residing in the MAC

---

[36] Interviewees 51, 58, 59, and 60.

[37] See the *Law on Assemblies, Processions, and Demonstrations* and *Regulations on How Public Security Agencies Should Handle Mass Incidents.*

[38] Interviewee 35.   [39] Interviewee 46.

[40] "Homeowners of the MAC Community Take Rational Actions to Protect Homes." *Southern People Weekly.* January 1, 2010. http://news.sina.com.cn/c/sd/2010-01-01/214819383652_2.shtml.

Community, the protest enjoyed the privilege of using media as a means of attracting public attention, influencing public opinion, and monitoring government actions. In my interviews, several activists expressed the opinion that the resistance was actually mobilized by the media.[41] It was the media that first learned of the incineration project and publicized the news. Massive reports laying out concerns about incineration's environmental consequences unnerved the local residents and stimulated the struggle. Except for a short period of silence because of official bans on media coverage, a number of newspapers, magazines, television programs, and mainstream websites – at both local and national levels in mainland China and Hong Kong – closely followed the protest campaign, the local government's reactions, and the incineration project. Further, S City residents also used their community online forum to help monitor police action. When activists were taken away to the police station, other residents would quickly post the news in cyberspace, and the media would follow up and report on it. After being released, the activist would write about the experience and post it on the online forum. In this way, the public as well as other residents could soon learn of police brutality, if any. Against this backdrop, authorities were wary of using force and were pressured to abide by accommodating informal norms.

Although it received less coverage than the S City case, the N City protest still attracted substantial media attention, through which later protests learned from its experience. In addition, taking full advantage of their social networks, N City resisters obtained a wide range of external support from a retired head of SEPA and members of the National Committee of Chinese People's Political Consultative Conference as well as environmental and technical experts. The support helped legitimize this grassroots objection, urged the local government to take dissenters' ideas more seriously, and protected them from harsh treatment. Furthermore, several of the protest leaders used to work in the central government agencies. Their familiarity with the structure and operation of government made it relatively easy for them to navigate the complex bureaucratic system and directly visit relevant government offices to express their opinions. Calling their actions "visiting" (*baifang*) rather than "petitioning" (*shangfang*) was strategic: "visiting" implied that protest leaders were the equals of the officials, with no need to make appointments or go through the petition system; they could simply "open the door and enter" the officials' offices (*tuimen jiujin*). Admittedly, they could not visit all government departments in this way; they could pay direct visits to the officials of the SEPA, for example, but not the municipal government, which was much more heavily guarded and less accessible.[42]

In contrast, because rural protesters usually lack these resources, police brutality is less publicized. Banana Villagers had little access to the media.

---

[41] Interviewees 34, 42, and 45.   [42] Interviewee 36.

Although they invited journalists to their village and posted their grievances on the Internet, no mainstream media reported the case owing to local government intervention. The Apple Village protest managed to receive some mainstream media coverage, but most reports came *after* the villagers had won the lawsuit against authorities and the number of reports was much fewer than those written about the two urban cases. Additionally, while both rural cases, like the urban cases, received help from environmental experts and NGOs, unlike the N City case, they lacked direct endorsement from people with political influence. Hence, the absence of the media spotlight and political allies meant that local authorities had fewer qualms about getting tough on resisters.

Identity politics matters as well in explaining the urban–rural disparity. Police in China are disproportionately located in the urban areas.[43] Until quite recently, police officers simply did not live in rural villages.[44] For this reason, officers are less willing to identify themselves as *villagers* than as *urbanites*. In particular, as mentioned earlier, if they live in the same communities as urban protesters, they may share the latter's concerns and feel sympathetic. This is exemplified in the N City case in which the police confessed to resisters their similar opposition.

Even so, villagers with fewer media resources, less social capital, and less police sympathy can still use another avenue to impel officials to follow accommodating informal norms: solidarity among protesters, especially, the sheer number of challengers. Although large protests usually pose a greater challenge to local stability than small ones, it is more costly and difficult to repress the large ones; thus, authorities may handle them with extra caution and sometimes bend the rules.[45] Banana Villagers tested the limits of toleration by staging a 10,000-people sit-in, which was considered as transgressive and taboo by Apple Villagers. On April 1, 2011, thousands of Banana Villagers blocked the gates of the incineration plant and built shacks so that they could stay there day and night (see Figure 4.5). The sit-in lasted for two weeks, bringing the plant operation to a complete halt. To end the conflict, district government officials came to the village on April 8 and held a meeting with the villagers. Around 200 villagers were permitted to attend the meeting held in the building of village committee, while thousands more waited outside. Approximately 300 police were called in to maintain order. The meeting did

---

[43] China's police/citizen ratio decreases dramatically from urban to rural areas (Tanner and Green 2007).

[44] Currently, the government is implementing the "one-village one-police" policy to strengthen policing capacity in the rural regions. *Reference News*. September 9, 2015. www.cankaoxiaoxi.com/china/20150909/932495.shtml.

[45] The statistical analysis in Chapter 2 reveals that although larger protests tend to attract police presence more than smaller protests, they do not necessarily increase the chances of a police coercive response (see regression results in Chapter 2—Tables A 2.5 and A 2.6): police may frequently show up to monitor and control large protests while remaining wary of employing coercion.

FIGURE 4.5 Banana Villagers sit-in in April
(Faces of demonstrators have been blurred to protect their identity. Courtesy of a protest activist.)

not go well. Villagers felt that the officials had no intention of listening to their objections, so they prevented them from leaving until they promised to cancel the project. Eventually, the officials compromised, and in the evening the leader of the district government announced through a loudspeaker that the plant would not resume its operation without the masses' agreement. On April 12, the district government issued a document formally suspending the incineration project. On April 15, villagers' shacks were dismantled and the two-week sit-in was over.

Both interfering with the operation of the incinerator and preventing district officials from leaving pushed the boundaries of tolerance, yet villagers were quick to point out that their actions were peaceful and that they did not damage the property of the plant. At their sit-in, they displayed Mao's picture as well as signatures of protesters under environmental protection slogans, in the hope of legitimizing their action and avoiding repression. At this point, the government had not yet resorted to coercion.

Compared with the boundary-pushing actions of the Banana Villagers, the Apple Village protest was much more restrained. Resisters cautioned against public demonstrations, owing largely to the much smaller number of resisters and the local political atmosphere. In fact, the Apple Villagers' largest collective action included no more than 60 people. Many villagers were reluctant to jump on board for fear of offending the village's strongman, who was in favor of the incineration project. Fewer participants gave authorities less incentive to adhere to accommodating informal norms, which translated to a more limited space for action for the protesters. When I asked the protest leaders whether they had ever gathered at the city government building, one promptly answered: "You cannot do that! That would be trouble-making behavior, and you would get arrested ... You cannot pressure the government by gathering the masses."[46] Apple Villagers did not obstruct the construction of the incineration plant

[46] Interviewee 49.

either. When construction began, "thugs" were employed to guard the construction site, holding sticks and knives to prevent possible disruptions from villagers. Rather than engaging in direct confrontation with them, peasants petitioned the township and county governments. Deng, a protest leader, explained: "They [authorities] were looking for excuses to arrest us. If we came to the plant, we would do them a favor by giving them such an excuse." Another protest leader echoed: "We wouldn't go, no matter who else went there [the incineration plant]!"[47] Deng added, "Let them build. Ultimately, [the case] should follow legal procedure. The law has the final say about whether the plant should be built or not. We just wait and see!" Indeed, in this struggle, even using the petition channel, an institutional channel, might have incurred repression. After their lawsuit victory, the head of the county government to which the village belonged confessed to Deng that if he and others had simply petitioned the government without filing the lawsuits, the government would have arrested them to quell their resistance,[48] probably adopting some of the dirty tricks illustrated in Chapter 3.

Change Over Time

The government's attitude toward a protest can change over the course of a struggle, which is influenced by the way authorities and protesters interact with each other. In the N City case, as in the Shining Hospital case, officials and resisters gradually relaxed over time. "In the beginning," one of the N City protest leaders recalled, "both sides were nervous. Later on, we both became more relaxed because we were more familiar with each other."[49] Protesters noticed the shift in the officials' attitudes throughout the process from initially trying to resolve the dispute by pressure, to gradually attempting to persuade protesters, to finally treating protest representative as equals in negotiations. As one dissenter put it: "Toward the end, we even talked to each other like friends."[50] Police intervention in this case occurred mostly at the initial stage. Clearly, as time went on, the government generally conformed to accommodating informal norms in handling the case.

Officials' reactions to protests do not necessarily move in a linear pattern but may shift in a more complex fashion. The S City protest, for example, was initially allowed to unfold in a relatively wider space; police did not intervene, and the media were allowed to keep watchful eyes on the incineration project and the resistance. However, the relatively liberal atmosphere underwent a shift in early November 2009 when the media turned silent owing to the city government's enactment of three strict bans on any report about incineration. Furthermore, the police intervention brought the protest to a halt. Due to these reactions, early November was dubbed "white terror" (*baise kongbu*) by protesters.[51] Frustration and pessimism pervaded the MAC Community. To reverse the

---

[47] Interviewee 50.   [48] Interviewee 49.   [49] Interviewee 44.   [50] Interviewee 35.
[51] Interviewee 45. "White terror" is a Chinese Communist Party term, referring to counterrevolutionary repression during the Republican era before 1949.

FIGURE 4.6 An S City protester displays anti-incineration banner in the subway[52] (To protect privacy, faces and other identifying marks have been blurred.)

situation, Tian, a young white-collar employee of a foreign company, spent several hours touring around S City using the subway, wearing a terrifying gas mask and displaying anti-incineration banner (see Figure 4.6). In the end, she was taken to the police station for questioning but soon released. That day, Tian posted her experience online. Her witty observations went viral on the Internet. Traditional media immediately picked up the story, interviewed Tian, and reported her unusual experience. As a result, the ban on reporting about incineration began to break down. A week later, two young ladies, riding bicycles around the MAC Community to display anti-incineration banners that they wore, were also stopped and questioned by the police. Although they were not taken to the police station, the incident created a second stir in the community's online forum. The three ladies' heroic actions in the "white terror" inspired and emboldened other S City dissenters. The protest then regained momentum and two weeks later hit its zenith when hundreds of residents gathered in front of the S City Hall.

ORGANIZATION

The case studies herein further confirm that organization has an influence on the way the state reacts to contention. In cases in which protests took

[52] Homeowners' online forum. November 8, 2009.
　　www.rg-gd.net/forum.php?mod=viewthread&tid=175684&extra=page%3D1&page=1.

boundary-pushing actions (large-scale demonstrations or sit-ins, for example), resisters tend to downplay the role of organization, describing them as totally spontaneous events. The N City demonstration on World Environment Day 2007 was clearly well organized: around 1,000 demonstrators showed up at the same time, many wearing the same T-shirts. Yet demonstrators still insisted that the principle of their struggle was "without organization but with discipline,"[53] which meant avoiding organizing their collective action in a formal way but practicing self-discipline. The reason for this insistence was, as one activist put it, to "avoid arrest."[54]

That being said, authorities sometimes tolerate low-level involvement of formal organizations and cross-region, cross-community alliances among challengers. This helps explain why the effects of organization on repression are not quite significant (see regression results in Chapter 2). In regard to formal organization, at least one environmental NGO gave support to protesters in all four cases, providing consultation on the hazards of incineration and putting resisters in touch with lawyers, experts, and journalists. As mentioned previously, an environmental NGO also grew out of the S City protest: it obtained official approval in 2012 and has been active in promoting waste sorting and recycling since then. Additionally, authorities also allowed a low-level alliance between the protesters of the two urban cases. Besides communication through the homeowners' online forums, a few S City protesters also attended a meeting held by N City activists, with anti-incineration experts in attendance as well. Moreover, at its peak, the two-week sit-in in Banana Village drew around 10,000 people, including residents from neighboring villages. The multi-village sit-in incurred no coercive response. Hence it can be said that, while authorities are certainly sensitive to the forms of protest organization, low-level formal and linked protests will not necessarily result in repression; officials' reactions also depend on other factors, such as their prediction of how severe the "trouble" protesters potentially can cause. The effect of organization becomes more clear in the Falun Gong case to be discussed in Chapter 5.

By contrast, when actions are largely institutional, protest leaders do not attempt to hide their roles in resistance. In Apple Village, three villagers took the lead in filing the lawsuits against the government as well as in organizing collective petitions to the government. Yet, for standing out as leaders of the generally institutional actions, the villagers still paid a high price – the leaders had to endure tremendous pressure from authorities, who employed "soft" tactics of repression to overcome resistance. The primary leader, in his sixties, suffered a stroke and became paralyzed at the height of government pressure.[55]

---

[53] Interviewee 35. See also "Pictures: The Mass Movement against Building an Incineration Plant in the PC Community Reaches New Height" (Homeowners' online forum, June 6, 2007.
  http://house.focus.cn/msgview/1396/85473593.html).
[54] Interviewee 47.   [55] Interviewees 59 and 60.

WHEN ACCOMMODATING INFORMAL NORMS BREAK DOWN

Even in regime-engaging protests, accommodating informal norms do not always play a part in regulating the actions of either the authorities or the protesters. As discussed earlier, authorities may abide by these informal norms at one phase of a struggle but not at another. On top of that, officials have devised a series of soft forms of repression to counter grassroots challenges. On the flip side, protesters themselves occasionally cease to follow accommodating informal norms and fail to enforce self-censorship.

Soft Forms of Repression

While protesters are pushing the envelope, local officials at times remind them of the limits of toleration. In addition to outright violence, authorities – regardless of regime type – have a broad array of subtler means that can be employed to address behavioral challenges; focusing merely on harsh means of punishment may lead to an underestimate of repression (Davenport 2007). Thus, to better comprehend repressive actions, this section focuses on relatively "softer" approaches – approaches that include intimidation, media censorship, Internet hacking, relational repression, and inducing compliance through the promise of material benefits. Many of these means are intended to demobilize opposition and pre-empt collective action.

Protesters in my cases received police phone calls or home visits warning them against actively broadcasting anything about the hazards of incineration or collecting petition signatures. To pre-empt a planned demonstration in October in S City, law enforcement summoned its organizers to the police station at midnight. After being released and returning home, one of the organizers used the homeowner's Internet forum to announce the cancellation of the demonstration. Police also intercepted buses carrying peasants to the S City Hall to join their urban neighbors' demonstration on November 23, 2009.[56] To hinder mobilization, police prohibited a third party from renting an auditorium to N City protesters when they invited an anti-incineration expert to give a speech in the community.[57] Law enforcement officers also forbade the homeowners to hang banners on residential buildings or display posters against incineration in the community compound. The media, such as newspapers and TV programs sometimes received official bans on reporting anything about incineration.[58] Moreover, the government did not shy away from technological interventions, such as hacking homeowners' online forum, so as to impede communication among residents.[59]

---

[56] Interviewee 56. See also posts on the online community forum, e.g., one by "Villager" (November 23, 2009, www.rg-gd.net/forum.php?mod=viewthread&tid=177739).
[57] Interviewees 40, 36, and 55.   [58] Interviewees 40, 35, and 34.   [59] Interviewee 45.

In addition, it is not rare for authorities to take advantage of personal connections to defuse activism (Deng and O'Brien 2013; Luo, Andreas, and Li 2017; O'Brien and Deng 2015a). The state can force protesters' relatives, friends, advisors, employers, and the like, to put pressure on protest leaders and activists to desist. A protest activist in Apple Village, for example, was forced to quit because, his wife, who worked at the local public security bureau, was threatened with losing her job if her husband continued participating in the struggle. The lawyer who brought the Apple Village lawsuit also endured pressure both from his former advisor and from D City officials, who attempt to persuade him to give it up.[60] Sometimes, high-ranking officials come in person to visit protest leaders to discourage opposition. A vice mayor of D City paid a visit to the homes of the protest leaders of Apple Village just a couple of days before the court ruling. In his visit, the vice mayor tried to bribe the protest leaders and promised them and their families economic benefits from job opportunities to new apartments, on the condition that the protesters withdraw their suits.[61]

These soft forms of repression increase the cost of mobilization and resistance. For instance, they led to the "white terror" of the S City struggle, the nadir of the protest campaign. What's more, soft repression, although appearing less harsh, can still take a toll on resisters. Shu, the primary protest leader of Apple Village, was a victim of this. Daily visits by officials from the city, county, and township governments just ahead of the court ruling, placed him under substantial psychological pressure, the result of which was that he suffered a serious stroke; as of 2016, he still could not walk. Nonetheless, the government's attempts at repression failed to smother the protest: other villagers picked up the torch and carried on.

Protesters Losing Self-Control

While regime-engaging protests are often characterized by self-discipline among the resisters, this does not mean that, at some point, they might not lose control of themselves. Studies have shown that when state repression is perceived as unjust or excessive, it can facilitate further protest and push it toward radicalization (Hess and Martin 2006; O'Brien and Deng 2015b; Opp and Roehl 1990; Rasler 1996). This was the case in the police–villager confrontation in Banana Village. On the morning of May 27, 2011, a group of 20 to 30 elderly villagers walked toward the township government offices bearing a petition. On their way, a van approached and pulled over. Several policemen jumped out of the van and attempted to stop the seniors from going. The argument between the seniors and the police in the street attracted larger and larger audiences. The police then arrested two villagers using the excuse that they were blocking

---

[60] Interviewee 57.   [61] Interviewees 49 and 50.

traffic. The arrest took the villagers by surprise. They felt it was "illegal," a set-up by authorities to crush their opposition. This feeling, in turn, provoked a backlash and escalation. News of the arrest quickly spread throughout the village, and by noon a growing number of villagers had taken to the streets, indignant and outraged. When the villagers identified the police captain as the one who had led the failed arrest of Meng (the activist who printed anti-incineration posters) in March, they vented their anger on him, triggering the violent clash described at the start of this chapter. It was at precisely this moment that accommodating informal norms ceased to function.

IMPACT ON REGIME LEGITIMACY

The government's diverse responses to contention have distinct effects on regime legitimacy. Generally speaking, harsh repression alienates citizens and damages regime legitimacy, whereas tolerance helps preserve it.

Repression and Regime Legitimacy

Resentment of the May 27th crackdown still lingered in Banana Village one year afterwards when I was conducting fieldwork there. In my interviews, many villagers drew a parallel between the Communist Party and the Japanese invaders who ruled the region in World War II. An old male villager, highly respected in the area, told me, "The government was just as bad as bandits and the Japanese ... The Communist Party caused just as much trouble as used to be made by the Japanese."[62] Similarly, a villager in his forties, remarked,

Let me make a joke, partly true, partly false: neither the Japanese nor the Nationalist Party beat the masses [in our village]. The masses helped the Communist Party seize state power. Now, the Communist Party beat the masses up!!! ... Didn't you see the scene last year [the May 27th incident; see Figure 4.7]. Really cruel! At midnight or 2am, the police forced their way into people's houses and made arrests. Bandits *and* robbers!! I would never have thought that the Communist Party could be even worse than the Japanese!![63] (emphasis added)

As for those who got arrested or wounded in the crackdown, they felt even more aggrieved and indignant. "I loathe seeing the words of Communist Party [now]," said Bing, an elderly male villager who was detained for several days.

My brain has been poisoned. I know it is inappropriate to think so, but I can't help myself ... If the incumbent cadres and the Communist Party are good, how come fifty or sixty thousand people came here to 'make trouble'?! If we [my wife and I] are bad guys and anti-revolutionaries, then the fifty or sixty thousand other people should be anti-revolutionaries as well! The country is filled with bad guys. Very few are good!![64]

[62] Interviewee 51.   [63] Interviewee 37.   [64] Interviewee 54.

FIGURE 4.7 Banana Villagers clash with police on May 27
(Faces have been blurred to protect actors' identity. Courtesy of a protest activist.)

Bing's wife, Bu, in her sixties, was the first arrested on May 27, and she told me that both she and her husband could not fall asleep during the night whenever they thought about what they had been through.[65] When she was arrested, police raised her blouse to cover her head, leaving her breasts and stomach exposed. This was a truly humiliating experience, especially in a Chinese village. Bu also recalled that when she was arrested, four policemen threw her into a vehicle and stepped on her shoulders. The pain lasted for several months afterwards. On the same day, her husband was put into criminal detention, a more severe penalty than Bu's, because he was accused of leading the protest. Bing had high blood pressure and suffered a stroke in jail; although he was released soon thereafter, he was restrained from leaving the locality.

Bu said that, for a while after he returned home, her husband cried every day – he felt so badly treated, "Indeed, all through my life, I have worked so hard in the collective farms," said Bing. "I am not a bad guy. I have never done a bad thing all my life ... In prison, you were not treated as a human being – you were being treated like a criminal, required to give thumbprints, footprints,

[65] Interviewee 53.

and have pictures taken from every side." Still when asked whether the couple would continue resisting the operation of the incineration plant, the answer was a definite "yes." "We would not be afraid of protest," said Bing. Another villager then added, "If the plant continued operating, we would take the iron sticks or other tools with us. If you hit us, we would hit you too. Just like that. Why? You beat us first and we fight back!"[66] All these comments suggest the defiance of the government's authority.

Villagers were especially irritated that people in their sixties and seventies were beaten by law enforcement and this provoked condemnation: "Where is the justice?! Don't forget this is a Communist regime!" At present, local people's grievances, criticism, and anger remain unvented: "In our small village, over 100 people went to arrest a woman at night. Are you bandits or robbers? If you [the government] are so strong, why do small countries in the South China Sea dare to bully China? Why not turn your force against these countries?!"[67] In this quote, it is interesting to see that the interviewee used nationalist rhetoric, a source usually employed as a means of legitimizing the Communist Party rule, to satirize the regime.

Given the protesters' resentment against authorities and their clash with police, can the Banana Village struggle be considered regime-engaging? By and large, yes. First, despite harsh repression, the government made concessions and did not resume the incineration project after the clash – as of fall 2016, the project has been under suspension. In the aftermath of the clash, the government sent working groups of 300 bureaucrats to Banana Village to help pacify villagers and alleviate contention.[68] In a news article from 2014, the official media blamed the project's suspension on the local government which, it claimed, overlooked local residents' questions and shirked its responsibilities in sufficiently explaining the project to the residents.[69] The news report, copied by the Party website later, did not blame villagers at all. That is to say, the state media regarded the villagers' objection as legitimate.

Second, after the May 27th incident, villagers did not use force either. Instead, they employed their social connections in an attempt to report their grievances to the central government. Thus, it is largely the local government that lost its legitimacy, not the central government. Protest activists shared the view that the central government was kept in the dark about the May 27th repression. In their opinion, the local government had deceived the higher-level government, exaggerated the scale of the protest, and reported it as a "riot." According to the villagers, this explained why as many as five or six thousand policemen were able to be sent to the village. One protest activist expected that the local government would not dare to clamp down on future resistance

---

[66] Interviewee 59.   [67] Interviewee 37.   [68] Interviewee 52.
[69] The article had no mention of the May 27th incident. "Why Was an Incineration Plant, Representing a Hugh Investment, Lying Idle?" *Chinese Environmental News*. July 7, 2014. http://gx.people.com.cn/n/2014/0707/c347804-21597325-4.html.

because, if the central government learned about further crackdown, local leaders would be removed from office. Many blamed particular leaders of the municipal government and investors in the incineration plant for the suppression. In this sense, when distinguishing the local from the central government, the legitimacy of the central government could be maintained. This confirms Yongshun Cai's (2008) thesis that decentralization helps preserve regime stability because *local* government can be blamed when repression occurs. In addition, interviewees sometimes singled out corrupt officials for denunciation: "The Communist Party is good, yet corrupt officials are bad."[70] It is fair to argue that protesters expressed such views for the sake of self-protection; nevertheless, criticizing individual officials does not fundamentally challenge regime legitimacy.

Moreover, despite the violent clash, some protesters still recognized that many policemen were good. They divided the cops into "real" and "fake" ones (thugs). Some argued that law enforcement officers were not allowed to have tattoos. But villagers recalled that some men in police uniform, in fact, had tattoos on their arms, supporting the idea that not all the officers sent in were legitimate. In the villagers' view, the real policemen disapproved of the brutal suppression yet could do nothing about it. "Of course, they didn't verbally express objection to repression, but you could see [their disapproval] in their faces. When I saw them on the road, I greeted them, 'You've had a hectic day.' They smiled to me."[71] When the masses cursed the police, one activist spoke up on their behalf saying that the repression was the fault of the municipal government and the incineration plant, not the police.[72]

In my field research in the village, I asked victims and their families what they wanted after the May 27th incident. Many of them answered that they wanted justice: economic compensations and rehabilitation. The family of the man who was beaten to the point of disability petitioned different levels of the local governments and eventually got loans from the village committee for his treatment and recovery.[73] However, the government did not accept the family's demand of full compensation. The family thought about filing a lawsuit against the local government, but no lawyers would take on the case as they saw little chance of success. On the other hand, we see that even after the crackdown the victim's family still turned to the government for help and the government gave the loans, an indication that the contention was still regime-engaging. Nevertheless, if the government should choose to move forward with the incineration project and employ force in the future, it would further push the protest toward transgressive. As a protester put it, villagers might resort to violence against the repression. Yet another scenario is that due to "white terror" – arrests and interrogation – they might be too scared to resume their struggle and therefore

[70] Interviewee 58.   [71] Interviewee 37.   [72] Interviewee 61.
[73] Interviewees 41, 55, and 58.

give in. After witnessing the arrests of their fellow villagers for speaking out about police assault, some villagers were unwilling to talk about the opposition and a few declined my interviews. Both scenarios would threaten regime legitimacy and resilience in the long run.

Tolerance and Regime Legitimacy

All four cases abound with examples of negotiations between protesters and officials. In the two urban and Banana Village cases, authorities created a special communication channel, called the "liaison system" or "coordination group" (*xietiao xiaozu*), appointing a few local residents (especially party members) as liaisons to bridge the communication between officials and residents. Although resisters regarded the channel as serving the government's interest, i.e., to dissuade people from acting upon their opposition, it at least revealed the government's willingness to keep the dialogue channel open. Under the pressure of grassroots opposition, local governments also held meetings with local residents as pacification measures (see Figure 4.8). Not all meetings

FIGURE 4.8 A meeting between officials and Banana Villagers in April 2011
(On the stage of the theater where the meeting is held, officials and experts give speeches to the villagers; meanwhile, a banner, which reads, "Garbage incineration wrecks the country and ruins the people," is allowed to be displayed on the stage. Courtesy of a protest activist.)

alleviated conflicts, though. In a meeting with Apple Village protesters, officials of the local environmental protection department, who were supposed to educate peasants, lost their debate with protest leaders on the consequences of incineration, and this fanned the flames of grassroots opposition even more. Eventually, three protests (excluding the Banana Village struggle) ended with state concessions without naked force.

When authorities abide by accommodating informal norms and cave in to protesters' demands, does this indicate a weakness of the state? It seems not. Tolerance and concessions can be interpreted in favor of the regime, showcasing its accountability and responsiveness to grassroots opinion.[74] In this sense, regime legitimacy is sustained rather than undermined.

Given the Apple Villager's victorious lawsuit against the government, it is tempting to attribute the victory to progress made in the rule of law in China. In our interview, however, the lawyer in charge of the case told me he does not think this is true; instead he attributes the success to "enlightened officials," who did not intervene in the judicial process nor used brutal means to stifle the protest. In his view, the law was useless: the court, lacking independence from the government, could have contrived reasons that would render the litigation moot. Instead, the lawyer gave credit to the leaders of the provincial environmental protection department who withdrew their approval of the incineration project, leading to the peasants' victory. In other words, even though the government lost the suit, the legitimacy of the government was not undermined.

Reviewing the anti-incineration protests, urban professionals expressed their acknowledgement of a widening space for claim-making, improvement in governance, and an increasingly accountable government. Sa, an S City protester, frankly admitted, "Many activities today would have been doomed if they had taken place 20 years earlier, even in S City."[75] Juan, an anti-incineration expert, added, "Government officials have gradually realized that you cannot neglect the masses (*laobaixing*). In the past, they could dismiss them, be repressive, impose martial law in a village, and then make arrests. These were the routines previously, but they no longer dare to do so now."[76] Recognizing the growth of protest space, another anti-incineration expert detected "progress" with respect to both activism and the government. As he put it:

Chinese citizens have changed from fearing to speak out to daring to express a view and then further to insisting upon action. When the protests took place, I was worried because, ten years earlier, the protest would have not ended in this way … However, in recent years with increasing contact with the outside world after the reform and opening up, citizens' awareness of environmental and rights protection has increased … They have taken rights protection more and more seriously. The government is improving as well; it doesn't dare to act as insolently as before … On the whole, China is

---

[74] Interviewees 35 and 48.   [75] Interviewee 42.   [76] Interviewee 47.

making progress. At least, these environmental NGOs are permitted to exist. Before, they were all banned. This is a sign of social progress. Many articles that could not be published in the past can be now.[77]

What has brought about such a change? Juan (the expert mentioned earlier) explained the change in the officials' mindset and the altered dynamics in their interactions with disgruntled citizens in this way:

The government no longer thinks that it can always hold back [challenges] because the results can be truly devastating. The very violent event that took place some years ago [the 1989 Tiananmen uprising] is the last thing that the government would like to see again. Neither does the government dare to [be repressive] now. In this way, both sides [protesters and officials] make some compromise. One side says 'I don't create big trouble,' while the other says 'I don't seriously prevent you from expressing grievances.' Both sides take a step back. Thus, they both have a certain buffer space. It is not like in the past when we shouted at each other and whatever the other side said landed on deaf ears. At least, we can engage in face-to-face dialogue now, even though the problems cannot be solved. So there seem to be some communication opportunities.[78]

Others factors, such as the media, matter as well in the shifting landscape of protest. As Sa (the S City protester) stated, "The historical background [of S City], the growth of traditional media, and the birth of social media have formed a joint force. In this context, these [protest] activities are able to produce the strongest effect [for change]." After their struggle, Sa formed an NGO for waste sorting and recycling (noted above). "Although we have a lot of complaints against the S City government," said Sa, "we have to depend on it. [After all,] It has the generosity (*xionghuai*) to listen to our suggestions, and many of them have been accepted. When we offer officials advice, even though they may not give a clear response, they take it back and consider it. If the advice is feasible, they will follow it."[79]

These remarks suggest that the urban middle class welcomes and embraces the change in China's contentious politics: an enlarging protest space that is allowed through accommodating informal norms of contention. And they give credit to the regime's progress in governance, which, in turn, helps build regime legitimacy.

CONCLUSION

In telling the stories of the four anti-incineration protests, this chapter elaborates on how and why accommodating informal norms of contention vary across regions, social groups, and time. Generally speaking, compared to the urban middle class, villagers have fewer resources (such as political connections and media access), which reduces officials' incentive to conform to the informal

---

[77] Interviewee 40.   [78] Ibid.   [79] Interviewee 42.

norms and thus leaves the dissidents with a narrower space for protest. Yet, if villagers manage to demonstrate the solidarity of their community, they can create more space for resistance as well. S City protesters had the largest protest space, thanks to the relatively liberal political context and convenient access to the media. Apple Villagers felt themselves restrained in such a limited protest space that they had to resort to lawsuits to address their grievances. The variations occur not only because of distinctions in local political environments, identity politics, and the resources available to protesters, but also due to dynamic interactions between resisters and authorities – how dissenters perceive the boundaries of protest space and push the limits and how officials enforce the limits of protest space.

The cases depicted here are by no means representative of all anti-incineration protests nor even all regime-engaging protests in China. Protesters in these four cases called upon different resources and used all the leverage that they could mobilize and apply. S City protesters relied more on the media, while those in N City relied more on social capital and connections with political elite. These resources were the envy of other protesters. Apple Village's victory in its lawsuit is probably not applicable to other cases because villagers in this case were able to find the fatal flaw in the project's environmental impact assessment report – the fabricated surveys – whereas such "hard" evidence is difficult, if not impossible, to find in other cases. In Banana Village, the majority of local residents were mobilized and actively participated in the struggle; the extent of its solidarity and participation is not quite often to be seen in other places. All of these cases attracted media attention in varying degrees (with Banana Village garnering the least) and gained support from anti-incineration experts and environmental NGOs. Therefore, each case had its unique leverage and experience, which may not be duplicated in other anti-incineration protests.

It is worth noting that protesters in all four cases strived to push the limits regarding actions and organization but not for claims. Enjoying the largest protest space of all the cases, S City protesters only raised NIABY and anti-corruption claims; the other three cases strictly confined themselves to NIMBY demands. As for actions, each case involved some extralegal actions (with Apple Village involving the least), such as demonstrations, sit-ins, and collective petitions exceeding the maximum permitted number of representatives. With regard to the form of organization, an environmental NGO and anti-incineration experts got involved in all four protests. Two urban cases also established connections with each other. S City protesters went as far as establishing an environmental NGO, a formal organization, on the heels of the success of the struggle. These boundary-pushing efforts were generally tolerated by the state, although local authorities at times reminded protesters of the limits of protest space and resorted to various means of soft repression to demobilize dissent.

By and large, these cases were regime-engaging protests and played a positive role in building regime legitimacy. In the Banana Village protest, police arrests of villagers – considered illegitimate by the local residents – led to conflict escalation and triggered the police–villager clash. State repression provoked resentment among local people. Nonetheless, it was largely the local government that lost legitimacy and many villagers still had faith in the central government. The mechanisms and dynamics of this protest were quite different from those in regime-threatening protests, to be introduced in the next chapter.

5

Antagonistic Informal Norms in Regime-Threatening Protests

If the people do not fear death, how can execution frighten them?

Dao De Jing (fourth century BC)

Wherever there is oppression, there is resistance.

Mao Zedong

Accommodating informal norms of contention are volatile by nature. Due to a lack of the enforcement imperative that formal laws and regulations have, neither officials nor protesters are bound to adhere to those norms, which may break down even in a regime-engaging protest (see Chapters 3 and 4). The primary reason for the government to bend the rules for challengers is the concern of legitimacy; the reason for protesters to exercise self-censorship is the fear of repression. If either of these pre-requisites is unavailable, accommodating informal norms will become impossible. In particular, when conflicts and grievances are mixed with such factors as ethnicity, religion, ideology, a history of animosity, and linkage to the West, reconciliation becomes considerably more difficult, the chance that accommodating informal norms will not work increases, and *antagonistic* informal norms instead is likely to come to the fore. These are the central topics of Chapter 5.

Antagonistic informal norms of contention are characterized by transgressive resistance *and* unlawful repression. Under these norms, *resisters* are not afraid to adopt "forbidden forms of claim-making," in Tilly's (2003 and 2006) term. Examples include the Mau Mau revolt in Kenya in the 1950s and the Philippine Yellow revolution in the 1980s (McAdam, Tarrow, and Tilly 2001). Additionally, *authorities* are determined to use any means – including illegal or extralegal ones – to crush dissent. The state's use of illicit force in social control does not merely prevail in non-democratic settings (X. Chen 2017; Johnston 2012; Levitsky and Way 2010), but can also be observed in countries where the rule of law is ostensibly in place (Punch 2011). For instance, extralegal police shootings are common in nations such as India and Brazil (Belur 2010; Huggins 2010); in the "War on Terror," the US government adopted a variety of legal, illegal, and extralegal tactics, including widespread domestic surveillance programs, detention of citizens without trial, and auxiliary courts that operated with little transparency or oversight (Moustafa 2014; Williams 2015). In China, as will be demonstrated, torture, mass arrests, and extrajudicial detention are among the various unlawful sanctions.

Antagonistic informal norms typically occur in regime-threatening protests. Although some regime-engaging protests are neither completely immune from unlawful repression nor from unruly resistance, they are not at the fore. By contrast, when both the state and the challengers regard each other as enemies, antagonistic informal norms arise. In regime-threatening protests, the protest space defined by antagonistic informal norms is even more limited than that allowed by the legal mandates. Excessive force can delegitimize repression, increase dissent, and encourage persistent contention (e.g., Franklin 2015; Hess and Martin 2006; Opp and Roehl 1990). With the absence of accommodating informal norms, contention of such a kind frequently sets in motion a vicious cycle of repression and transgression, thereby intensifying conflict and challenging regime stability.

This chapter selects three high-profile regime-threatening struggles: the 2009 Uyghur ethnic unrest, the Falun Gong (a quasi-religious group) protest campaign, and the Charter 08 campaign (a pro-democracy protest). These cases illustrate important characteristics of regime-threatening protests, particularly as pertains to claims, actions, and organization. In contrast to the regime-engaging protests, cases herein each transgressed boundaries that the Chinese Communist Party (CCP) has made red lines: Uyghur protesters desiring independence from the Chinese rule turned violent; the Falun Gong formed an autonomous national organization, which became political and staged protest events targeting Chinese leaders, albeit peaceful ones; and the Charter 08 campaign, in a peaceful, non-disruptive manner, called for doing away with the single-party system. Therefore, each of these regime-threatening protests involved one type of political grievance or another that the CCP has perceived as transgressive, even though the forms of protest action and organization varied. In each case, officials responded in the same way – a heavy-handed crackdown, combined with a mixture of legal, illegal, and extralegal measures.

Why is unlawful coercion part of the repressive repertoire? For one thing, in regime-threatening protests, it is the top leadership that pushes officials to crush the unrest, rendering repression a political task that is placed above the law. This is particularly visible in crackdown campaigns when the order of suppression typically comes from state leaders and authorities at all levels and from all departments – including the judiciary system – are urged to take part in the campaigns. As a result, cases such as mass arrests and rapid sentencing procedures abound. This mechanism will be elaborated on when discussing the

Uyghur case and the anti-Falun Gong campaign. For another, compared to legal sanctions, unlawful punishments are usually less noticeable by the public and permit more flexibility for law enforcement. In this sense, authorities sometimes resort to these means to facilitate the quelling of dissent. The Charter 08 campaign is an example of this.

None of the cases in this chapter are isolated incidents: they all have historical roots. For this reason, I used second-hand sources to trace the growth and evolution of these cases through time, paying particular attention to the ways they moved in a regime-threatening direction. Studying these cases allows a more comprehensive examination of informal norms of contention, the boundaries of protest space, and the diverse indications of distinct types of informal norms on regime legitimacy and durability.

UYGHUR UNREST IN XINJIANG

The two pillars of accommodating informal norms of contention are the government's informal tolerance and protesters' active imposition of self-censorship. Both of them were missing in the Uyghurs' protest in 2009 – arguably the worst eruption of ethnic violence in the history of the People's Republic of China (PRC).

2009 Uyghur Unrest in Urumqi

On the afternoon of July 5, 2009, over 200 Uyghurs gathered at People's Square, in the center of Urumqi – the capital of Xinjiang, the Uyghur autonomous region.[1] The demonstrators were calling for a full investigation of the Shaoguan incident, in which a violent fight erupted between Han and Uyghur workers at a factory in Guangdong province (southern China) on June 25 and 26, leaving at least two Uyghurs dead and 118 people injured.[2] Police moved in, removed over 70 demonstrators, and dispersed the crowd.[3] A few hours later, hundreds of Uyghurs – armed with knives, stones, and the like – launched brutal attacks against Han Chinese residents, including women, children, and the elderly (Human Rights Watch 2005). The crowd also ransacked shops and set houses and vehicles on fire.[4] It was not until the early hours of July 6 that

---

[1] "Scores Killed in China Protests." *BBC News*. July 6, 2009. http://news.bbc.co.uk/2/hi/asia-pacific/8135203.stm.

[2] "Man Held Over China Ethnic Clash." *BBC News*. June 30, 2009. http://news.bbc.co.uk/2/hi/asia-pacific/8125693.stm.

[3] "Record Atrocities: A Review of the Horrific Night." Chen Gang. *China Radio International*. July 7, 2009. http://news.cri.cn/gb/27824/2009/07/06/Zt1965s2554780.htm.

[4] Ibid.

security forces were able to re-establish control.[5] On July 7, hundreds of Han Chinese marched through the streets in Urumqi, armed with homemade weapons to take revenge on the Uyghur. Law enforcement used tear gas to disperse the Han demonstrators.[6] Government sources reported a total of 197 deaths and 1,721 injuries. Most of the victims were Han Chinese,[7] and Chinese police shot dead 12 Uyghurs.[8] Property damage was considerable: 331 shops and 1,325 motor vehicles were destroyed or burned, and many public facilities were ruined.[9]

The bloody incident took the Chinese leadership by surprise, compelling President Hu Jintao to cut short his G8 (Group of Eight) meeting in Italy and return to Beijing to manage the crisis.[10] The Party leadership ordered offenders from the July 5th incident to be punished heavily and quickly.[11] Xinjiang's governor, Nur Bekri, claimed that the government would use *all means* to maintain control in Urumqi.[12] The Xinjiang People's Procuratorate operated under the "three-fasts" principle – fast review, fast arrest, and fast prosecution – when handling cases related to the incident (Human Rights Watch 2009). In the ensuing weeks, thousands of people were arrested,[13] and mosques were temporarily closed. By November 2009, over 400 individuals faced criminal charges.[14] Nine were executed that same month and, by February 2010, at

[5] "Over 100 Han Chinese Killed in Xinjiang and the Western Media Tragically Misreading the Event." Yang Gang, Guo Zhongxiao, and Zhang Jieping. *Yazhou Zhoukan*. 2009. Vol. 23, No. 28.

[6] Ibid.

[7] Initial figures (announced on the morning of July 7) counted 156 dead, 123 of them Han Chinese and 33 Uyghurs (Bovingdon 2010: 168). See also "Chinese President Visits Volatile Xinjiang" (Edward Wong and Jonathan Ansfield, *The New York Times*, August 25, 2009, www.nytimes .com/2009/08/26/world/asia/26china.html?_r=0).

[8] "Xinjiang Widens Crackdown on Uyghurs." Kathrin Hille. *Financial Times*. July 19, 2009. www.ft.com/cms/s/0/5aa932ee-747c-11de-8ad5-00144feabdco.html.

[9] "Development and Progress in Xinjiang." The Information Office of the State Council. September 21, 2009. www.gov.cn/english/official/2009-09/21/content_1422566.htm.

[10] "Hu Quits G8 Trip to Tackle Xinjiang Crisis." Kathrin Hille and Richard McGregor. *Financial Times*. July 8, 2009. www.ft.com/intl/cms/s/0/dbd76e6a-6abo-11de-ado4-00144feabdco.html #axzz43ZE4c7bE.

[11] "Zhou Yongkang: Offenders from the July 5th Incident Will Be Punished Heavily and Quickly." *Xinhuanet*. July 13, 2009. http://news.southcn.com/china/zgkx/content/2009-07/13/content_ 5361830.htm.

[12] "Is China Fraying? Racial Killings and Heavy-Handed Policing Stir Up a Repressed and Dangerous Province." *The Economist*. July 9, 2009. www.economist.com/node/13988479#foot note1.

[13] "Xinjiang Arrests 'Now Over 1,500'." BBC News. August 3, 2009. http://news.bbc.co.uk/2/hi/ asia-pacific/8181563.stm. "Xinjiang Widens Crackdown on Uyghurs." Kathrin Hille. *Financial Times*. July 19, 2009. www.ft.com/cms/s/0/5aa932ee-747c-11de-8ad5-00144feabdco.html.

[14] "Riot Woman Sentenced to Death for Killing." Cui Jia. *China Daily*. December 5, 2009. www.chinadaily.com.cn/cndy/2009-12/05/content_9122992.htm.

least 26 had received death sentences, including 24 Uyghurs and two Han Chinese.[15] Security was tight in Xinjiang, and Internet access within Urumqi remained restricted for nearly a year following the unrest.[16]

In its early hours, the July 5th incident had looked like a regime-engaging event but rapidly moved to a different track later on. Lack of dialogue between the government and protesters and, after one-third of the demonstrators were taken away, Uyghur resistance turned transgressive, resorting to unrestrained violence. In response, authorities were resolved to relentlessly crush the unrest, employing whatever means it took. It is important to note that neither protesters nor officials see the July 5th incident in isolation but rather treat it as part of Uyghur unrest that has existed in Xinjiang for the past several decades. Hence, the protest dynamics of this incident were heavily influenced by the norms of contention established in this area between the two sides: one, a stern-faced government that often overstepped the law to put down unrest and, the other, persistent dissidents who frequently turned aggressive and radical.

A Brief Introduction to Xinjiang

To better understand the July 5th incident and the characteristics of Uyghur unrest in general, it is necessary to give a brief introduction to Xinjiang's demography, history, and geopolitics. Xinjiang is one of China's 31 provincial administrations, lying on the northwestern frontier of the country.[17] With abundant oil reserves, this region is China's most important energy base (Becquelin 2000). Xinjiang has a total population of 21.82 million. Uyghurs, a Turkic ethnic group numbering around 10 million,[18] make up the largest portion. Most Uyghurs believe in Islam and live in southern Xinjiang. With consistent migration to the province over the past few decades, Han population today numbers 8.83 million; in Urumqi, the capital city located in northern Xinjiang, Han Chinese outnumber Uyghurs.[19]

Xinjiang has 5,500 km of international borders – including one with the former Soviet Union – and lies near the center of the Eurasian landmass

---

[15] "Nine Executed over Xinjiang Riots." *BBC News.* November 9, 2009. http://news.bbc.co.uk/2/hi/asia-pacific/8350360.stm. "China Sentences Four More to Death for Urumqi Riot." Le Yu. *Reuters.* January 26, 2010. http://uk.reuters.com/article/2010/01/26/uk-china-xinjiang-idUKTRE60P3HM20100126.

[16] "Security Tight in Xinjiang." Radio Free Asia. June 24, 2011. www.rfa.org/english/news/uyghur/security-06242011134728.html.

[17] Xinjiang occupies a sixth of China's landmass, making it the largest administrative unit in the country.

[18] *2010 China Census Data.* National Bureau of Statistics of China. 2011. www.stats.gov.cn/tjsj/tjgb/rkpcgb/.

[19] Nearly 75 percent of the Urumqi's population (a total of 3.11 million) are Han Chinese. "Bulletin on the 2010 China Census of Urumqi." *Tianshan.cn.* September 16, 2011. http://news.ts.cn/content/2011-09/16/content_6173591.htm.

(Becquelin 2000; Bovingdon 2010). In the era of the Republic of China (1912–1949), two short-lived East Turkestan Republics existed in Xinjiang, one from 1933 to 1934 and the other from 1944 to 1949. After the Sino–Soviet split in the late 1950s, the history of the Uyghurs' struggle for independence was constantly stressed in Soviet propaganda targeting Xinjiang's Muslim population (Han 2013). Since the dissolution of the Soviet Union and the independence of the Central Asian countries, closer political and religious connections were forged with Turkic Muslims throughout Central Asia, which reinforced the Uyghurs' religious and ethnic identity and their sense of distinction from the Chinese (Dillon 2004: 166).

Antagonistic Informal Norms and a Vicious Cycle of Repression and Transgression

Even before the July 5th incident, Xinjiang was a turbulent region in China, witnessing numerous protests by Uyghurs since the 1980s. Accommodating informal norms are rarely seen in these struggles; instead, the lack of self-censorship among dissenters combined with the absence of state leniency characterizes Uyghur unrest. First, protesters normally fail to stay within the bounds set by the regime in terms of claims, actions, and organization. Some have called for more autonomy for Xinjiang, while others have aimed to establish an independent state. These viewpoints are reflected in shouted slogans such as "Down with the Han/Chinese government" and "Long Live Xinjiang's Independence" (Bovingdon 2010: 110; Dillon 2004: 59). Uyghur actions have taken the form of demonstrations, armed insurrections, and gun battles with police. Many of these events were premeditated, involving formal organizations – some Uyghurs received military training in rural southern Xinjiang, Pakistan, or Afghanistan – and the events tended to establish linkages across regions as seen in cases in which demonstrations spread swiftly across multiple regions (Bovingdon 2010).

The other part of the norms in Uyghur resistance concerns state repressive responses. Here, Uyghur dissent is often politicized, equated with separatist contention, and regarded as CBOEs (contradictions between ourselves and the enemy; see Chapter 3). While Uyghurs have their unique grievances, such as ethnic discrimination and government restrictions on religious practice, they also share many of the same grievances as Han Chinese, including official corruption, environmental degradation, and objections to the family-planning policy (Hastings 2005). Yet, in almost every case in which protesters explicitly raised such matters, officials insisted that they were openly challenging the Party rule or aiming at secession and depicted their contentious actions as riots, hooliganism, or sabotage (Bovingdon 2010: 119; Dillon 2004: 51). With few exceptions, the regime has shown no tolerance for these protests and has refused to negotiate any resisters' claims (Bovingdon 2010: 8 and 153–154; Hastings 2005: 131). Even though some local officials do understand and sympathize with protesters, the politicization of Uyghur resistance and the ideologically charged climate have compelled them – especially ethnic minority officials – to take a tough stance on dissidents in order to prove their loyalty to the Chinese regime and to display their full compliance with the leaders' concern over maintaining order and the unity of the nation (Hillman 2016: 6). As a result, repression is the decisive element in state reaction.

What follows will demonstrate how antagonistic informal norms have been gradually established in Uyghur unrest, in parallel with a course of conflict exacerbation. Actually, in the early days of the reform era, Xinjiang witnessed a brief period of political toleration toward religious practice and social protests when Hu Yaobang was the General Secretary of the Communist Party. After the 1980 disturbances in Aksu, which involved inter-ethnic riots (Clarke 2011), the state offered a concession by re-establishing the Xinjiang Islamic Association, allowing the partial revival of traditional customs (Dillon 2004: 59; Hierman 2007). Many mosques were constructed afterwards, and the number of Uyghur officials in the government also increased. By and large, Uyghur protests had been peaceful during the 1980s (Bovingdon 2010: 106).

Nonetheless, from the early 1990s onward, political violence gradually spread throughout Xinjiang (Becquelin 2000; Dillon 2004; Mackerras 2004). The protest that contributed most to the reversal of the government's 1980s policy was the 1990 Baren Insurgency in southern Xinjiang. The Islamic Party of East Turkestan, a rebel group, planned a series of synchronized attacks on government buildings (Dillon 2004: 93; Millward 2004: 14). Armed with rifles, rebels took police officers hostage, killed and injured officers, and attacked the town hall with hand grenades and other explosives (Dillon 2004: 64). The underlying issues of this uprising included Chinese migration to Xinjiang and the forthcoming family-planning policy (Millward 2004: 15); it appears that some protesters propagated separatist ideologies (Dillon 2004: 73; Han 2013).

The Baren Insurgency then ushered in an era of transgression and repression, with antagonistic informal norms playing a significant role in the protest dynamics. The contention not only grew in severity but also became more organized (Dillon 2004; Hastings 2011). Armed insurrections, bombings, and assassinations of "pro-Chinese clergy" in the pursuit of independence took place throughout the 1990s (Bovingdon 2010; Dillon 2004). In retaliation, in 1996, the state launched "Strike Hard" anti-crime campaigns in Xinjiang (Dillon 2004: 85; Han 2010). Mass arrests and the confiscation of weapons occurred across the region. Meanwhile, authorities imposed increased pressure on the practice of Islam: all Islamic publications were required to get state approval, non-registered mosques and religious schools were closed down, and all imams were required to declare their loyalty to the government in writing (Hierman 2007). The 1996 Strike Hard campaign created a backlash, marked by escalating conflict and increasing instability, which reached its peak at the time of the Ghulja (Yining) Uprising in 1997, a violent pro-independence protest relentlessly put down by authorities (Bovingdon 2010; Hierman 2007).

In the aftermath, there were thousands of arrests and incommunicado detentions as well as many alleged cases of abuse or torture of prisoners (Millward 2007: 334).

Prior to July 2009, state crackdown led to the eventual decline of *open* anti-state claim making in the region, but, at the same time, encouraged clandestine resistance. Uyghurs turned to "everyday resistance" – avoiding outright collective defiance but using songs, jokes, satire, and political fantasy – to express their dissatisfaction and criticism of the political system, with some wishing for independence (Bovingdon 2002).

Despite going underground, Uyghurs' grievances against Han rule remained strong, and several rounds of Strike Hard campaigns in the 2000s played a key role in fueling the resentment. In the campaigns, authorities have frequently overstepped laws when imposing penalties. Chinese law requires that police must display an arrest warrant at the time of arrest, with the approval of the procuratorate or court.[20] However, during the political campaigns, these procedures were typically ignored or streamlined. For instance, in the 2001 campaign, Wang Lequan, then-Xinjiang Party Secretary, gave instructions on the principle of "two basics": "As long as the *basic truth* is clear and as long as the *basic evidence* is verified, *prompt* approval of arrest, prosecution, and court decisions is required" (emphasis added; Human Rights Watch 2005: 67). Under this principle, formal procedures were compromised and unlawful arrest seemed to be common (Human Rights Watch 2005). Further, local officials, who were anxious to show their superiors that they were absolutely on board with the Strike Hard campaigns, put the pressure on local police to solve cases quickly, resulting in a spike of torture cases in police interrogations (Tanner 2002b). Yet, torture and maltreatment of detainees are punishable offenses under China's laws.[21]

On the whole, the lack of accommodating informal norms and the prominence of antagonistic informal norms of contention resulted in the exacerbation of contention and the increasingly deteriorating relationship between Uyghurs and authorities. This was the background of the July 5th incident. It in part explains why a conflict between Uyghurs and Han Chinese 2,000 miles away became the proximal cause of one of the largest violent protests in China in decades.

Why Antagonistic Informal Norms

The July 5th incident clearly demonstrates the protest dynamics when antagonistic informal norms are at play: an exchange of extreme resistance with excessive coercion. Building on previous discussion, this section illustrates that

---

[20] *Criminal Procedure Law*, Articles 66, 71, and 72.
[21] *Criminal Procedure Law*, Article 43; *Criminal Law*, Article 247.

a number of factors – especially, ethnicity, religion, a history of animosity, and foreign support – help explain the contentious dynamics in Uyghur unrest.

Actions

Although violence and bloody confrontations are commonly associated with the July 5th incident, it actually started with a peaceful demonstration. Why did the demonstration promptly descend into a deadly anti-Chinese riot? Although it is still unclear which side – the police or demonstrators – is to blame for initiating the violence, most sources agree that Uyghur protesters attacked and killed Han residents and engaged in violent confrontations with security forces. In this sense, the July 5th incident is indicative of the intense relationship between the Uyghurs and the Han Chinese. In recent decades, despite a modest absolute rise in living standards, Uyghurs still experience discrimination in the labor market and suffer a higher poverty rate than the Han (Becquelin 2004). Growing economic inequality between the two groups has been coupled with a dramatic increase in Han migration into the region, government restrictions on religious practices, and anxiety over the survival of Uyghur cultural attributes in a Han-majority society (Millward 2009). Mutual distrust and discrimination between the Han and the Uyghurs make intergroup communication difficult and limited, thereby making the intergroup dynamic extremely susceptible to violence (Han 2010). Against this backdrop, Uyghurs' hatred was inflamed by the deaths of Uyghurs in Shaoguan and, ultimately, they turned to bloodshed as seen on July 5.

Claims

At the outset of the July 5th rally, protesters demanded authorities to impartially handle the Shaoguan incident. Seemingly no secession claims were raised at this point. However, once the protest spiraled out of control, separatist claims followed. Unlike Han protests, Uyghur grievances are usually viewed through an ethnic lens by both resisters and authorities (Hastings 2005). Uyghurs share the historical memory of their struggle for independence from Chinese rule; lately, Uyghur diaspora organizations frequently evoked such memory and stoke the fires of the desire for Uyghur autonomy. When specific grievances such as economic or environmental ones are combined with ethnic nationalism, religion, and a history of animosity, the chance of escalating conflict increases if the state does not respond appropriately. While separatism might not be the primary issue for most Uyghurs, it does exist and once petitions for redressing grievances seemingly unrelated to separatism have been rejected, it rises to the fore (Hastings 2005: 33). This aids in explaining the rapid move to put forth the radical political claims in the July 5th event.

Organization

The initial demonstration on July 5 was planned, and Uyghurs from other parts of Xinjiang joined the rally (Millward 2009). Following the Shaoguan incident,

Uyghur diaspora organizations circulated videos of the brawl on the Internet along with the accusation of slow actions by the police and an under-reported death toll.[22] In early July, Uyghurs planned a march to Urumqi's People's Square in response to perceived government inaction and mishandling of the Shaoguan incident. Prior to the demonstration, many Uyghurs from other parts of the region, especially southern Xinjiang, came to Urumqi (Millward 2009). Hence, it is quite clear that the Urumqi protest had links across regions and probably across social groups. Yet, it is still unclear whether formal organizations were involved in the protest. The Chinese government accused Rebiya Kadeer, president of the World Uyghur Congress (WUC), an organization of exiled Uyghur groups, of instigating the July 5th incident.[23] While most Western observers have challenged the government's allegation, independent evidence revealed that Rebiya appeared to have had some involvement in the unrest (Mackerras 2012).[24]

Putting the above disagreement aside, the existence of many Uyghur diaspora groups that oppose Chinese rule makes the authorities sensitive and suspicious of all Uyghur protests in the country. The formation of Uyghur exile communities dates back to the Mao era when hundreds of thousands of Uyghurs and other Turkic peoples, including leaders and supporters of the East Turkestan Republics, fled to the Soviet Union and Turkey (Han 2013: 60–62). In the past three decades, Uyghur diaspora organizations, with support from countries such as Germany, Turkey, and the United States, have been active in mobilizing and sustaining the Uyghur nationalist movement in Xinjiang (Han 2013: 60–63). Against this backdrop, even though the July 5th disturbance might not have been orchestrated by the WUC or other exile organizations, the potential connection between the Urumqi protest and overseas anti-China forces could make the Chinese government paranoid and prod them to respond harshly.

Because both protesters and authorities were unwilling to engage in dialogue – Uyghurs crossed all the red lines in terms of actions, claims, and organization, and authorities responded with heavy-handed repression – the July 5th demonstration can truly be defined as a regime-threatening protest.

---

[22] "Old Suspicions Magnified Mistrust into Ethnic Riots in Urumqi." Jonathan Watts. *The Guardian*. July 10, 2009. www.theguardian.com/world/2009/jul/10/china-riots-uighurs-han-urumqi.

[23] "Eligen Imibakhi, Chairman of the Standing Committee of the Xinjiang Regional People's Congress, Discusses about Urumqi's Severe Criminal Violent Incidents." *Xinhuanet*. July 6, 2009. http://news.xinhuanet.com/legal/2009-07/06/content_11660959.htm.

[24] Another unofficial source suspected that Hizb ut-Tahrir, an international political organization whose goal is to re-establish the Islamic Caliphate or Islam state, was involved in the unrest. "Uyghur Senior Correspondent Gheyret Niyaz: Rioters Yell 'Building the Islamic Caliphate; Hizb ut-Tahrir Might be the Planners.'" Han Yonghong. *Lianhe Zaobao*. July 27, 2009. www.zaobao.com.sg/special/feature/story20090727-29025.

Impact on Regime Legitimacy and Stability

Without accommodating informal norms in play and when antagonistic informal norms became the only game in town, Uyghur unrest is caught in a vicious cycle that rotates between suppression and radicalization. Excessive repression has put the legitimacy of the Chinese rule in jeopardy, alienated many Uyghurs, and expanded the grievances among the Uyghur population. Increasing restrictions on Uyghurs' religious practices could help build a Uyghur front that will be unified by a shared bitterness over Han rule. Some indications appear that anti-state resistance has spread from small, dedicated radical groups to larger segments of the Uyghur population (Hierman 2007). On the state side, there is a recent tendency in China to apply the "terrorist" label to all forms of ethnic protest; this practice, which rejects the legitimacy of ethnic dissent, can further exacerbate resentment among Uyghurs and undermine the CCP's nation-building efforts in Xinjiang (Terrone 2016: 48).

Relying heavily on undue force to deal with resistance has failed to preserve security and stability in China's far west. When the deep-seated contention exploded on July 5, the result was devastating, both to the state and ordinary citizens. After 2009, a number of violent outbreaks in both Xinjiang and other places in China saw Uyghurs attacking law enforcement officers, cadres, imams, and ordinary citizens.[25] Yu Zhengsheng, a top Party leader, warned in 2015, "Xinjiang faces a very serious situation in sustaining long-term social stability."[26] Abroad, Uyghur exile groups became ever more active in pressing for independence from China and in sharply criticizing the Chinese government.[27] Attempts by authorities to blame the Uyghur diaspora for the July 5th incident succeeded only in inflaming nationalism among the Uyghur diaspora

---

[25] For example, see "Eight Police Killed in Revenge Attacks in Hetian, Xinjiang; Urumqi Increases Police Forces, Searching Uyghurs' Homes Unexpectedly" (Radio Free Asia, October 13, 2014, www.rfa.org/mandarin/yataibaodao/shaoshuminzu/ql1-10132014094340.html), "Chief Imam at Kashgar Mosque Stabbed to Death as Violence Surges in Xinjiang" (Tania Branigan, *The Guardian*, July 31, 2014, www.theguardian.com/world/2014/jul/31/china-jume-tahir-imam-kashgar-xinjiang-mosque-stabbed-death-violence), "Kunming Rail Station Attack: China Horrified as Mass Stabbings Leave Dozens Dead" (Barry Neild and agencies, *The Guardian*, March 2, 2014, www.theguardian.com/world/2014/mar/02/china-mass-stabbings-yunnan-kunming-rail-station), and "China Security Chief Blames Uighur Islamists for Tiananmen Attack" (Megha Rajagopalan, *Reuters*, November 1, 2013, www.reuters.com/article/us-china-tiananmen-idUS BRE9A003L20131101).

[26] "Massacre at Chinese Coal Mine: Knife-Wielding Separatists Blamed for Attack in Xinjiang that Killed at Least 50 as Racial Tensions Flare." *South China Morning Post*. October 1, 2015. www.scmp.com/news/china/policies-politics/article/1863165/least-50-reportedly-killed-september-xin jiang-attack.

[27] "Hundreds of Uighurs Lobby China for Independence." *The Telegraph*. May 14, 2012. www.telegraph.co.uk/news/worldnews/asia/china/9263756/Hundreds-of-Uighurs-lobby-China-for-independence.html.

online community while increasing the international awareness of Rebiya Kadeer and the WUC (Culpepper 2012).

Overall, constant reliance upon excessive coercion to ensure popular compliance is not a long-term solution, as it is not only an inefficient and expensive strategy but probably ultimately a self-defeating one (Shue 1991: 218). Hence, as long as the vicious cycle continues, further destabilization of Xinjiang and other regions of the PRC might be inevitable.

THE FALUN GONG PROTEST

In a prolonged protest struggle, the norms that shape the behavior of the state and protesters can change from accommodating to antagonistic. When this happens, the protest shifts from regime-engaging to regime-threatening. This type of transition is exemplified by the Falun Gong case, and the turning point was the April 25th incident.

Besieging Zhongnanhai – April 25th Incident

On the morning of April 25, 1999, more than 10,000 Falun Gong practitioners from several provinces of China gathered in front of Zhongnanhai, the central Party and state headquarters where China's top leaders live and work. The orderly crowd stayed peaceful and silent: they did not hold up placards or shout slogans, nor did they obstruct or occupy any part of the street (Chan 2004). Instead, they stood close to one another in three or four rows along the street, and those behind sat on the ground, some resting while others read the *Zhuan falun*, the Falun Gong bible. Throughout the day, negotiations took place between the National Petition Bureau officials and practitioner representatives who complained about the hurt feelings caused by criticism of the Falun Gong and the restrictions placed on fellow Falun Gong disciples (Palmer 2007). Representatives demanded official recognition of their religious association (Junker 2014b; Perry 2002a). In the process, the demonstrators waited patiently and quietly; they were not harassed or dispersed by law enforcement (Ownby 2008). Before they left in the late evening, they cleaned up, leaving neither a single scrap of paper nor a single cigarette butt behind (Chan 2004).

A Brief History of Falun Gong

The Falun Gong was founded by Li Hongzhi in May 1992 in Changchun, a northeastern city.[28] It was initially a *qigong* association, focusing on body

---

[28] Li was born in the early 1950s. At the height of the Cultural Revolution, he applied to join the Communist Youth League (Thornton 2010). After high school graduation, Li spent eight years as a trumpet player in the army and police institute and then took up a position at a state-owned

training, health, and healing.[29] Early practitioners usually characterized the Falun Gong as a cultivation system, a practice involving physical movement, mental discipline, and moral tenets that together could affect positive changes in the nature of the human body (Penny 2012). Yet around 1994, Li began to change the nature of the Falun Gong, replacing physical training with ideology as its chief object. He argued that the purpose of practicing Falun Gong was to purify one's heart and attain spiritual salvation. His writings stress that he himself, Master Li, is the omniscient and omnipotent savior of the entire universe (Palmer 2007; Thornton 2010). The Falun Gong spread rapidly across the country and reached its pinnacle between late 1998 and early 1999, with millions of adherents and thousands of practice sites (*liangong dian*) scattered all over China (Chan 2004; Palmer 2007; Perry 2001). Its adherents came from a wide range of social backgrounds, including government officials, university professors, businessmen, and housewives.

Accommodating Informal Norms in Place: Pre-April 25th Resistance

At the outset, the government did not intervene in the spiritual movement and, in fact, provided some support. However, the state's favorable attitude changed in the mid-1990s, when the Falun Gong organization was legally disbanded and its publications banned (Junker 2014b; Ownby 2008: 165–174; Palmer 2007: 249–256). Additionally, the Falun Gong also came under increasing media criticism. Against this backdrop, adherents mounted around 300 peaceful demonstrations between June 1996 and April 1999, demanding apologies from the media (Ownby 2008: 169; Palmer 2007: 251–254).

Take the *Guangming Daily* incident as an example. On June 17, 1996, an article published in the *Guangming Daily* (an influential official newspaper) derided Li Hongzhi as a "swindler," denounced *Zhuan falun* (the Falun Gong bible) as propagating feudal superstition, and called for a thorough criticism of the spiritual group. The article triggered wider anti-Falun Gong propaganda in the media, with around 20 major newspapers following suit, and the central government also issued an order banning all Falun Gong books (Junker 2014a; Palmer 2007: 249). In response, practitioners staged mass demonstrations – frequently with more than 1,000 participants – around the offices of media outlets that published or broadcast critical reports (Thornton 2010: 227). Li Hongzhi encouraged such actions, calling practitioners who rose up to defend his organization the true disciples and chiding those who were inactive (Ownby 2008; Palmer 2007: 249–250). In the end, there was no follow-through to the

company. He received training from multiple *qigong* masters, some of whom were Buddhists while others were Daoists (Palmer 2007; Thornton 2010).

[29] *Qigong* is a practice of integrating physical postures, breathing techniques, and focused intentions for health and meditation. "What is *Qigong*?" (The National Qigong Association, http://nqa.org/resources/what-is-qigong/).

Guangming Daily's call, and so the ban on Falun Gong publications was not implemented consistently (Ownby 2008).

A result like this was not atypical prior to April 1999 when both state authorities and the dissidents generally conformed to accommodating informal norms. On the one hand, officials and most media institutions regularly yielded to Falun Gong protesters and issued apologies as demanded (Ownby 2008: 16; Palmer 2007: 256), although their protest rallies were probably unauthorized. In fact, the government carried out a "three-nots" policy on media reporting about spiritual groups like the Falun Gong: media should *not* be for it, *not* be against it, and *not* label it good or bad.[30] On the other hand, while Li Hongzhi repeatedly called for his followers to publicly defend the Falun Gong, he simultaneously emphasized that the practice was *non-political* (Junker 2014a).

Nonetheless, things began to change. In mid-April, 1999, when Falun Gong adherents gathered in Tianjin to protest against an article published in a magazine of Tianjin Normal University (a limited-circulation journal), the magazine editor refused to give in, police beat demonstrators and made 45 arrests, and the municipal government declined to release those arrested. The Falun Gong followers then decided to head towards Beijing. Eventually, the event developed into what came to be known as the April 25th incident.

Antagonistic Informal Norms and a Vicious Cycle of Repression and Transgression

The siege of Zhongnanhai became a watershed in the Falun Gong movement: it propelled the conflict into a bitter spiral of repression and radicalization. This is exactly the opposite of the learning curve of accommodating informal norms as seen in regime-engaging protests, in which both the government and challengers work on *de-escalating* the conflicts. In what follows, I show how the code of behavior of the state and protesters transformed from accommodating to antagonistic.

In the post-April 25 period, the state launched a full-fledged campaign against the Falun Gong. Authorities, claiming that the spiritual group was seeking to overthrow the government and establish a theocracy (Ownby 2008: 179), banned its practice on China's soil, arrested its key leaders, and issued an international arrest warrant for Li Hongzhi.[31] A massive propaganda

---

[30] "China's Blind-Eye Policies Helped, Then Hurt, Falun Dafa Movement." Ian Johnson. *The Wall Street Journal.* December 13, 2000. www.wsj.com/articles/SB976673635142213846. The reasons for acquiescence varied. A large number of CCP members were Falun Gong followers or sympathizers; some high-level officials saw the Falun Gong as a healing organization, while others feared its influence and dared not take the risk of alienating the organization's tens of millions of followers (Palmer 2007: 254–255).

[31] "A Ministry of Public Security Spokesperson Accepts Interview on Ordering the Arrest of Criminal Suspect Li Hongzhi." *People's Daily.* July 30, 1999. www.people.com.cn/GB/channel1/10/20000706/132339.html.

campaign against the group was launched across all media, and Falun Gong Internet sites were blocked (Palmer 2007: 275–276). In reaction, between April 25 and July 22, over 300 demonstrations took place across the country (Thornton 2010). Afterwards, protests continued in the form of petitioning, public displays of Falun Gong exercises and banners, and distributions of pro-Falun Gong literature (Junker 2014a; J. Tong 2009). At the onset of the crackdown, Li Hongzhi warned the government not to treat the Falun Gong masses like enemies (Palmer 2007: 276), but soon afterwards he disappeared for over a year (Chan 2013; Junker 2014a).

Initially, protesters were often treated relatively lightly and sent home with few lasting repercussions (Junker 2014a). Nonetheless, as resistance persisted, repression practices escalated, ranging from fines and job termination to multi-year incarceration (Junker 2014a; J. Tong 2009). The four chief leaders under Li Hongzhi received heavy sentences and thousands of followers were detained.

State crackdown also involved unlawful tactics. The regime established a Party-led security apparatus known as the "610" Office (named after its inaugural date, June 10, 1999) to lead the anti-Falun Gong campaign (Noakes and Ford 2015), but its establishment had no formal legal mandate and should be considered as an extralegal, extra-ministerial security force (Cook and Lemish 2011). Furthermore, Falun Gong practitioners could be sentenced to the reeducation-through-labor camps (Human Rights Watch 2002), an extra-legal system discussed in Chapter 3. After the reeducation-through-labor system was abolished in 2013, Falun Gong detainees were sent to prisons or to reeducation centers overseen by the 610 Office (Noakes and Ford 2015).

Similar to other political campaigns in China, the anti-Falun Gong campaign was highly centralized. It followed orders from top-echelon Party leaders who headed a "central leading group" created for this campaign and the organization's executive branch was the 610 Office. The central authorities issued transformation quotas for the numbers of Falun Gong practitioners who had to renounce their beliefs; the quotas were then disseminated to local authorities (Noakes and Ford 2015). To reach the ideological transformation quotas, local authorities were incentivized to use any means necessary, including extralegal or illegal ones. Indeed, physical abuse and torture of Falun Gong inmates to force recantations appeared to be widespread in the detention facilities (Palmer 2007: 223).

With the anti-Falun Gong campaign moving on, Falun Gong protesters turned radical. On one occasion, they tried to hang a giant portrait of Li Hongzhi over the painting of Mao Zedong in Tiananmen Square (Perry 2002a; Thornton 2010), an open defiance of the Communist rule. Li Hongzhi himself also launched a direct attack on the CCP. In a 2005 article, he denounced the Party as an "evil cult," characterized the official suppression as an "enormous sin of the ages," and called for people to withdraw from the Party and any of its associated organizations (Penny 2012: 222–223). In this sense, the Falun Gong struggle has become forthrightly regime-threatening and overtly politicized.

Why Antagonistic Informal Norms

In many cases, even after breaking down, accommodating informal norms of contention can be re-established as in the cases of Hill Factory and Banana Village (see Chapters 3 and 4). Why was this not the case in the Falun Gong struggle? The answers are multifaceted and complex but lie mostly in the state leaders' growing suspicion of the Falun Gong – its heterodox ideology, overseas expansion, and organizational capacity. What's more, the spiritual group's warning messages and its adherents' fearless resistance strengthened the mistrust. Hence, once the repression machine started up, it was difficult for either side to shut it off, back down, and return to the negotiating table.

The nature of this quasi-religious organization made it difficult to obtain the CCP's trust. Historically, there has been no lack of suppression of heterodox groups in PRC as seen in various campaigns to eradicate "feudal superstitions" and religious sects (like the Yiguan Dao). It was disturbing to the Chinese leaders when they saw an ideological competition grow up between the Falun Gong and the CCP, whose official doctrine requires its members to believe in no religion. Around 1994, the quasi-religious group began to require its practitioners to devote themselves exclusively to its own doctrine and to eschew all other spiritual, philosophical, and religious dogmas; meanwhile, Li Hongzhi changed his birthday registration from July 7, 1952 to May 13, 1951 (celebrated as the birthday of Shakyamuni Buddha).[32] The official press accused him of making the change in order to claim himself as "a reincarnation of Shakyamuni." The regime found it alarming and intolerable that many Party members,[33] including high-level officials in the government and army, became followers of the Falun Gong (Perry 2002a; J. Tong 2009). This unprecedented embracing of an alien religious ideology by Party members was perceived as a real threat to the Communist regime.

The overseas development of this heterodox religious group also made the CCP leadership uncomfortable. In the late 1990s, the Falun Gong expanded globally and had main stations in numerous countries. In 1996, facing increasing official criticism, Li Hongzhi and his family immigrated to the United States (Palmer 2007: 249).[34] Despite being abroad, Li exercised absolute control over the group via telephone, email, and so forth (Ownby 2008: 165–174; Palmer 2007: 249–256). Being abroad rendered it difficult for authorities to take control of Li's activities and his organization.

In addition, the leaders' vexation was intensified by the extraordinary organizational capability of the Falun Gong, which had an effective pyramid leadership structure (with Li Hongzhi at the top as the paramount authority)

---

[32] "Life and Times of Li Hongzhi." *People's Daily*. July 23, 1999. www.people.com.cn/english/199907/23/enc_19990723001032_TopNews.html.

[33] It was estimated that 15.6 per cent of the officially announced 2.3 million Falun Gong followers were Party members (Chan 2004).

[34] After applying for investor immigrant status, the Lis settled in New York in 1998.

and maintained an absolute centralization of thought and money. Despite its failure to obtain legal recognition, the Falun Dafa Research Society, the highest institution of the Falun Gong, was able to issue notices and circulars about the training stations until the end of July 1999.[35] The group's exceptional organizational capacity was clearly demonstrated in the April 25th incident.

What made the authorities further resolved to launch a comprehensive crackdown was the Falun Gong's warning messages against the imminent repression. On June 2, 1999, Li Hongzhi released a statement on the Internet, hinting that 100 million Falun Gong cultivators might rise up in the face of repression (Palmer 2007: 272). A blunter threat appeared on the Falun Gong online bulletin board: "The authorities should quickly sober up to avoid an even more severe consequence ... Isn't the act of imperiously pushing 100 million good people to the opposite side producing another 'June 4th Incident'?"[36] (Palmer 2007: 272).[37]

State repression was then met with fearless resistance by faithful followers. The suppression was perceived as illegitimate when disciples saw nothing wrong in practicing Falun Gong, the purpose of which was simply to improve their personal health and life quality. Unlawful repression (such as torture), in turn, confirmed the perception of illegitimacy. What's more, the guru, Li Hongzhi, also encouraged fights against coercion. Some practitioners even saw tougher suppression – especially incarceration – as a kind of martyrdom and a means of self-cultivation (Junker 2014a). In this way, the state crackdown did not subdue resistance but instead made devoted believers more determined in their struggle.

Impact on Regime Legitimacy and Durability

In the face of ruthless crackdowns, many practitioners abandoned the Falun Gong, whereas others remained loyal. While its activities seem to have decreased in the PRC, its continued resistance remains a matter of grave concern to the CCP (Noakes and Ford 2015). Through the Falun Gong's vast telecommunications network, Li Hongzhi's message can be continuously conveyed to mainland China where, since 2002, its activities have largely gone underground, as seen in covert meetings in the form of small groups or larger conferences (J. Tong 2012). Pro-Falun Gong slogans appeared on walls and

---

[35] The Falun Gong was composed of a vertical point-to-point connection, with the connection among the main stations (*zongzhan*), branch stations (*fenzhan*), guidance stations (*fudao zhan*), and informal leaders of practice sites (Chan 2004). The organization structure helped reinforce notions of discipline and selfless sacrifice among practitioners and facilitated rapid mobilization and collective action.

[36] This refers to the 1989 Tiananmen uprising, which ended on June 4.

[37] These menacing messages were followed up by demonstrations and sending petitions with tens of thousands signatures to President Jiang Zemin and Primer Zhu Rongji (Palmer 2007: 273–274).

Chinese currency, Falun Gong pamphlets and CDs are secretly distributed in public spaces, and anonymous phone calls are made to persuade people to withdraw from Party organizations.

Moreover, the Falun Gong has prospered overseas, staging and sustaining well-organized and persistent resistance against the Chinese state. Disciples have orchestrated large-scale public demonstrations to accuse and denounce brutal and unlawful repression and human rights violations in China; they have also filed formal lawsuits against Chinese officials, lobbied foreign governments for support, and made a bid to nominate Li Hongzhi for the Nobel Peace Prize (Junker 2014b; Palmer 2007: 278; Thornton 2010: 231). Currently, the Falun Gong issue has become a component of general discourse among international human rights groups and Western governments criticizing human rights violations in China (Palmer 2007: 281). Additionally, media outlets (including television stations and newspapers) run by the organization consistently deliver attacks on the Chinese regime; among them, *Epoch Times*, one of the largest overseas Chinese news outlets, has even initiated a campaign for readers to disavow their affiliations to any CCP organizations. No doubt, these activities keep embarrassing the Chinese government in the world, pose a challenge to its legitimacy, and constantly foster hatred against the state among Falun Gong practitioners and sympathizers. Last but not least, the widespread practice of unlawful means to punish the practitioners also adversely affects rule-of-law in contemporary China (Keith and Lin 2003).

CHARTER 08

As discussed in previous chapters, the government bends the rules for protesters out of legitimacy concerns. Yet once resisters question state legitimacy, there can be little room left for leniency and negotiations; rather, both sides play their cards according to antagonistic informal norms. This is exemplified in the Charter 08 campaign; here, pro-democracy ideology became a core element that challenged the one-party system.

Charter 08 is a manifesto for democratic reform, published online on December 10, 2008, the 60th anniversary of the Universal Declaration of Human Rights. The charter called for 19 changes, including the end of the single-party system, the establishment of an independent legal system, and the realization of freedom of association.[38] Initially, it was signed by 303 Chinese intellectuals, lawyers, journalists, and retired Party officials, among others;[39] by October 2014, more than 13,000 people inside and outside China had signed the charter.[40] Charter 08 was hailed as the most significant act of public dissent

[38] "Charter 08." www.2008xianzhang.info/chinese.htm.
[39] "A Nobel Prize for a Chinese Dissident." *The New York Times.* September 20, 2010. www.nytimes.com/2010/09/21/opinion/21iht-edhavel.html?_r=1.
[40] "Charter 08." www.2008xianzhang.info/chinese.htm.

against the CCP and one of the boldest calls for political change since Tiananmen.[41] In fact, many of the charter signers had participated in the 1989 Tiananmen movement. The state's relentless suppression of this movement had turned a number of its participants into veteran dissidents, whose numbers included Liu Xiaobo and Zhang Zuhua, the main authors of Charter 08.

The Seed of Charter 08: 1989 Tiananmen Movement

In spring 1989, Beijing witnessed mass demonstrations led by college students. Disgruntled by economic injustice, rapid inflation, and official corruption, demonstrators took to the streets and occupied Tiananmen Square (Calhoun 1989); the number of participants – from all walks of lives – reached a million at its zenith (Zhao 2001). The movement lasted from mid-April to early June, and spread to hundreds of other cities in China.[42] Protesters pushed for pro-democratic political reform, yet they also urged the government to tackle the economic problems (Zhao 2001). During the demonstrations, many student organizations were established. Some student leaders were more inclined to engage in dialogue with the government, whereas others preferred a more radical approach. In general, student leaders all agreed to keep the protest movement peaceful (Liu 1992; Zhao 2001).

At the outset, the government condemned student marches and demonstrations as anti-Party, anti-government disturbances.[43] This harsh attitude, however, failed to intimidate students, outraging them instead and stimulating several large-scale marches to the Tiananmen Square. Feeling the pressure, the government began to soften its tone and took a more conciliatory stance. The state held several dialogues with student leaders. In early May, Zhao Ziyang, then-General Secretary of the Communist Party, acknowledged the concerns of students as legitimate and praised the movement as patriotic and supportive of the Party.[44] The state media also started to cover the movement in a positive way. Yet government conciliation was unable to put a stop to the protest movement. On the contrary, a few hundred students took more radical action and started a hunger strike, which won them broad social support and gave the movement more momentum. Eventually, hardliners within the state

[41] "Beijing Strikes at Dissidents." David Stanway. *The Guardian*. January 3, 2009. www.theguardian.com/world/2009/jan/04/china-human-rights-charter-08. "Charter 08: A Bold Call for Change." Catherine Sampson. *The Guardian*. December 12, 2008. www.theguardian.com/commentisfree/2008/dec/12/china-humanrights.

[42] "Five Things You Should Know about the Tiananmen Square Massacre." Noah Rayman. *Time*. June 4, 2014. http://time.com/2822290/tiananmen-square-massacre-anniversary/.

[43] "We Must Take a Clear-Cut Stand against Disturbances." *People's Daily*. April 26, 1989. http://news.xinhuanet.com/ziliao/2005-02/23/content_2609426.htm.

[44] "Zhao Ziyang's Speech in a Meeting with Officials of the Asian Development Bank." Xinhua News Agency. May 4, 1989. http://1989report.hkja.org.hk/site/portal/Site.aspx?id=A27-126.

sent troops and tanks to quell the movement. The death toll is in dispute, ranging from several hundred to several thousand.[45]

Was the 1989 movement regime-threatening? Yes and no. Indeed, given its scale, organization, and claims, the movement contained elements that were threatening to Party rule. Some activists also saw democracy as a primary goal in the movement (Zhao 2001). On the other hand, while claims such as "democracy" and "free press" were raised, most of the protesters did not intend to topple the state.[46] Instead, as Liu Xiaobo (1992) recalls, many of them demanded an acceleration of the political reform to be *led by* the CCP. Most of those who participated in the movement did so in reaction to the economic problems brought about by market reform (Calhoun 1989; Zhao 2001). Although it ended in bloody repression, both authorities and protesters made an effort to negotiate and participate in dialogue at some point in the movement. For this reason, the Tiananmen incident cannot be seen as clearly regime-threatening.

However, ruthless suppression of a nonviolent movement not only severely undermined the legitimacy of the state and alienated its people but also turned a number of protest activists and sympathizers into professional pro-democracy fighters, many of whom took part in the Charter 08 campaign. The stories of the two initiators of the campaign – Liu Xiaobo and Zhang Zuhua – are telling in this regard.

Liu Xiaobo, then a university professor, initiated a four-man hunger strike (himself included) at the end of the Tiananmen movement and was arrested in the wake of the crackdown. He was detained in jail until January 1991.[47] After being released, Liu was dismissed from his profession. He then went freelance and, in the 2000s, became president and board member of the Independent Chinese PEN Center (ICPC).[48] Due to his persistent political activism, including

---

[45] "Hong Kong Recalls Tiananmen Killings, China Muffles Dissent." Adam Rose and Ben Blanchard. *Reuters*. June 4, 2014. www.reuters.com/article/2014/06/04/us-china-tiananmen-idUSKB NoEFoDV20140604. Most casualties took place outside of Tiananmen Square when Beijing residents attempted to prevent the military force from pushing into the Square, while on the Square most people were able to retreat to safety after negotiations with the troops.

[46] As a side note, the 1989 Tiananmen movement was largely an urban affair, and surveys reveal that, in May 1989, 50% of the urban residents wanted to slow down market reform and return to the old socialist system, whereas merely 20% of them wanted to speed up the reform and expand it to political democratization (Tang 2005).

[47] Liu was convicted of "counter-revolutionary propaganda and incitement" but exempted from criminal punishment for his "major meritorious action" (*zhongda ligong biaoxian*), i.e., helping persuade students to withdraw from Tiananmen Square to avoid possible bloodshed ("Liu Xiaobo Deserves the Nobel Prize," Chinese Contemporary Prisoners of Literary Inquisition, Case 64 of Volume 1, Independent Chinese PEN Center, Issue 13, www.penchinese.org/blog/archives/9653).

[48] ICPC claims to dedicate itself to the promotion of freedom of expression and publications to counter censorship (ICPC, www.penchinese.org/english/about-icpc). For years, ICPC received funding from the National Endowment for Democracy, funded largely by the US Congress (National Endowment for Democracy, www.ned.org/where-we-work/asia/china).

writing numerous articles, launching campaigns, and authoring declarations advocating the values of freedom and demanding multi-party elections,[49] he was frequently put under house arrest (especially, during sensitive times such as the anniversary of the 1989 movement)[50] or sentenced to years in the reeducation-through-labor camp.

The 1989 movement also changed the life of Zhang Zuhua, the other primary drafter of Charter 08. Zhang had been a high-ranking official in the Communist Party Youth League.[51] Because he actively participated in the 1989 movement and organized his fellow colleagues to support the students, Zhang was stripped of his official positions. Since then, Zhang has pursued a career promoting human rights and democratic reform in China through organizing civil society forums and writing books on constitutional democracy.[52] Like Liu Xiaobo, Zhang has often lived under police surveillance and has been put under house arrest at sensitive moments.[53]

After 20 years living as political dissidents, Liu and Zhang started the most influential pro-democracy protest since Tiananmen: Charter 08.

Antagonistic Informal Norms at Play

To spur officials to follow accommodating informal norms of contention, regime-engaging protesters typically make an effort to desensitize their claims and avoid contesting the authority of the government (see Chapters 3 and 4). Charter 08 campaigners did just the opposite. The charter unequivocally denounced the legitimacy of the regime by declaring that the CCP rule "has stripped people of their rights, corroded the humanity, and destroyed their dignity"[54] and condemned the CCP's approach to modernization as "disastrous." As a solution, Charter 08 demanded direct elections and regime change – from an authoritarian to a democratic regime. In so doing, in terms of claims, the Charter 08 clearly transgressed the boundaries of the protest space allowed by the state.

---

[49] "Recommendations about Major National Affairs of Our Country – October 10th Declaration." Wang Xizhe and Liu Xiaobo. *The Independent Review*. August 11, 1996. www.duping.net/XHC/show.php?bbs=10&post=1017959.

[50] "Police Cars Wait Outside while Being under House Arrest for Years." *Apple Daily*. October 9, 2010. http://hk.apple.nextmedia.com/news/art/20101009/14535145.

[51] "The Life of the CCP's Former Rising Star Was Changed by the June 4th Incident." *Mingpao*. December 8, 2010. http://dailynews.sina.com/gb/chn/chnpolitics/mingpao/20101208/1315206 5376.html.

[52] "Charter 08 Co-Organizer Zhang Zuhua Abducted by Police ahead of Nobel Ceremony." Chinese Human Rights Defenders. December 9, 2010. http://chrdnet.com/2010/12/charter-08-co-organizer-zhang-zuhua-abducted-by-police-ahead-of-nobel-ceremony/.

[53] "Zhang Zuhua, a Drafter of Charter 08 and Scholar of Constitutionalism, Was Abducted." *ChinaAid*. December 10, 2010. www.chinaaid.net/2010/12/blog-post_10.html.

[54] "Charter 08." www.2008xianzhang.info/chinese.htm.

The Chinese regime then responded promptly with repression, labeling Charter 08 a "counter-revolutionary platform."[55] The evening before the charter was published, Beijing police raided the houses of Liu Xiaobo and Zhang Zuhua and took them into custody. Zhang was released after 12 hours, but Liu remained in detention.[56] At least 70 of the 303 original signatories were summoned or interrogated by police.[57] On December 25, 2009, Liu Xiaobo was sentenced to 11 years in prison for "inciting subversion of state power."[58] While incarcerated, Liu was awarded the 2010 Nobel Peace Prize.[59]

Following the award announcement, law enforcement took immediate action to forestall or disrupt celebration activities organized by political dissenters. Scores of dissidents were detained, harassed, or put under surveillance.[60] Liu Xiaobo's wife, Liu Xia, was placed under house arrest, and her communication with the outside world was severely restricted.[61] Yu Jie, a well-known dissident writer and a friend of Liu Xiaobo, alleged that prior to the 2010 Nobel ceremony, he was forcibly taken from his home to an undisclosed location where he was stripped naked and kicked and slapped by security officers.[62]

The aforementioned police actions have no legal basis but have become routine tools for dealing with political dissidents. Compared to formal sanctions, these informal means allow more latitude in exerting control over dissent and, because they are deployed in a low-key fashion, authorities hope to avoid negative publicity and criticism both domestically and internationally.

Analysis of the case of Charter 08 reinforces the findings of earlier chapters that the state is rigid about the rules set for the space of protest *claims*, allowing

[55] "Beijing Strikes at Dissidents." David Stanway. *The Guardian*. January 3, 2009. www.theguardian.com/world/2009/jan/04/china-human-rights-charter-08.

[56] A New Call for Chinese Democracy." Austin Ramzy. *Time*. December 10, 2008 http://content.time.com/time/world/article/0,8599,1865510,00.html.

[57] "Beijing Acts to Stifle Dissident Call for Reform." Jamil Anderlini. *Financial Times*. January 3, 2009. www.ft.com/cms/s/0/705dc080-d938-11dd-ab5f-000077b07658.html#axzz3F7YdjWDp.

[58] "Chinese Human Rights Activist Liu Xiaobo Sentenced to 11 Years in Jail." *The Guardian*. December 25, 2009. www.guardian.co.uk/world/2009/dec/25/china-jails-liu-xiaobo.

[59] Liu died in custody in July 2017, two months after he was diagnosed with late-stage liver cancer ("Liu Xiaobo, Nobel Laureate and Political Prisoner, Dies at 61 in Chinese custody," Tom Phillips, *The Guardian*, July 13, 2017, www.theguardian.com/world/2017/jul/13/liu-xiaobo-nobel-laureate-chinese-political-prisoner-dies-61).

[60] "China, Angered by Peace Prize, Blocks Celebration." Andrew Jacobs. *The New York Times*. October 9, 2010. www.nytimes.com/2010/10/10/world/asia/10china.html?_r=1&partner=rss&emc=rss. "Viewing the Liu Xiaobo Response through Twitter." David Bandurski. *Mingpao Daily*. October 10, 2010. http://cmp.hku.hk/2010/10/11/7990/.

[61] "Five Years on, Liu Xiaobo's Wife Stays Silent, under House Arrest." Xin Lin (translator: Luisetta Mudie). Radio Free Asia. October 8, 2015. www.rfa.org/english/news/china/silence-10082015111519.html.

[62] "Chinese Dissident in U.S. Tells of Harassment, Torture." *Los Angeles Times*. January 18, 2012. http://latimesblogs.latimes.com/world_now/2012/01/china-beijing-dissident-chinese-writer-yu-jie-torture-washington.html.

little room for maneuver in this regard. Although Charter 08 was largely a peaceful online campaign that did not create much disruption, demanding the termination of Party rule *per se* was enough to trigger undue coercion.

Impact on Regime Legitimacy

Excessive force has been unable to wipe out pro-democracy dissent in China. Ironically, unlawful measures to silent and punish political dissidents actually help reinforce their belief in democracy and justify the necessity to fight for it. In the pro-democracy global atmosphere, harsh reaction to peaceful pro-democracy resistance can easily draw criticism from Western governments and human rights organizations, casting doubt on the legitimacy of the authoritarian regime. Liu's Nobel Prize caused acute embarrassment to the Chinese government, putting China's human rights issue in an international spotlight. The Nobel Prize galvanized foreign leaders (including US President Barack Obama), other Nobel laureates, and human rights groups, to call for Liu's release.[63] Inside China, news of Liu's award was censored. Nonetheless, the award was an affirmation of the efforts of those who were fighting for democracy in China and was a big morale boost for Chinese democracy dissidents. Wang Dan, a prominent student leader of the 1989 movement, took the sanguine view that the prize would encourage more people to participate in the pro-democracy movement inside and outside of China.[64] Yet although the majority of human rights activists applauded Liu's award, a few objected to it. Wei Jingsheng, a famous dissident known for his bold call for democracy and criticism of Deng Xiaoping during the Democracy Wall movement of 1978, believed that other dissidents deserved the award more than Liu;[65] a group of 14 overseas Chinese dissenters even called on the Nobel Committee to deny the prize to Liu.[66] The varied reactions reflect the competition and fractured relations among the dissident groups. Nevertheless, by and large, Liu's Noble Prize played a positive role in raising the reputation of and bringing more sympathy to Chinese human rights dissidents. What's more, the Prize further delegitimized the repression of political dissidents within China.

---

[63] "Nobel Peace Prize Given to Jailed Chinese Dissident." Andrew Jacobs and Jonathan Ansfield. *The New York Times.* October 8, 2010. www.nytimes.com/2010/10/09/world/09nobel.html?pagewanted=all.

[64] "Overseas Chinese Dissidents Had Varied Reactions to Liu Xiaobo's Award." *BBC News.* October 8, 2010. www.bbc.co.uk/zhongwen/simp/china/2010/10/101008_liuxiaobo_overseas_reaction.shtml.

[65] Ibid.

[66] "Unusual Opposition to a Favorite for Nobel." Andrew Jacobs and Jonathan Ansfield. *The New York Times.* October 6, 2010. www.nytimes.com/2010/10/07/world/asia/07china.html?_r=0.

"Different Reactions: Behind Liu Xiaobo's Nobel Prize." *Jinggang Station.* October 9, 2010. www.backchina.com/news/2010/10/09/108629.html.

CONCLUSION

This chapter has focused on conditions in which accommodating informal norms are absent and antagonistic informal norms play out. It illustrates that important factors – including ethnicity, religion, ideology, a history of animosity, and international linkage – can complicate the interaction dynamics of resisters and the state, deepen mistrust between them, and hinder the application of accommodating informal norms. Furthermore, in regime-engaging protests, local officials often avoid excessive coercion due to state leaders' calls for leniency and protesters' self-censorship. In regime-threatening protests, by contrast, the top leadership is in favor of a ruthless crackdown, and local officials may then step outside the law to deal with challengers who enter forbidden zones.

To be clear, ethnicity and religion do not inevitably lead to repression. The analysis in Chapter 2 shows that protests by minorities in general do not necessarily incur a greater chance of repression. As an example, while there is a strong sense of ethnic identify among the Koreans in China, relations between Han Chinese and Koreans seem comparatively free of serious tensions (Mackerras 2004: 222). With respect to religion, the majorities of Uyghurs are practitioners of Islam; so are the Hui, but the state is more tolerant of protests by the Hui than by Uyghurs (Gladney 2004; see Chapter 2). A recent study shows that Communism and Islam in China are *not incompatible* belief systems; rather, the Islamic law and the Chinese state are reconcilable and manage to work together (Erie 2016). In this sense, it is only when ethnicity and religion entangle with other issues (such as history and politics) that accommodating informal norms may fail, as demonstrated in the Uyghur and Falun Gong protests.

Cases in this chapter (especially Charter 08) confirm that the type of claims represents the most rigid red line in determining whether or not it will bring about state repression. When claims were seen as challenging the CCP's monopoly on political power, there was little room for tolerance in terms of actions and organization. Although my regime-engaging cases pushed the limits of the space for organization and actions, they never pushed the limits for claims, e.g., raising goals targeting the one-party system. The Falun Gong case also proves that organization is a critical factor in determining state reaction to protest, especially when an autonomous organization demonstrates high mobilization capacity.

The three cases also illustrate the shift from regime-engaging to regime-threatening protests. During the 1980s, Uyghurs' claim for more autonomy in Xinjiang resonated with the top Chinese leaders, resulting in a relatively permissive environment for Uyghur religious and cultural practice. Yet, entering the 1990s, Uyghurs' violent and organized uprisings brought about unrelenting crackdowns. While Uyghurs' protests against Han rule turned mainly underground during the 2000s, bloody protest broke out on July 5, 2009 in Urumqi.

Likewise, authorities were relatively lenient towards Falun Gong resistance at the outset and generally tolerated hundreds of demonstrations by its practitioners. However, the April 25th incident was a turning point. Since the state initiated comprehensive repression in 1999, the Falun Gong resistance has been galvanized into a true political opposition campaign. In the case of Charter 08, brutal suppression of the 1989 Tiananmen uprising radicalized pro-democracy dissidents and created long-term fighters against the regime. In all three cases, when contention becomes regime-threatening, it tends to descend into a vicious cycle of transgression and repression, with both authorities and protesters contributing to the escalation of conflict.

Excessive force has failed to eliminate protests by Uyghurs, Falun Gong adherents, and pro-democracy dissidents. Nowadays, Xinjiang remains one of China's most unstable regions. Ethnic tensions and violent attacks on ordinary citizens have also gone beyond Xinjiang and spread to other provinces in China. Abroad, Uyghur exile groups continue pressing their case for independence from China. The Falun Gong resistance persists in mainland China, although it has largely gone underground; drawing on its extensive media network and endorsement from the foreign governments, the Falun Gong prospers overseas and has launched long-term campaigns to condemn the legitimacy of the CCP and its leaders. The clampdown on Charter 08 was unable to deter pro-democracy dissidents. On the contrary, Liu Xiaobo's Nobel Prize heartened the dissenters and has called regime legitimacy into question. Outside the PRC, all these protests consistently attack the human rights records of the Chinese government, embarrassing the regime on the international stage. All in all, these protests, under the influence of antagonistic informal norms, jeopardize social stability, erode regime legitimacy, and pose a real challenge to authoritarian durability in the long term. In this sense, while regime-threatening protests are relatively infrequent in China now, their detrimental influence on regime stability should not be underestimated.

6

Conclusion

The ruler is like a boat and the people are like the water. The water can float or overturn the boat.

Xunzi (third century BC)

Since a ruler, then, must know how to act like a beast, he should imitate both the fox and the lion, for the lion is liable to be trapped, whereas the fox cannot ward off wolves. One needs, then, to be a fox to recognize traps, and a lion to frighten away wolves. Those who rely merely upon a lion's strength do not understand matters.

Niccolò Machiavelli, *The Prince* (1532: 61)

Playing by the Informal Rules explores a crucial issue: What is the impact of rising protests on the durability of an authoritarian regime? Using the case of China, this book throws light on authoritarian resilience by stressing how the state has been able to control and contain protests through accommodating informal norms of contention. This approach is different from most studies on the stability of authoritarian regimes, which center on *formal* institutions, economic resources, international linkages, and so forth.[1] In addition, despite a recent growth in interest in *informal* institutions, most observers tend to focus on how these unwritten rules affect the quality and performance of *democracy* or *liberal* politics (e.g., Azari 2012; Bratton 2007; Carlson 2006; Darden 2008; Helmke and Levitsky 2004 and 2006b; Lauth 2000; Siavelis 2006; c.f. L. Tsai 2007; K. Tsai 2007). Relatively less has been written about the effects of informal institutions on *authoritarian* resilience, especially at times of growing dissent.[2] As this work shows, examining informal norms of contention is

---

[1] For reviews, see Brownlee, Masoud, and Reynolds (2015) and Hess (2016).

[2] For instance, Fjelde and Hegre (2014) have argued that political corruption is an informal institution that allows non-democratic leaders to build political support and acts as a substitute

helpful in elucidating the resilience of the Chinese regime amid surging unrest and expanding our understanding of the complexity of authoritarian politics.

In addition, this book suggests that scholarship about contentious politics in authoritarian settings, which has tended to focus on transgression and repression, would be advanced by devoting more attention to ways in which these regimes engage protesters in negotiation and attempt to manage – rather than simply repress – protests. Existing research on contentious politics in non-democratic settings has overwhelmingly centered on transgressive protests and harsh repression, i.e., regime-threatening protests. This type of resistance tends to be a zero-sum game: either the regimes are overthrown or the protests are smothered. Relatively few studies have examined the non-zero-sum game between government and challengers (like regime-engaging protests). Overlooking the distinctions between these types of contention largely leads to the myth that associates proliferating protests with the decline of authoritarian states.[3] Thus, discussions on the political impact of contention should disaggregate types of protests, considering their contrasting indications on regime stability.

Empirically, this work enhances our understanding of authoritarian resilience in China. Current explanations for the durability of this one-party state have highlighted its ability to incorporate the burgeoning private sector, to accommodate the emerging civil society organizations and media commercialization, to maintain an appropriate mixture of carrots (welfare provision) and sticks (political repression), to manage urbanization through internal migration restrictions (hukou system), to recruit, monitor, and reward the political elite and local cadres, and to rebuild the Party's organizational apparatus and government institutions (Brødsgaard 2004; Chen and Dickson 2008 and 2010; Dickson 2007 and 2008; Gallagher and Hanson 2013; Holbig 2009; Landry 2008; Manion 2015 and 2017; Naughton and Yang 2004; Saich 2016; Shambaugh 2008;[4] Stockmann 2013; Stockmann and Gallagher 2011; Teets 2014; Truex 2018; K. Tsai 2007 and 2013; Tsang 2009; Walder 2004 and 2009a; Wallace 2014; Yang 2004). Other explanations for regime resilience in China include an emphasis on the positive roles of community solidary groups and patronage politics in facilitating the functioning of China's political system (Hillman 2014; L. Tsai 2007). Through a variety of analytic lenses, previous studies allow a deeper understanding of the endurance of the Chinese regime.

---

for liberalizing concessions in the formal institutions of the state, thereby extending the longevity of non-democratic regimes. But their discussion has little to do with contention and protest control.

[3] For similar criticism, see Ulfelder (2005: 313).

[4] Shambaugh has more recently changed his position and now contends that Chinese Communism has reached its final phase, although he does not predict when it will collapse ("The Coming Chinese Crackup," *The Wall Street Journal*, March 6, 2015, www.wsj.com/articles/the-coming-chinese-crack-up-1425659198).

However, these works do not directly address the question of why the state manages to remain stable *despite mounting protests*. As the coexistence of the two is at odds with existing theories, providing a systematic answer to this question contributes to a better understanding of governance and authoritarian resilience in this single-party state.

CONTENTIOUS POLITICS AND REGIME STABILITY IN CHINA

Due to rigid institutional arrangements that serve to forbid protests, the majority of resisters in present-day China, who seek state intervention, support, or concessions, often fail to comply completely with the harsh legal requirements in spite of their self-censorship in claim making and mobilization. The fact that the government rarely approves contentious actions, such as marches, renders nearly all protest activities illegal in China. Nonetheless, when an unauthorized march takes place, authorities typically respond using an informal procedure, e.g., "diplomacy-first, force as backup" – that is, they monitor the protest closely, react according to protesters' further activities, and do not take forceful measures in the first place. In fact, a common practice is an attempt to direct the public contestation to the negotiation table and to convert it into an institutional act (e.g., a petition). Such unwritten rules, which I call "accommodating informal norms of contention," plays an essential role in the actual interaction between government officials and aggrieved citizens at the grassroots level.

While not disputing the importance of formal institutions, this book stresses that examining accommodating informal norms of contention can provide invaluable insights into the political implications of contention. As we have seen, these informal norms not only result in an extralegal space in which citizens can express their grievances but also serve as a social safety valve, help channel street protests to the negotiation table, and stimulate self-censorship among dissenters. When both officials and protesters play according to the informal rules and work on resolving conflicts through dialogue not force, it prevents the contention from becoming a zero-sum contest and contributes to regime resilience. One element that is missing in most studies on contentious politics in non-democratic states is a discussion of accommodating informal norms of contention and their implications. Solely centering on formal institutions that restrict citizens' rights of protest merely reveals part of the whole picture of contentious politics in China while overlooking a gray zone in which some activities bypassing the law are *de facto* tolerated. This protest space is full of contentious actions and saves contentious politics in China from being largely transgressive and repressive.

Why does a strong authoritarian state allow the existence of accommodating informal norms? The research argues that the Chinese authorities have deep concerns about preserving regime legitimacy and stability in the face of surging protests. Because of these concerns, the political elite have been calling for government officials to distinguish between different types of contention and calling for leniency when dealing with "contradictions among the people" (CAP). These directives are often at odds with the rigid formal laws that virtually prohibit all non-state-sponsored collective action. The inconsistent mandates combined with protesters' boundary-pushing yet self-limiting efforts can pressure local authorities to bend the rules for challengers. In particular, when local officials are embedded in their own jurisdictions or when popular resistance is in line with the local government's interests, politicians in the localities are more likely to sympathize with protesters and be willing to apply informal tolerance.

The mechanisms and dynamics of accommodating informal norms only work with regime-engaging protests. However, even with such protests, these informal norms can break down. By and large, regime-engaging protesters self-discipline their claim making and endeavor to avoid transgression; yet, when protesters continuously push the envelope, their protests have the potential to turn transgressive at any point. On the other hand, authorities constantly monitor protests and at times remind challengers of the limits through informal or formal means of punishment. Nonetheless, as long as both officials and protesters can return to dialogue, these protests can still be considered regime-engaging. This was true in the cases of both the Hill Factory struggle (Chapter 3) and Banana Village protest (Chapter 4). In addition, the application and perception of accommodating informal norms may differ across regions, social classes, and time owing to identity politics, local political environment, and resources mobilized by protesters.

Accommodating informal norms barely appear in regime-threatening protests. Instead, what I call "antagonistic informal norms of contention" play a central role here. Under the latter norms, authorities bend the laws *against* dissidents who impose little self-censorship. More often than not, the top leadership issues orders for repression and the local authorities, under pressure to complete the crackdown task, may employ whatever means at their disposal. Regime-threatening protests tend to sink into a vicious cycle of transgression and repression, which is in line with the conventional depictions of contentious politics in non-democratic settings. This kind of contention is inclined to jeopardize regime stability and legitimacy, as exemplified in the cases of Uyghur unrest, the Falun Gong protest, and the Charter 08 pro-democracy campaign (Chapter 5). These case studies also illustrate that the chance that antagonistic informal norms will play out increases when conflicts and grievances are mixed with factors such as ethnicity, religion, ideology, a history of animosity, and international linkage.

Then, which type of social protest is more prevalent in China today? According to my quantitative research, regime-engaging protest is the dominant form of contention in the country. Based on a unique nationwide dataset of protest events across China, my analysis reveals a wider space for protest than the one constrained by legal mandates and shows that self-control in claims, actions, and organization is popular among protesters. This result reinforces the findings of my qualitative studies, suggesting that bending the rules in favor of resisters and dissenters' self-censorship is widespread across the country. This finding aids in explaining why the one-party state remains resilient amid a mounting number of social protests. That being said, I caution against underestimating the potential destructive effect of regime-threatening protests on regime survival, even though they comprise only a tiny proportion of total contentious events. Failure to curb that type of protest always poses a challenge to the incumbents.

Stressing accommodating informal norms and protest space by no means downplays the repressive environment for collective action that exists in China. Protest is still a sensitive issue for the government and a precarious endeavor for dissenters. In the reform era, the Chinese government has taken various measures to strengthen its control over protest, from increasing the amount of money and personnel devoted to preserving social stability (X. Chen 2013; Fewsmith 2016; Wang and Minzner 2015) to censoring online discussions of collective action (King, Pan, and Roberts 2013). Officials have the final say in dealing with contention and may not respect accommodating informal norms that have been established. Besides heavy-handed repression, the regime can also employ unlawful means (e.g., hiring thugs and using extralegal detention facilities) or adopt soft forms of repression (e.g., intimidation and Internet hacking) to discourage activism. In this context, most challengers have to contain contention within a narrow space for resistance. Although the space for protest *actions* is relatively broad, the regime imposes sharp limits on the types of *claims* that can be made, and there is little room for formal *organization* or links among protests.

On the flip side, protesters are always pushing the envelope, and it is this kind of grassroots resistance that contributed to the formation of accommodating informal norms in the first place. Hence, contentious politics in contemporary China is part of an ongoing process of "tactical interaction," in which collective action involves an evolving interplay between challengers and rulers, produces a chess-like sequence of interactions between the two (McAdam 1983: 736). In this way, tactical interaction gives rise to these informal norms of contention and subsequently extralegal legitimate protest space.

Once again, this book does not contend that accommodating informal norms alone contribute to regime resilience, but rather that state capacities – both to curb dissent by force and to accommodate protesters' demands – are key factors that ultimately determine regime stability. Even when a state has lost a great deal of legitimacy, it can remain quite stable and be invulnerable to revolution if "its coercive organizations remain coherent and effective" (Skocpol 1979: 32). Furthermore, when protesters expect that officials are able to respond to their demands in a positive manner, they may censor themselves and pose no direct challenge to the regime.[5]

---

[5] As an example, in the early eighteenth century, when the Qing state had the resources and incentives to protect local communities from natural disasters, peasants hit by the disasters would use peaceful petitions to make their claims; by contrast, one century later, when the capacity of

The picture of contentious politics depicted in this book spans the time period largely from the late Jiang to the Hu administrations. To what extent do the findings extend to the Xi Jinping era? To be sure, since Xi took office in November 2012, the space for political *criticism* and civil society groups seems to have become even more limited. The new leadership has been deeply concerned with the spread of liberal ideas – such as "constitutional government" and "judicial independence"[6] – and has tightened its control over the Internet and social media, cracked down on non-governmental organizations (NGOs) such as labor and women's rights organizations, arrested hundreds of human rights lawyers, put intellectuals under tighter scrutiny, and the like (Fewsmith 2016; Fu and Distelhorst 2018; Human Rights Watch 2015; Shambaugh 2016). According to a report by Freedom House (2015), the overall level of repression in China has indeed increased since Xi came to power, and this is particularly true for online opinion leaders, labor activists, journalists, scholars, and Uyghurs, among other groups. Nevertheless, when it comes to groups such as protest participants and political dissidents, the degree of suppression has remained *consistent* with the final years of the Hu era; petitioners even suffer slightly less coercion, as the report reveals. At the top, the Xi administration has reiterated its predecessor's calls for security agents to avoid the use of force when possible (Freedom House 2015). At the grassroots level, tacit tolerance is still observed in many cases; resisters, more often than not, self-limit their claim making.[7] In fact, an annual research report reveals that the level of violence in mass incidents fell substantially across the country in 2016, reversing a growing trend since 2008, and meanwhile negotiations and peaceful means in dispute resolution increased nationally (Zhang and Liu 2017). Moreover, it is worth mentioning that the crackdowns on NGOs in the Xi era differ in the *types* of NGOs. For instance, while *labor* organizations tended to be the targets of state attacks, few *environmental* NGOs were reported to suffer harsh treatment.[8] In this sense, we may tentatively conclude that even though the current leadership has become less tolerant of political critics and some types of grassroots NGOs, the dynamics of contentious politics revealed in this book have not undergone drastic changes. For a more decisive answer, further systematic research into the protest space in the Xi era is necessary.

---

the Qing state – including its economic resources – was in substantial decline, peasants would resort to confrontational and violent collective action (Hung 2007).

[6] These concerns are enumerated in a memo referred to as Document No. 9. For more details about this document, see "China Takes Aim at Western Ideas" (Chris Buckley, *The New York Times*, August 19, 2013, http://www.nytimes.com/2013/08/20/world/asia/chinas-new-leadership-takes-hard-line-in-secret-memo.html).

[7] Observations from my fieldwork between 2013 and 2016, including dialogues with protest leaders and activists and environmental NGO staff members (e.g., Interviewees 49, 90, 100, and 107).

[8] "Are China's NGOs Another Kind of Rights-Protection Movement?" Chen Honglei. *The Reporter*. August 24, 2016. https://www.twreporter.org/a/china-ngo.

Looking forward, can accommodating informal norms hold in China in the future? In history, such unwritten rules as those discussed in this work appeared in the Soviet Union in the 1960s and 1970s but vanished after 1979 when domestic and international conditions changed and the incumbents became more intolerant of dissent (Karklins 1987). Will this be the case in China? Apparently, this is difficult to tell, especially considering the vagaries of historical contingency. Unforeseen events or factors – e.g., economic crises and wars with foreign countries – could affect the state's willingness and capacity to permit some space for protest. It is also worth mentioning that accommodating informal norms have limitations in keeping unrest under control. Their positive effect of absorbing contention may be more evident in the short run, and it is questionable whether the containing effect can be sustainable over time.[9] State tolerance and compromises may motivate more protests. Given that contentious actors constantly push the envelope and local officials have discretion over handling contention, there is always a chance that a regime-engaging protest can shift in the regime-threatening direction. Although the unwritten rules help the government manage conflicts in an expedient and flexible way, the lack of effective and well-established formal institutions to stabilize actors' expectations about upcoming interactions has the potential to cause the interactions deviate from regime-engaging routes.

Will the Chinese regime remain stable in the time ahead? Again, there is no crystal ball to gaze into. The incumbents, regarding preserving stability as an "overriding task,"[10] are most anxious to seek an answer to this million-dollar question. Their anxiety is clearly manifested in their paranoid reactions to the "Jasmine Revolution" (as described at the start of this book), in the consistently rising domestic security expenditure over decades (Greitens 2017; Xie 2013), and in the development of an umbrella organizational structure overseeing social stability in the central and local governments alike (Biddulph 2015; Wang and Minzner 2015; Xie 2012). Indeed, while the great majority of protests today are regime-engaging, this does not guarantee the future, especially when we take the fluidity between regime-engaging and regime-threatening protests into consideration. In the Falun Gong protest and the Uyghur unrest, both authorities and protesters played a part in escalating the conflict and pushing the protests in a regime-threatening direction. The dominant pattern of protests in the country might also shift if a negative cycle of repression and transgression spreads, even with protests that begin with economic and environmental claims. This potential can be seen in the Hill Factory and Banana

---

[9] According to my dataset, violent protests did not show a clear pattern of either growth or decline during the researched time period – from 2001 to 2012 (see Figure A 2.1).

[10] For instance, in 1989, Deng Xiaoping proclaimed: "Of China's problems, the need for stability overrides all else. Without a stable environment, nothing can be achieved, and whatever achievements have been made will be lost." ("Stability Overrides All Else," *News of the Communist Party of China*, http://cpc.people.com.cn/GB/64162/64170/4467121.html)

Village cases. This shift seems to be truer for the lower classes (workers and peasants) than for the middle class, who seem to have more protest space and more robust respect for the legitimacy of the state. Despite the fluidity, the model of regime-engaging and regime-threatening protests provides a valuable tool for observing the trajectory of political challenges and assessing their impact on regime stability. For a reliable evaluation, we need to watch the interactions between the state and protesters carefully and closely.

CONTENTIOUS POLITICS AND REGIME STABILITY BEYOND CHINA

Accommodating informal norms as explored in this book are not unique for China. They were seen in the USSR during the 1960s and 1970s (as noted) when the Communist regime allowed some unsanctioned dissent as long as it refrained from exceeding prescribed limits (Karklins 1987). Elsewhere, even though by law the Moroccan government required permits for public gatherings and licensing of all NGOs (Tilly 2006), incumbents showed an increasing tolerance for public expression of discontent in the two decades before the Arab Spring when activism of citizens and NGOs did not directly challenge the monarchy (Albrecht 2013; Benchemsi 2014; Lust-Okar 2005). In Vietnam today, while workers seldom follow strike procedures prescribed by law, the Communist regime rarely enforces the law and punishes illegal strikers but, instead, frequently acts in the interests of the workers (Chan 2011; Kerkvliet 2010). To be sure, these informal norms may not last forever but they are instrumental in coping with popular resistance and in bolstering authoritarian stability during the period when they are in place.

For a more sophisticated understanding of contentious politics in authoritarian regimes, this research calls for more attention to be focused on the varieties of such regimes. Non-democratic regimes can range from almost complete social control based on fear and terror to regimes that are repressive yet provide limited opportunities for dissent and allow a greater degree of freedom (Johnston 2011). A "closed authoritarian" regime like China's differs from a "competitive authoritarian" regime or a "hybrid" regime like Russia's with respect to political pluralism and civic space (Diamond 2002; Levitsky and Way 2002 and 2010; Robertson 2011); and even within the same category of closed authoritarian regime, the extent of protest space in China is dramatically distinct from that in North Korea. The term "liberalized autocracy" has been coined to refer to a specific subtype of authoritarianism in which regimes are distinguished from one another by the degree of pluralism granted toward society (Albrecht 2013: 14–15; Brumberg 2002). Furthermore, the levels of regime durability vary by regime type. By and large, a single-party state is regarded as relatively stable, compared with other kinds of authoritarianisms, such as military and personalist regimes (Brownlee 2007; Geddes 1999 and 2003; Magaloni 2008). When studying reasons behind such variation, in addition to scrutinizing formal institutions, future research may pay more attention to how *informal* institutions can work to absorb contention and thus assist in sustaining authoritarian rule.

Indeed, when an authoritarian state starts to liberalize, the state may face a cascading sequence of popular uprisings that are initiated by a small group of individuals who begin pushing the envelope and then expand into broader and broader sectors of society until a full-scale mobilization is underway (O'Donnell and Schmitter 1986: 49; Rigger 2014: 45). As Samuel P. Huntington (1991: 137) famously remarks, "liberalized authoritarianism is not a stable equilibrium; the halfway house does not stand." Nevertheless, political liberalization does not necessarily lead to radical change but may instead play a role in inducing self-censorship among opposition forces. As a divide-and-rule strategy, granting some opposition groups limited opportunities to participate in elections while excluding others can produce moderation among the included parties (Lust-Okar 2005). While political opposition challenges incumbents, it may also comply with the overall rules of the political game; both regime incumbents and opposition groups may refrain from questioning the other's existence, injecting a significant dose of stability to the political system (Albrecht 2013). This is indeed akin to the logic of regime-engaging protests, in which neither authorities nor resisters challenge the legitimacy of the other.

The conceptual model of regime-engaging and regime-threatening protests that I have developed in this book can be employed to monitor the trajectory of political contention in authoritarian regimes beyond China. In order for a protest to be regime-engaging, both authorities and protesters must be open to negotiation. State toleration, which provides the opportunity for negotiation, is the prerequisite for regime-engaging protests. It is critical that authorities permit some room, formal or informal, for engagement and dialogue. In addition, we can detect protesters' attitudes toward negotiation from the forms of protest claims, actions, and organization, examining whether or not these cross the red lines set by the state. Every political order is characterized in part by the size and features of a "legitimate protest space;" the boundaries of the space, as reflected by the tolerated forms of claims, actions, and organization, may differ among regimes.[11] Nonetheless, as long as protesters do not transgress the bounds set by their own regime, they establish that they are willing to negotiate with authorities and have some expectation that authorities are willing to negotiate with them as well. When both authorities and protesters do not refuse reconciliation through dialogue, the protest can be manageable. I would propose that a state is probably in relatively stable condition even when it abounds with regime-engaging protests, whereas a regime is in danger when

---

[11] What constitutes "political" in one setting may be non-political in another (Weiner 1971: 163). In a totalitarian state, even the most trivial matter can be political (Zhao 2001:11): Food, for instance, became a political issue in France before the French Revolution because the Old Regime took responsibility for the bread supply (Mann 2012).

regime-threatening protests prevail. In China today, we see the former situation; in Eastern Europe in 1989 and in some Arab countries (such as Tunisia and Egypt) in 2011 the latter situation prevailed.

Historically, it is not rare to see changes from regime-engaging protests to regime-threatening ones in illiberal states other than China. Solidarity in Poland in 1980 began with predominantly economic demands: pay raises and a return to the old meat prices (Kubik 1994). Yet, as the movement proceeded, workers' claims became increasingly political: a call for the right to establish free trade unions and free elections. Eventually, what had begun as an isolated strike of shipyard workers with limited goals created the first noncommunist government in a socialist regime (Tarrow 2011: 122). Moreover, there is always a chance of protests moving *en masse* from regime-engaging to regime-threatening. This is what happens in revolutionary moments. Protests are not isolated; they follow examples and patterns, or what Tilly calls "repertoires." Meanwhile, connections between acts of mobilization can be forged as well. As Mark Beissinger (2002: 450) has demonstrated, prior to the collapse of the Soviet Union, multiple national groups simultaneously contested the national order *interactively* and a successful challenge by one group was followed by further challenges by others. In this sense, the emergence of a tide of nationalism (accompanied by increasingly bold calls for secession) overwhelmed the Soviet state and resulted in its collapse (Beissinger 2002).

More recently, the move from regime-engaging to regime-threatening unrest was seen in the Arab world. In 2011, protests in countries such as Tunisia and Egypt actually started out as peaceful demonstrations calling for economic and political reform but rapidly escalated to regime-threatening protests, openly demanding regime change (Brownlee, Masoud, and Reynolds 2015; Chomiak 2014; Fahmy 2012: 350; International Crisis Group 2011a and 2011b; Lynch 2012). The prevalence of regime-threatening protests in a country, however, does not inevitably mean the end of a regime: the regime's fate, to a great extent, depends on its capacity for repression (Levitsky and Way 2010; Skocpol 1979). Indeed, in the 2011 Arab upheaval, the coercive apparatus proved paramount to determining the durability of authoritarian regimes (Bellin 2012). Although regime-threatening protests dominated six countries – Tunisia, Egypt, Bahrain, Syria, Libya, and Yemen – not all regimes were toppled. Peaceful protests fell rapidly to state crackdown, replaced in Bahrain by low-key civil activism and in Syria by full-scale civil war (Brownlee, Masoud, and Reynolds 2015: 4).

*

On the whole, while a rise of political contention in authoritarian regimes has, in many cases, led to regime crisis and possibly to regime change (e.g., Acemoglu and Robinson 2006; Kurzman 1996; McAdam, Tarrow, and Tilly 2001; Opp 1994; Rasler 1996; Seidman 2009; Slater 2010), studies of authoritarian stability need to go beyond a focus on the number of protests (or of protesters) alone.

Of equal – if not more – importance in the understanding of authoritarian durability is the differentiation between the types of protests and the need to take a closer look at the dynamics and trajectories of dissent, in particular, the way how authorities react to protests and the way how resisters interact with authorities. Rather than downplaying the repressiveness of authoritarian states, *Playing by the Informal Rules* calls attention to a variety of tactics, more nuanced and sophisticated than commonly thought, that can be used by such regimes to handle contention. In this sense, informal norms of contention can provide a new perspective on the diverse ways in which power is employed in the face of grassroots resistance. The concept of informal norms of contention and the theoretical model of regime-engaging and regime-threatening protests may not only provide essential tools in advancing the discussion of contentious politics and authoritarian resilience, but they may also inspire new approaches to the study of power, rules, legitimacy, and resistance in modern societies.

Appendix I

Data and Technical Details

CHAPTER 2

Data Reliability and Biases

While my dataset might be criticized in terms of reliability and potential biases, I believe that these issues do not affect my results in any major way. First, apart from reprinting news from other media sources, Boxun takes the form of citizen journalism: citizens play an active role in collecting, reporting, analyzing, and disseminating news and information (Bowman and Willis 2003). In my dataset, a total of 1,110 protest events are reprinted news or confirmed by reports from other media channels, including the Western media (e.g., BBC and VOA) and websites of human rights groups (e.g., China Labor Bulletin and Information Center for Human Rights & Democracy), whereas the remaining 308 events do not list their information sources other than Boxun. Reports of the 1,110 events are, indeed, more reliable, but since a number of reports of the 308 Boxun-specific events include attached photos or videos, which usually display protesters' demands and the sites of events, and this evidentiary support helps confirm the basic information of the events. I also made an effort to cross-check these Boxun-specific reports. As a robustness check, I ran regression analyses on 2 different sets of events: one including all 1,418 events and the other exclusively comprising the 1,110 events. Their results are almost identical.[1] Therefore, I am confident that the accuracy of my dataset is acceptable for the purposes of this research.

Moreover, my dataset is probably not truly representative of protests in China during the researched period because events were not selected based on random sampling but largely relied upon news reports reprinted by Boxun and

---

[1] See Table A 2.10 in Appendix I.

on citizen journalists' contributions. Since Boxun tends to collect information on the more repressive events as noted in Chapter 2, my dataset is probably skewed towards protests that are repressed. It is also fair to question the quality of news reports collected by Boxun. As the sources of information are mainly from protesters, these reports are likely to exaggerate the severity of repression. These potential biases, however, are not a severe problem for this research. If a real protest space can be detected based on a dataset that is skewed toward repressed events, this should strengthen my argument.

Police Reactions to Protest Events

Definitions of Police Actions When They Are Present at Protest Events
Limited action comprises erecting barricades, maintaining the order of traffic, observing, monitoring, or recording protesters' action, negotiating with protesters, and coordinating conflicts between protesters and a third party.

Violence refers to all violent physical actions taken to obtain or achieve something. It includes pushing, shoving, hitting, grappling, or beating. Moreover, violence takes place if police use weapons or equipment, such as guns, tear gas, and batons, to attack protesters or cause damage to property. Dispersing a crowd is also counted as violence, unless news reports explicitly state that no police–protester conflicts occurred. Coercive interrogation after arrest is also treated as violence.

Arrest includes house arrest or any other actions restraining the freedom of protesters. Being summoned for interrogation is also included. Being taken away by police from the protest spot and sent back to the residential community is not treated as arrest. Nevertheless, being taken away but no mention of the destination is considered as arrest.

Statistical Description of Police Reactions
Table A 2.1 illustrates a high rate of police presence at protest events: 63.5 percent of events. This is in accord with the state regulations,[2] which requires that police have the missions of timely discovering, reporting, and controlling a mass incident. Further, after the police showed up, they took limited or no action at 36.1 percent of events, used violence at 16.7 percent, made arrests at 19.5 percent, and used violence along with arrests at 27.8 percent (see Table A 2.2).

According to Table A 2.3, police or thugs turned up at 64 percent of events, 0.5 percent higher than not considering thugs. When the police/thug were present, as seen see in Table A 2.4, they took no or limited action at 35.5 percent of the events (0.6 percent less than not considering thugs), used violence at 17.6 percent (0.9 percent more), made arrests at 19.3 percent (almost no

---

[2] See *Regulations on How Public Security Agencies Should Handle Mass Incidents.*

TABLE A 2.1 *Police presence (=1) vs. absence*

Police Presence	Freq.	Percent
0	517	36.46
1	901	63.54
Total	1,418	100

TABLE A 2.2 *Policing actions*

Police Actions	Freq.	Percent
1 = no or limited action	325	36.07
2 = violence	150	16.65
3 = arrests	176	19.53
4 = violence and arrests	250	27.75
Total	901	100

TABLE A 2.3 *Police/thug presence (=1) vs. absence*

Police Presence	Freq.	Percent
0	510	35.97
1	908	64.03
Total	1,418	100

TABLE A 2.4 *Policing/thug actions*

Policing Actions	Freq.	Percent
1 = no or limited action	322	35.46
2 = violence	160	17.62
3 = arrests	175	19.27
4 = violence and arrests	251	27.64
Total	908	100

change), and used violence along with arrests at 27.6 percent[3] (nearly no change). That is, policing became a bit more aggressive after including thugs.

[3] The percentages are rounded off, so a total of them may not add up 100 percent. More precise figures are available in Table A 2.4.

Definitions of Key Independent Variables

Claims

Economic claims include (1) defending material goods, monetary resources, or property rights and (2) calling for increasing economic resources. Examples include laid-off workers demanding higher severance pay and homeowners opposing house demolition. *Environmental claims* include resistance to any project that is expected to impair or endanger the local environment or anything that has caused environmental damage. It can be an objection to a power plant or a demand to relocate a polluting factory. *Political claims* concern demands with an explicitly political nature. However, protesters with moderate rather than radical goals may receive distinct responses from the state. *Moderate* political claims are issue-specific and usually target particular government decisions, officials, or officers, which include disclosing corruption of an individual official, exposing misconduct of a specific government department, and demanding to improve the performances of a certain institution (e.g., the court system). By contrast, *radical* political claims target the central government, seek comprehensive political change, regional autonomy, autonomous political participation, and challenge the regime as a whole. Examples of radical political claims include a call for the independence of Tibet and a demand for an end to one-party rule. The residual category, "other" claims, include pro-Chinese nationalist protests, religious protests, and medical disputes. While pro-Chinese nationalist protests are also "political" in nature, they are not categorized into political claims because I have decided to focus on political claims that target the Chinese government, whereas these nationalist protests largely target foreign governments.

Actions

Violent actions refer to using physical force (such as hitting, shoving, and beating) or weapons (such as rocks, bombs, guns, and bricks) to take confrontational actions (e.g., attacks, riots) or other actions that cause damage to people or property. *Peaceful disruptive actions* include civil disobedience, demonstrations, strikes, rallies, marches, sit-ins, and the like. When both violent and peaceful disruptive activities took place in an event, this event is counted as violent. *Peaceful non-disruptive actions* include circulating petition letters, publishing protest letters, and performing innovative contentious actions such as shaving one's head bald.

Estimation Techniques

Binary Logistic Regression

In the first step, the dependent variable, whether police attend an event or not, is a binary variable. I employ binary logistic regression (BLR), the most popular model for binary data (Agresti 2007), to analyze my data. The BLR model is specified as follows:

$$\log\left[\frac{\text{Police presence}}{\text{Police absence}}\right] = \beta_0 + \beta_1 \text{Economic}$$
$$+\beta_2 \text{Environmental} + \beta_3 \text{Moderate political}$$
$$+\beta_4 \text{Other claims} + \beta_5 \text{Peaceful disruptive}$$
$$+\beta_6 \text{Peaceful nondisruptive} + \beta_7 \text{Isolated}$$
$$+\beta_8 \text{Informal} + \beta_9 \text{Protest size} + \beta_{10} \text{Peasants}$$
$$+\beta_{11} \text{Minorities} + \beta_{12} \text{County} + \beta_{13} \text{Township}$$
$$+\beta_{14} \text{Village} + \beta_{15} \text{Duration}$$

In this model, the dependent variable is the log odds of police presence at a given protest event. To ease the interpretation of BLR results, I present the odds ratios (rather than coefficient estimates), which represent the odds of observing a police presence at a given event versus not observing its presence. An odds ratio for a particular explanatory variable having a value higher than 1 signifies an increase in the odds associated with a one-unit increase in the particular independent variable; whereas an odds ratio for a particular explanatory variable between 0 and 1 indicates a decrease in the odds associated with a one-unit increase in the particular independent variable (Davenport, Soule, and Armstrong 2011: 161).

Table A 2.5 reports a series of BLR results.[4] In Model 1, police presence is estimated simply by measures regarding the character of protest. Most of the character measures (except informal organization) are significant and in the expected direction. These results hold after entering control variables – protest locations and duration (Model 2). Model 3 only examines the impact of social groups on policing: it indicates that both peasants and minorities increase the odds of police presence as expected. These results remain constant after introducing control variables (Model 4). The influence of social groups, however, is weakened after incorporating character measures: the effect of minority protests becomes insignificant (Model 5). Yet, the impact of peasant protests remains robust. Building on Model 5, Model 6 adds control measures. The two models show striking continuity and the impact of protest character and social groups holds in Model 6. Overall, the full model (Model 6) confirms most of the hypotheses regarding protest character and groups.

As I am also interested to know whether police discriminate against Uyghurs and Tibetans, I ran regression analysis for them as well. Model 7 resembles Model 6 except that environmental and moderate political protests become non-significant. That is to say, Uyghurs and Tibetans, like minorities as a whole, do not significantly invite police presence.

---

[4] See Table A 2.8 for descriptive statistics and correlation for variables in Table A 2.5.

TABLE A 2.5 *BLR models predicting police presence at protest events in China, 2001–2012*

	Model 1 Protest Character	Model 2 Character +Control	Model 3 Social Groups	Model 4 Group +Control	Model 5 Character +Groups	Model 6 Full Model	Model 7 Uyghurs & Tibetans
Protest character							
Claims^{R1}							
Economic	0.800***	0.811***			0.795**	0.800**	0.808*
	(0.0461)	(0.0503)			(0.0646)	(0.0655)	(0.0720)
Environmental	0.844*	0.849*			0.829*	0.835*	0.844
	(0.0598)	(0.0635)			(0.0753)	(0.0766)	(0.0836)
Moderate political	0.832**	0.842**			0.833*	0.836*	0.844
	(0.0514)	(0.0546)			(0.0683)	(0.0688)	(0.0746)
Other claims	0.816**	0.829*			0.826*	0.830*	0.837
	(0.0576)	(0.0610)			(0.0712)	(0.0719)	(0.0775)
Actions^{R2}							
Peaceful disruptive	0.745***	0.748***			0.754***	0.751***	0.751***
	(0.0235)	(0.0240)			(0.0239)	(0.0240)	(0.0240)
Peaceful non-disruptive	0.657***	0.666***			0.661***	0.665***	0.666***
	(0.0493)	(0.0507)			(0.0497)	(0.0505)	(0.0506)
Organization							
Isolated	0.926**	0.924**			0.918**	0.920**	0.920**
	(0.0245)	(0.0247)			(0.0244)	(0.0246)	(0.0246)
Informal	0.978	0.970			0.967	0.964	0.964
	(0.0611)	(0.0610)			(0.0605)	(0.0606)	(0.0605)
Protest size (log)	1.034***	1.035***			1.032***	1.034***	1.034***
	(0.00681)	(0.00733)			(0.00685)	(0.00734)	(0.00733)

	(1)	(2)	(3)	(4)	(5)	(6)	(7)
Social groups							
Peasants			1.157***	1.124**	1.103**	1.118**	1.118**
			(0.0364)	(0.0453)	(0.0342)	(0.0433)	(0.0427)
Minorities			1.194***	1.149*	1.017	1.030	
			(0.0600)	(0.0672)	(0.0684)	(0.0745)	
Uyghur & Tibetan							1.042
							(0.0871)
Control variable							
Locations[R3]							
County		1.016		1.055		0.983	0.982
		(0.0451)		(0.0529)		(0.0471)	(0.0469)
Township		1.042		1.096		0.997	0.996
		(0.0527)		(0.0609)		(0.0533)	(0.0532)
Village		1.058		1.010		0.976	0.977
		(0.0434)		(0.0527)		(0.0486)	(0.0480)
Duration (log)		0.994		1.014		0.993	0.993
		(0.00751)		(0.00729)		(0.00749)	(0.00749)
Log likelihood	-876.917	-875.565	-956.089	-952.294	-871.927	-871.323	-871.282
N	1,418	1,418	1,418	1,418	1,418	1,418	1,418

Note: Main entries are odds ratios with standard errors in parentheses.
[R1] reference group: radical political claims; [R2] reference group: violence; [R3] reference group: city.
* $p < 0.05$, ** $p < 0.01$, *** $p < 0.001$ (two-tailed tests)

Multinomial Logistic Regression

I scrutinize police actions after they show up at the protest events by analyzing the model of multinomial logistic regression (MLR). I divide "police actions" into four mutually exclusive categories: (1) taking no or limited action, (2) using violence only, (3) making arrests only, (4) using violence and making arrests together. Then I use MLR models to estimate coefficients for the impact of explanatory variables on particular outcomes of the dependent variable, relative to a baseline outcome (Long 2012). The MLR model is specified below, where π_j denotes the last three kinds of police actions, and π_J indicates the baseline – the first kind of action:

$$\log\left(\frac{\pi_j}{\pi_J}\right) = \beta_{0j} + \beta_{1j}\,\text{Economic} + \beta_{2j}\,\text{Environmental}$$
$$+\beta_{3j}\,\text{Moderate political} + \beta_{4j}\,\text{Other claims}$$
$$+\beta_{5j}\,\text{Peaceful disruptive} + \beta_{6j}\,\text{Peaceful nondisruptive}$$
$$+\beta_{7j}\,\text{Isolated} + \beta_{8j}\,\text{Informal} + \beta_{9j}\,\text{Protest size}$$
$$+\beta_{10j}\,\text{Peasants} + \beta_{11j}\,\text{Minorities} + \beta_{12j}\,\text{County}$$
$$+\beta_{13j}\,\text{Township} + \beta_{14j}\,\text{Village} + \beta_{15j}\,\text{Duration} \qquad j = 1,2\ldots,J\text{-}1$$

Like the BLR analysis, I also present the odds ratios (rather than coefficient estimates) for the MLR model. The MLR models shown in Table A 2.6 illustrate consistent results to the BLR models.[5] Models 8 and 9 lend strong support to a series of hypotheses regarding protest character. Compared with Model 8, protest character in Model 9 becomes even more important after entering the control variables, for the effect of moderate political claims also becomes significant and in the expected direction while the effect of the rest explanatory variables remains constant.

As I am also interested to study police reaction to Uyghurs and Tibetans, I ran MLR analysis for them as well. Results of Model 10 resemble Model 9 except that the impact of moderate political protests on arrests alone becomes insignificant. Findings from the two models suggest that, Uyghurs and Tibetans, like minorities as a whole, have no influence on police coercion.

Unexpected Regression Results

I have analyzed the unexpected regression results for formal organization and minorities in the text of Chapter 2. Below I provide a detailed discussion on other unexpected results and discrepancies between BLR and MLR results illustrated in Table A 2.7 (in bold and italic).

A discrepancy between BLR and MLR models is that larger protests and protests linked to others tend to attract police presence than smaller and isolated protests; yet, they are not more likely to suffer coercive response than the latter. I assume that police place a high priority on monitoring large and

---

[5] See Table A 2.9 for descriptive statistics and correlation for variables in Table A 2.6.

TABLE A 2.6 *MLR models predicting police reactions at protest events in China, when police were present, 2001–2012*

Protest character claims^{R_1}	Model 8 Protest character +social groups			Model 9 Full model			Model 10 Uyghur & Tibetan		
	Violence	Arrests	Violence & Arrests	Violence	Arrests	Violence & Arrests	Violence	Arrests	Violence & Arrests
Economic	1.013	0.204*	0.310*	0.971	0.177*	0.218*	0.597	0.186*	0.220*
	(0.767)	(0.136)	(0.182)	(0.743)	(0.120)	(0.132)	(0.514)	(0.130)	(0.140)
Environmental	1.515	0.124**	0.487	1.359	0.100**	0.292	0.839	0.104**	0.299
	(1.236)	(0.0977)	(0.316)	(1.128)	(0.0806)	(0.196)	(0.777)	(0.0858)	(0.212)
Moderate political	1.117	0.280	0.424	1.100	0.253*	0.333	0.693	0.267	0.336
	(0.848)	(0.187)	(0.249)	(0.841)	(0.171)	(0.201)	(0.591)	(0.184)	(0.210)
Other claims	0.248	0.105**	0.240*	0.233	0.0905**	0.165**	0.158	0.0939**	0.169**
	(0.212)	(0.0756)	(0.148)	(0.202)	(0.0661)	(0.105)	(0.149)	(0.0700)	(0.111)
Actions^{R_2}									
Peaceful disruptive	0.152***	0.571*	0.157***	0.155***	0.587	0.163***	0.158***	0.587	0.163***
	(0.0379)	(0.161)	(0.0357)	(0.0390)	(0.166)	(0.0377)	(0.0396)	(0.166)	(0.0378)
Peaceful Non-disruptive	1.54e-14	3.641*	0.271	2.10e-15	3.467	0.232	3.81e-17	3.474	0.233
	(4.56e-08)	(2.372)	(0.221)	(1.66e-08)	(2.287)	(0.195)	(2.27e-09)	(2.291)	(0.195)
Organization									
Isolated	1.179	1.195	1.019	1.181	1.169	0.981	1.208	1.161	0.986
	(0.266)	(0.252)	(0.203)	(0.269)	(0.248)	(0.199)	(0.275)	(0.246)	(0.200)
Informal	0.957	0.605	0.956	0.973	0.628	1.021	1.007	0.621	1.028
	(0.597)	(0.282)	(0.498)	(0.610)	(0.295)	(0.539)	(0.630)	(0.291)	(0.542)
Protest size (log)	0.967	0.949	1.113*	0.940	0.920	1.067	0.945	0.919	1.069
	(0.0565)	(0.0509)	(0.574)	(0.0597)	(0.0541)	(0.0602)	(0.0599)	(0.0540)	(0.0603)

(continued)

TABLE A 2.6 (continued)

Protest character claims R_1	Model 8 Protest character +social groups			Model 9 Full model			Model 10 Uyghur & Tibetan		
	Violence	Arrests	Violence & Arrests	Violence	Arrests	Violence & Arrests	Violence	Arrests	Violence & Arrests
Social groups									
Peasants	1.430	1.094	1.632*	1.158	0.833	0.942	1.098	0.849	0.919
	(0.349)	(0.276)	(0.367)	(0.358)	(0.265)	(0.279)	(0.336)	(0.267)	(0.269)
Minorities	1.758	0.444	1.848	1.631	0.396	1.699			
	(1.001)	(0.273)	(0.849)	(0.992)	(0.260)	(0.862)			
Uyghur & Tibetan							0.897	0.432	1.686
							(0.684)	(0.296)	(0.952)
Control variable Locations R_3									
County				1.003	0.985	0.630	1.112	0.966	0.640
				(0.388)	(0.377)	(0.232)	(0.430)	(0.371)	(0.238)
Township				1.703	1.398	2.322*	1.803	1.376	2.355*
				(0.735)	(0.655)	(0.891)	(0.778)	(0.645)	(0.905)
Village				1.412	1.718	2.632*	1.490	1.680	2.715**
				(0.592)	(0.747)	(0.998)	(0.621)	(0.725)	(1.020)
Duration (log)				1.069	1.081	1.151*	1.069	1.082	1.150*
				(0.0725)	(0.0652)	(0.0673)	(0.0725)	(0.0653)	(0.0673)
Log likelihood	−1108.991			−1097.303			−1097.303		
N	908			908			908		

Note: Main entries are exponentiated MLR coefficients with standard errors in parentheses.
R_1 reference group: radical political claims; R_2 reference group: violence; R_3 reference group: city.
Police doing nothing or taking limited action is the reference category.
* $p < 0.05$, ** $p < 0.01$, *** $p < 0.001$ (two-tailed tests)

TABLE A 2.7 *Comparing hypotheses with BLR and MLR results*

	BLR results	MLR results		
	Police presence	Violence	Arrests	Violence & arrests
Protest character				
Claims (hypothesis 1)				
Economic	–	o	–	–
Environmental	–	o	–	o
Moderate political	–	o	–	o
Actions (hypothesis 2)				
Peaceful disruptive	–	–	o	–
Peaceful non-disruptive	–	o	o	o
Organization (hypotheses 3 & 4)				
Isolated	–	o	o	o
Informal	o	o	o	o
Protest size (log) (hypothesis 5)	+	o	o	o
Social groups (hypotheses 6 & 7)				
Peasants	+	o	o	o
Minorities (Uyghur & Tibetan)	o	o	o	o
Control variable (hypotheses 8&9)				
Locations: rural	o	o	o	+
Duration (log)	o	o	o	+

Note: *"o" means the regression result is not statistically significant, "–" refers to significantly reducing policing, and "+" indicates significantly increasing it.*

linked protests, which impose a greater threat on maintaining order and controlling protests; on the other hand, police officers may often handle these protests with caution in case of escalating conflicts, since it is more costly and difficult to repress large and linked protests than small and isolated ones. Therefore, police may frequently show up at large and linked protests for monitor and control but are wary of employing coercion.

Why do peasant protests tend to bring police presence but not coercion compared with protests by others? This might be explained by the relatively high incidence of violence in peasant protests. In my dataset, violence occurs in 33 percent of peasant protests, compared with 22, 7, and 20 percent of protests by workers, middle class, and minorities, respectively. Hence, police may *perceive* peasant protests as potentially violent and tend to attend their events and take precautions against violence. On the other hand, if no violence takes place afterwards, police would then not adopt coercion in these events. This may explain why police did not single out peasants for repressive measures.

In addition, locations do not predict police presence, but show significant influence on police arrests along with violence. A possible explanation is that

TABLE A 2.8 *Descriptive statistics and correlation for Table A 2.5*

		Mean	SD	1	2	3	4	5	6	7	8	9	10	11	12	13	14	15
1	Economic	0.628	0.484	1														
2	Environmental	0.073	0.261	-0.37	1													
3	Moderate political	0.178	0.382	-0.6	-0.13	1												
4	Other claims	0.073	0.261	-0.37	-0.08	-0.13	1											
5	Peaceful disruptive	0.767	0.423	0.04	-0.06	-0.01	0.01	1										
6	Peaceful non-disruptive	0.031	0.173	-0.13	0	0.09	0.04	-0.32	1									
7	Isolated	0.595	0.491	0.3	0	-0.27	-0.08	0.06	-0.13	1								
8	Informal	0.961	0.193	0	0.01	0.05	-0.08	-0.02	-0.05	-0.06	1							
9	Protest size (log)	5.526	1.982	0.09	0.09	-0.08	-0.12	-0.28	-0.05	-0.14	0.01	1						
10	Duration (log)	2.089	1.792	0.15	0.07	-0.13	-0.08	-0.22	0.09	0.03	-0.05	0.39	1					
11	Peasants	0.207	0.405	0.14	0.12	-0.1	-0.14	-0.14	-0.02	0.12	0.06	0.13	0.18	1				
12	Minorities	0.069	0.254	-0.27	-0.04	-0.04	0.04	0	0	-0.05	0.04	0.05	-0.05	-0.14	1			
13	County	0.095	0.294	-0.11	-0.06	0.01	-0.01	-0.05	-0.02	-0.05	0.05	0.09	0	0.04	0.41	1		
14	Township	0.065	0.246	-0.08	0.1	0.02	-0.04	-0.06	-0.05	-0.09	0.04	0.12	0.06	0.16	0.13	-0.09	1	
15	Village	0.104	0.306	0.06	0.11	-0.08	-0.07	-0.13	-0.01	0.12	0.03	0.07	0.15	0.53	0	-0.11	-0.09	1

Note: N = 1,418.

TABLE A 2.9 *Descriptive statistics and correlation for Table A 2.6*

	Mean	SD	1	2	3	4	5	6	7	8	9	10	11	12	13	14	15
1 Economic	0.605	0.489	1														
2 Environmental	0.083	0.275	-0.37	1													
3 Moderate political	0.182	0.386	-0.58	-0.14	1												
4 Other claims	0.069	0.254	-0.34	-0.08	-0.13	1											
5 Peaceful disruptive	0.685	0.465	-0.01	-0.05	0.02	0.03	1										
6 Peaceful non-disruptive	0.024	0.154	-0.12	-0.02	0.07	0.04	-0.23	1									
7 Isolated	0.554	0.497	0.25	0.01	-0.26	-0.05	0.02	-0.06	1								
8 Informal	0.963	0.19	0.03	0.02	0.03	-0.11	-0.03	-0.08	-0.05	1							
9 Protest size (log)	5.859	2.013	0.1	0.11	-0.05	-0.13	-0.28	-0.13	-0.17	0	1						
10 Duration (log)	2.183	1.851	0.15	0.08	-0.14	-0.04	-0.22	0.05	0.02	-0.06	0.43	1					
11 Peasants	0.24	0.427	0.19	0.12	-0.14	-0.15	-0.12	-0.06	0.15	0.06	0.12	0.23	1				
12 Minorities	0.084	0.277	-0.31	-0.06	-0.04	0.06	0.03	0	-0.02	0.04	-0.02	-0.07	-0.17	1			
13 County	0.109	0.312	-0.13	-0.09	0.01	-0.01	-0.04	-0.01	-0.05	0.05	0.08	-0.02	0.02	0.44	1		
14 Township	0.078	0.269	-0.05	0.11	-0.02	-0.03	-0.07	-0.05	-0.05	0.06	0.09	0.07	0.15	0.1	-0.1	1	
15 Village	0.118	0.323	0.08	0.13	-0.09	-0.07	-0.13	-0.01	0.14	0.04	0.06	0.18	0.55	-0.05	-0.13	-0.11	1

Note: N = 908

Playing by the Informal Rules

TABLE A 2.10 *BLR model predicting police presence (events reported by both Boxun and other sources)*, N = 1,110

	Police Presence
Protest Character	
Claims	
Economic	0.801** (0.0686)
Environmental	0.818* (0.0793)
Moderate political	0.837* (0.0731)
Other claims	0.847 (0.0766)
Actions	
Peaceful disruptive	0.739*** (0.0249)
Peaceful non-disruptive	0.653*** (0.0552)
Organization	
Isolated	0.914** (0.0271)
Informal	0.946 (0.0628)
Protest size (log)	1.028*** (0.00819)
Social groups	
Peasants	1.124** (0.0463)
Minorities	0.991 (0.0757)
Controls	
County	0.985 (0.0501)
Township	0.976 (0.0563)
Village	0.985 (0.0515)
Duration (log)	0.993 (0.00834)
Log likelihood	−660.434
N	1,110

Note: Main entries are odds ratios with standard errors in parentheses.
* $p < 0.05$, ** $p < 0.01$, *** $p < 0.001$ (two-tailed tests)

the state keeps a watchful eye on protests and usually dispatches police to attend a protest event wherever it occurs, urban or rural. On the other hand, authorities are more hesitant to use coercion in urban than rural areas due to the concerns of public attention, in line with hypothesis 8.[6]

---

[6] As noted in Chapter 2, peasant protests do not necessarily take place in rural areas, but may occur in urban areas, and not all protests taking place in rural areas are staged by peasants, but may be by other social groups. This is why peasant protests and rural protests have distinct effects on protest policing.

TABLE A 2.11 *BLR model predicting police presence (only including events reporting the number of participants)*, N = 878

	Police Presence
Protest Character	
Claims	
Economic	0.795* (0.0862)
Environmental	0.871 (0.108)
Moderate political	0.801* (0.0867)
Other claims	0.921 (0.112)
Actions	
Peaceful disruptive	0.720*** (0.0291)
Peaceful non-disruptive	0.635*** (0.0645)
Organization	
Isolated	0.910** (0.0309)
Informal	0.951 (0.0802)
Protest size (log)	1.025** (0.00920)
Social groups	
Peasants	1.117* (0.0530)
Minorities	0.974 (0.0970)
Controls	
County	1.010 (0.0611)
Township	0.958 (0.0638)
Village	0.938 (0.0611)
Duration (log)	1.006 (0.0103)
Log likelihood	−528.7878
N	878

Note: Main entries are odds ratios with standard errors in parentheses.
* $p < 0.05$, ** $p < 0.01$, *** $p < 0.001$ (two-tailed tests)

TABLE A 2.12 *BLR model predicting police presence (only including social groups and protest claims)*, N = 1,418

	Police Presence
Social groups	
Peasants	1.160*** (0.0373)
Minorities	1.086 (0.0757)
Claims	
Economic	0.839* (0.0702)
Environmental	0.914 (0.0859)
Moderate political	0.886 (0.0760)
Other claims	0.855 (0.0774)
Log likelihood	−952.006
N	1418

Note: Main entries are odds ratios with standard errors in parentheses.
* $p < 0.05$, ** $p < 0.01$, *** $p < 0.001$ (two-tailed tests)

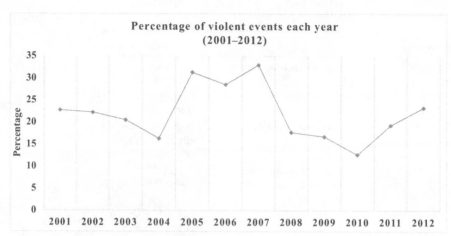

FIGURE A 2.1 Violent protests over time ($N = 1,418$)

Finally, regression results find no support for the hypothesis that protracted protests tend to bring police presence, but they do increase the probability of police violence along with arrests. There are at least two possible explanations for this discrepancy. First, police may be quite familiar with a lasting protest that is not considered threatening, and they feel they can afford to neglect it. On the other hand, once the patience of authorities runs out, police would then use whatever means to end it. A prolonged protest is assumingly difficult to terminate. Thus, police are more likely to employ violence in combination with arrests to reach its goal.

Appendix II

List of Interviewees

1. Zhang. A Hill Factory worker. Male.
2. Weng. A worker from an SOE factory, many employees of which joined the Hill Factory workers in the railway blockade. Male.
3. Chen. A middle-ranking cadre of the Hill Factory. Male.
4. Ye. A police officer of W District in D City. Male.
5. Li. An official of the D City People Congress. Female.
6. Wei. A middle-ranking official of the D City Federation of Trade Unions. Male.
7. Hai. A middle-ranking official of the D City Petition Bureau. Male.
8. Zhi. A leader of the Shining Hospital protest, retiree of the hospital. Male.
9. Hui. A leader of the Shining Hospital protest, retiree of the hospital. Female.
10. Liu. An activist in the Shining Hospital protest, retiree of the hospital. Male.
11. Fu. An activist in the Shining Hospital protest, retiree of the hospital. Male.
12. Cui. An activist in the Shining Hospital protest, employee of the hospital. Male.
13. Hong. An activist in the Shining Hospital protest, employee of the hospital. Female.
14. Mei. A worker from an SOE factory, many employees of which joined the Hill Factory workers in the railway blockade. Female.
15. Dai. A doctor from the hospital attached to Hill Factory. Male.
16. Gao. A taxi driver in D City. Male.
17. Che. A retired deputy director of the D City Petition Bureau. Male.
18. Pang. A vice-captain of the K District Public Security Bureau in D City. Male.

19. Yan. A captain of the K District Public Security Bureau in D City. Male.
20. Tou. A long-term petitioner in D City. Male.
21. Hao. A middle-ranking official of the petition office of the D City Politics and Law Commission of the Chinese Communist Party (CCP) in D City. Male.
22. Bao. A low-ranking official of the K District Petition Bureau in D City. Male.
23. Xiu. The head of a residents' committee. Female.
24. Xu. A detained taxi driver in D City, accused of inciting the taxi strike. Male.
25. Yong. A detained taxi driver in D City, regarded by authorities as a protest activist. Male.
26. Ping. A Hill Factory worker. Male.
27. Wu. A Hill Factory worker. Female.
28. Niu. A taxi driver in D City. Female.
29. Hou. The head of the W District Petition Bureau in D City. Male.
30. Jia. A middle-ranking official of the W District Petition Bureau in D City. Female.
31. Cao. A middle-ranking official of the D City Federation of Trade Unions. Male.
32. Zhao. A middle-ranking official of the D City Petition Bureau. Male.
33. Tong. A taxi driver in D City, a laid-off worker from Shining Factory. Female.
34. Xiang. A leader of an environmental non-governmental organization (NGO) that gave support to all four protests in Chapter 4. Male.
35. Xie. A leader of the N City protest. Male.
36. Bai. A leader of the N City protest. Male.
37. Xing. An activist in the Banana Village protest. Male.
38. Chang. An activist in the N City protest. Male.
39. Shan. An activist in an anti-incineration protest in another community in N City. Male.
40. Wang. A prominent anti-incineration expert, who endorsed all four cases in Chapter 4. Male.
41. Sao. A villager whose brother-in-law was severely beaten by police in the Banana Village protest. Female.
42. Sa. An activist in the S City protest. Male.
43. Xi. An activist in the S City protest. Male.
44. Jie. An activist in the N City protest. Female.
45. Tian. An activist in the S City protest. Female.
46. Hou. A leader of the N City protest. Male.
47. Juan. A senior engineer who provided professional consultancy to the two city protests in Chapter 4. Male.
48. Shi. A leader of an environmental NGO, which gave support to the Banana Villagers and S City protesters. Female.

49. Deng. A leader of the Apple Village protest. Male.
50. Qiang. A leader of the Apple Village protest. Male.
51. Shang. An activist in the Banana Village protest, an entrepreneur. Male.
52. Xia. A member of an environmental NGO, which gave support to all four cases. Female.
53. Bu. An elder villager who was the first arrested on May 27, 2011 in the Banana Village protest. Female.
54. Bing. An elder villager, Bu's husband, who was also arrested in the Banana Village protest. Male.
55. Ma. A villager whose son was severely beaten by police in the Banana Village protest. Interviewee 41, Sao's mother-in law. Female.
56. Tu. An activist in the S City protest. Female.
57. Qiu. A lawyer who filed lawsuits representing the N City and Apple Village protesters, respectively. Male.
58. Shuang. A villager whose brother was severely beaten by police in the Banana Village protest. Interviewee 41, Sao's husband. Male.
59. Jing. An activist in the Banana Village protest. Male.
60. Meng. An activist in the Banana Village protest. Male.
61. Duan. An activist in the Banana Village protest. Female.
62. Can. An official of the petition office of the D City Disabled Persons' Federation. Male.
63. Spring. A participant in the Shining Hospital protest, employee of the hospital. Female.
64. Ping. An activist in the Shining Hospital protest, employee of the hospital. Male.
65. Fang. A participant in the Shining Hospital protest, employee of the hospital. Male.
66. Yang. A participant in the Shining Hospital protest, retiree of the hospital. Male.
67. Ju. An activist in the Shining Hospital protest, retiree of the hospital. Female.
68. Sheng. An activist in the Shining Hospital protest, retiree of the hospital. Male.
69. Jian. The head of Shining Factory. Male.
70. Ge. An entrepreneur, interested in buying Shining Hospital in the take-over dispute. Male.
71. Zun. The director of Shining Hospital. Female.
72. Ning. A participant in the Shining Hospital protest, employee of the hospital. Female.
73. Nan. An observer of all three protests in D City. A D City resident, middle-class professional. Male.
74. Piao Fu. An Apple Villager, who did not participate in the protest. Male.
75. Piao Xiao. An Apple Villager, who did not participate in the protest. Male.

76. Piao Po. An Apple Villager, who did not participate in the protest. Female.
77. Zhong. An observer of Hill Factory protest. A D City resident, middle-class professional. Male.
78. Liu. A taxi driver in D City. Male.
79. Model. A taxi driver in D City. Male.
80. Ou. A taxi driver in D City. Male.
81. Ming. A taxi driver in D City. Male.
82. Gu. A taxi driver in D City. Male.
83. Chun. A staff of the D City Traffic Bureau. Female.
84. Professor, Sociology, Peking University. Female.
85. Professor, Sociology, Peking University. Male.
86. Professor, Sociology, Peking University. Male.
87. Professor, Sociology, Tsinghua University. Male.
88. Professor, China Institute of Industrial Relations. Male.
89. Professor, School of Government, Sun Yat-Sen University. Male.
90. Wen. A member of an environmental NGO, which gave support to all four cases. Female.
91. Den. Vice director of Shining Hospital. Female.
92. Xian. Vice director and head of the trade union of Shining Factory. Male.
93. Feng. Retiree of Shining Hospital, who did not participate in the protest. Male.
94. Gou. An official of petition office of the State-Owned Assets Supervision and Administrative Commission of D City. Female.
95. Dia. An official of petition office of the D City Chamber of Commerce. Female.
96. Huai. A middle-ranking official of the petition office of the D City Politics and Law Commission of the CCP. Male.
97. Shuai. A taxi driver in D City. Male.
98. Hua. An activist in the Apple Village protest. Male.
99. Yi. A participant in the Apple Village protest. Female.
100. Ke. An activist in an anti-incineration struggle in a city in central China. Female.
101. Cloud. A famous pro-incineration expert. Male.
102. Nang. A famous pro-incineration expert. Male.
103. Min. An official in charge of garbage disposal in N City, in favor of incineration. Male.
104. Niao. A leader of an environmental NGO. Male.
105. Long. A journalist and anti-incineration activist. Male.
106. Jiao. An official in charge of garbage disposal in N City, in favor of incineration. Male.
107. Chuan. An activist in an anti-incineration protest in another community in N City. Female.

108. Niang. A participant in an anti-incineration protest in another community in N City. Female.
109. Cong. An official of the land bureau of a county, with which Apple Village was affiliated. Male.
110. Lai. A lawyer, active in environmental NGOs. Male.
111. Ceng. An activist in an environmental protest in Northeastern China. Female.
112. Jiao. An activist in an anti-incineration protest in another community in N City. Female.
113. Huo. An activist in an anti-incineration protest in another community in N City. Male.
114. Jin. A participant in an anti-incineration protest in another community in N City. Female.

References

Acemoglu, Daron and James A. Robinson. 2006. *Economic Origins of Dictatorship and Democracy*. New York: Cambridge University Press.

Agresti, Alan. 2007. *An Introduction to Categorical Data Analysis* (2nd edition). Hoboken: Wiley-Interscience.

Albrecht, Holger. 2007. "Authoritarian Opposition and the Politics of Challenge in Egypt." In Oliver Schlumberger (ed.) *Debating Arab Authoritarianism: Dynamics and Durability in Nondemocratic Regimes*. Stanford: Stanford University Press, pp. 59–74.

2013. *Raging against the Machine: Political Opposition under Authoritarianism in Egypt*. Syracuse: Syracuse University Press.

Aldrich, Daniel P. 2008. *Site Fights: Divisive Facilities and Civil Society in Japan and the West*. Ithaca: Cornell University Press.

Almeida, Paul D. 2003. "Opportunity Organizations and Threat-Induced Contention: Protest Waves in Authoritarian Settings." *American Journal of Sociology*, Vol. 109, No. 2, pp. 345–400.

American Civil Liberties Union. 2013. *The War on Marijuana in Black and White*. New York: American Civil Liberties Union.

Amnesty International. 1999. *USA: Race, Rights and Police Brutality*. London: Amnesty International.

Azari, Julia R. and Jennifer K. Smith. 2012. "Unwritten Rules: Informal Institutions in Established Democracies." *Perspectives on Politics*, Vol. 10, No. 1, pp. 37–55.

Becquelin, Nicolas. 2000. "Xinjiang in the Nineties." *The China Journal*, Vol. 44, pp. 65–90.

2004. "Staged Development in Xinjiang." *The China Quarterly*, Vol. 178, pp. 358–378.

Beetham, David. 1991. *The Legitimation of Power*. Basingstoke: Macmillan.

Beinin, Joel and Frédéric Vairel. 2011. "Introduction: The Middle East and North Africa beyond Classical Social Movement Theory." In Joel Beinin and Frédéric Vairel (eds.) *Social Movements, Mobilization, and Contestation in the Middle East and North Africa*. Stanford: Stanford University Press, pp. 1–23.

Beissinger, Mark. 2002. *Nationalist Mobilization and the Collapse of the Soviet State*. New York: Cambridge University Press.

Bellin, Eva. 2012. "Reconsidering the Robustness of Authoritarianism in the Middle East: Lessons from the Arab Spring." *Comparative Politics*, Vol. 44, No. 2, pp. 127–149.

Belur, Jyoti. 2010. "Police 'Encounters' in Mumbai, India." In Joseph B. Kuhns and Johannes Knutsson (eds.) *Police Use of Force: A Global Perspective, Global Crime and Justice*. Santa Barbara: Praeger, pp. 52–62.

Benchemsi, Ahmed. 2014. "Morocco's Makhzen and the Haphazard Activists." In Lina Khatib and Ellen Lust (eds.) *Taking to the Streets: The Transformation of Arab Activism*. Baltimore: Johns Hopkins University Press, pp. 199–235.

Benney, Jonathan. 2016. "Weiwen at the Grassroots: China's Stability Maintenance Apparatus as a Means of Conflict Resolution." *Journal of Contemporary China*, Vol. 25, No. 99, pp. 389–405.

Bernstein, Thomas P. and Xiaobo Lü. 2000. "Taxation without Representation: Peasants, the Central and the Local States in Reform China." *The China Quarterly*, Vol. 163, pp. 742–763.

Biddulph, Sarah. 2015. *The Stability Imperative: Human Rights and Law in China*. Toronto: University of British Columbia Press.

Bierma, Paige. 1994. "Torture behind Bars: Right Here in the United States of America." *The Progressive*, July Issue.

Blaydes, Lisa. 2011. *Elections and Distributive Politics in Mubarak's Egypt*. New York: Cambridge University Press.

Blecher, Marc. 2010. "Globalization, Structural Reform, and Labour Politics in China." *Global Labour Journal*, Vol. 1, No. 1, pp. 92–111.

Bo, Yibo. 2008. *Review of Several Major Decisions and Events* (Ruogan zhongda juece yu shijian de huigu; Volume 2). Beijing: Chinese Communist Party History Publishing House. *In Chinese*.

Boudreau, Vince. 2004. *Resisting Dictatorship: Repression and Protest in Southeast Asia*. New York: Cambridge University Press.

   2005. "Precarious Regimes and Matchup Problems in the Explanation of Repressive Policy." In Christian Davenport, Hank Johnston, and Carol Mueller (eds.) *Repression and Mobilization*. Minneapolis: University of Minnesota Press, pp. 33–57.

Bovingdon, Gardner. 2002. "The Not-So-Silent Majority Resistance: Uyghur Resistance to Han Rule in Xinjiang." *Modern China*, Vol. 28, No. 1, pp. 39–78.

   2010. *The Uyghurs: Strangers in Their Own Land*. New York: Columbia University Press.

Bowman, Shayne and Chris Willis. 2003. *We Media: How Audiences Are Shaping the Future of News and Information*. Arlington: The Media Center at the American Press Institute.

Boykoff, Jules. 2007. "Limiting Dissent: The Mechanisms of State Repression in the USA." *Social Movement Studies*, Vol. 6, No. 3, pp. 281–310.

Brancati, Dawn. 2014. "Democratic Authoritarianism: Origins and Effects." *Annual Review of Political Science*, Vol. 17, pp. 313–326.

Bratton, Michael. 2007. "Formal versus Informal Institutions in Africa." *Journal of Democracy*, Vol. 18, No. 3, pp. 96–110.

Bratton, Michael and Nicholas van de Walle. 1997. *Democratic Experiments in Africa: Regime Transitions in Comparative Perspective*. New York: Cambridge University Press.

Brødsgaard, Kjeld Erik. 2004. "Management of Party Cadres in China." In Kjeld Erick Brødsgaard and Zheng Yongnian (eds.) *Bringing the Party Back In: How China Is Governed*. Singapore: Eastern Universities Press, pp. 57–91.

Brownlee, Jason. 2007. *Authoritarianism in an Age of Democratization*. New York: Cambridge University Press.

Brownlee, Jason, Tarek Masoud, and Andrew Reynolds. 2015. *The Arab Spring: Pathways of Repression and Reform*. Oxford: Oxford University Press.

Brumberg, Daniel. 2002. "The Trap of Liberalized Autocracy." *Journal of Democracy*, Vol. 13, No. 4, pp. 56–67.

Bulag, Uradyn. 2010. "Alter/Native Mongolian Identity: From Nationality to Ethnic Group." In Elizabeth J. Perry and Mark Selden (eds.) *Chinese Society: Change, Conflict and Resistance* (3rd edition). London; New York: Routledge, pp. 223–246.

Bunce, Valerie and Sharon L. Wolchik. 2006. "Favorable Conditions and Electoral Revolutions." *Journal of Democracy*, Vol. 17, No. 4, pp. 5–18.

Cai, Yongshun. 2002. "The Resistance of Chinese Laid-Off Workers in the Reform Period." *The China Quarterly*, Vol. 170, pp. 327–344.

2004. "Managed Participation in China." *Political Science Quarterly*, Vol. 119, No. 3, pp. 425–451.

2008. "Power Structure and Regime Resilience: Contentious Politics in China." *British Journal of Political Science*, Vol. 38, No. 3, pp. 411–432.

2010. *Collective Resistance in China: Why Popular Protests Succeed or Fail*. Stanford: Stanford University Press.

Calhoun, Craig. 1989. "Protest in Beijing: The Conditions and Importance of the Chinese Student Movement of 1989." *Partisan Review*, Vol. 4, pp. 563–580.

Carlson, Matthew M. 2006. "Electoral Reform and the Evolution of Informal Norms in Japan." *Asian Survey*, Vol. 46, No. 3, pp. 362–380.

Chan, Anita. 2011. "Strikes in China's Export Industries in Comparative Perspective." *The China Journal*, Vol. 65, pp. 27–51.

Chan, Cheris Shun-ching. 2004. "The Falun Gong in China: A Sociological Perspective." *The China Quarterly*, Vol. 179, pp. 665–683.

2013. "Doing Ideology amid a Crisis: Collective Actions and Discourses of the Chinese Falun Gong Movement." *Social Psychology Quarterly*, Vol. 76, No. 1, pp. 1–24.

Chan, Chris King-Chi and Elaine Sio-Ieng Hui. 2014. "The Development of Collective Bargaining in China: From 'Collective Bargaining by Riot' to 'Party State-Led Wage Bargaining.'" *The China Quarterly*, Vol. 217, pp. 221–242.

Chang, Kai. 2010. "A Legal Analysis of the Legality of Strike: A Case Study of Nanhai Honda Strike" (Guanyu bagong hefaxing de falü fenxi). *Strategy and Management*, No. 4. *In Chinese*.

Chang, Paul Y. 2015. *Protest Dialectics: State Repression and South Korea's Democracy Movement*. Stanford: Stanford University Press.

Chang, Paul Y. and Alex S. Vitale. 2013. "Repressive Coverage in an Authoritarian Context: Threat, Weakness, and Legitimacy in South Korea's Democracy Movement." *Mobilization: An International Journal*, Vol. 18, No. 1, pp. 19–39.

Chen, Chih-jou Jay. 2017. "Policing Protest in China: Findings from Newspaper Data." *Taiwanese Sociology*, Vol. 33: pp. 113–164. *In Chinese*.

Chen, Dan. 2017. "'Supervision by Public Opinion' or by Government Officials? Media Criticism and Central-Local Government Relations in China." *Modern China*, Vol. 43, No. 6, pp. 620–645.

Chen, Feng. 2000. "Subsistence Crises, Managerial Corruption and Labour Protests in China." *The China Journal*, Vol. 44, pp. 41–63.

2003. "Between the State and Labour: The Conflict of Chinese Trade Unions' Double Identity in Market Reform." *The China Quarterly*, Vol. 176, pp. 1006–1028.

Chen, Feng and Xin Xu. 2012. "'Active Judiciary': Judicial Dismantling of Workers' Collective Action in China." *The China Journal*, Vol. 67, pp. 87–108.

Chen, Hui. 2012. "Contradictions among the People and Studies of Social Stability in the New Era" (Xinshiqi renmin neibu maodun yu shehui wending yanjiu). *Study of Public Security*, Vol. 207, No. 3, pp. 19–30. *In Chinese.*

Chen, Jie. 2004. *Popular Political Support in Urban China*. Stanford: Stanford University Press.

Chen, Jie and Bruce J Dickson. 2008. "Allies of the State: Democratic Support and Regime Support among China's Private Entrepreneurs." *The China Quarterly*, Vol. 196, pp. 780–804.

2010. *Allies of the State: China's Private Entrepreneurs and Democratic Change.* Cambridge: Harvard University Press.

Chen, Xi. 2008. "Collective Petitioning and Institutional Conversion." In Kevin J. O'Brien (ed.) *Popular Protest in China*. Cambridge: Harvard University Press, pp. 54–70.

2012. *Social Protest and Contentious Authoritarianism in China*. New York: Cambridge University Press.

2013. "The Rising Cost of Stability." *Journal of Democracy*, Vol. 24, No. 1, pp. 57–64.

2017. "Origins of Informal Coercion in China." *Politics & Society*, Vol. 45, No. 1, pp. 67–89.

Chen, Yi-Da, Ahmed Abbasi, and Hsinchun Chen. 2009. "Framing Social Movement Identity with Cyber-Artifacts: A Case Study of the International Falun Gong Movement." *Security Informatics*, Vol. 9, pp. 1–23.

China Labour Bulletin. 2013. *A Report of China's Labor Movement: 2011–2012* (Zhongguo gongren yundong guancha baogao: 2011–2012). Hong Kong: China Labour Bulletin. *In Chinese.*

2015. *A Report on China's Labor Movement: 2013–2014* (Zhongguo gongren yundong guancha baogao: 2013–2014). Hong Kong: China Labour Bulletin. *In Chinese.*

China Labor Statistical Yearbook. 2005. Beijing: China Statistics Press. *In Chinese.*

Chomiak, Laryssa. 2014. "Architecture of Resistance in Tunisia." In Lina Khatib and Ellen Lust (eds.) *Taking to the Streets: The Transformation of Arab Activism.* Baltimore: Johns Hopkins University Press, pp. 22–51.

Chung, Jae Ho, Hongyi Lai, and Ming Xia. 2006. "Mounting Challenges to Governance in China: Surveying Collective Protestors, Religious Sects and Criminal Organizations." *The China Journal*, Vol. 56, pp. 1–31.

Clarke, Michael. 2011. *Xinjiang and China's Rise in Central Asia—A History*. London: Routledge.

Cook, Sarah and Leeshai Lemish. 2011. "610 Office: Policing the Chinese Spirit." *China Brief*, Vol. XI, No. 17, pp. 6–10.

Culpepper, Rucker. 2012. "Nationalist Competition on the Internet: Uyghur Diaspora versus the Chinese State Media." *Asian Ethnicity*, Vol. 13, No. 2, pp. 187–203.

Darden, Keith. 2008. "The Integrity of Corrupt States: Graft as an Informal State Institution." *Politics & Society*, Vol. 36, No. 1, pp. 35–60.

Davenport, Christian. 1995. "Multi-Dimensional Threat Perception and State Repression: An Inquiry into Why States Apply Negative Sanctions." *American Journal of Political Science*, Vol. 39, No. 3, pp. 683–713.

2007. "State Repression and Political Order." *Annual Review of Political Science*, Vol. 10, pp. 1–23.

2015. *How Social Movements Die: Repression and Demobilization of the Republic of New Africa*. New York: Cambridge University Press.

Davenport, Christian, Sarah A. Soule, and David A. Armstrong II. 2011. "Protesting While Black? The Differential Policing of American Activism 1960 to 1990." *American Sociological Review*, Vol. 76, No. 1, pp. 152–178.

Della Porta, Donatella and Herbert Reiter. 1998. "Introduction: The Policing of Protest in Western Democracies." In Donatella Della Porta and Herbert Reiter (eds.) *Policing Protest: The Control of Mass Demonstrations in Western Democracies*. Minneapolis: University of Minnesota Press, pp. 1–32.

Della Porta, Donatella and Olivier Fillieule. 2003. "Policing Social Protest." In David A. Snow, Sarah A. Soule, Hanspeter Kriesi (eds.) *The Blackwell Companion to Social Movements*, Malden: Blackwell Publishing, pp. 217–241.

Deng, Yanhua. 2017. "'Autonomous Redevelopment': Moving the Masses to Remove Nail Households." *Modern China*, Vol. 43, No. 5, pp. 494–522.

Deng, Yanhua and Guobin Yang. 2013. "Pollution and Protest in China: Environmental Mobilization in Context." *The China Quarterly*, Vol. 214, pp. 321–336.

Deng, Yanhua and Kevin J. O'Brien. 2013. "Relational Repression in China: Using Social Ties to Demobilize Protesters." *The China Quarterly*, Vol. 215, pp. 533–552.

2014. "Societies of Senior Citizens and Popular Protest in Rural Zhejiang." *The China Journal*, Vol. 71, pp. 172–188.

Diamant, Neil Jeffrey, Stanley B. Lubman, and Kevin J. O'Brien. 2005. "Law and Society in the People's Republic of China." In Neil J. Diamant, Stanley B. Lubman, and Kevin J. O'Brien (eds.) *Engaging the Law in China: State, Society, and Possibilities for Justice*. Stanford: Stanford University Press, pp. 3–27.

Diamond, Larry Jay. 2002. "Thinking About Hybrid Regimes." *Journal of Democracy*, Vol. 13, No. 2, pp. 21–35.

Dickson, Bruce J. 2007. "Integrating Wealth and Power in China: The Communist Party's Embrace of the Private Sector." *The China Quarterly*, Vol. 192, pp. 827–854.

2008. *Wealth into Power: The Communist Party's Embrace of China's Private Sector*. New York: Cambridge University Press.

2016. *The Dictator's Dilemma: The Chinese Communist Party's Strategy for Survival*. New York: Oxford University Press.

Dillon, Michael. 2004. *Xinjiang – China's Muslim Far North West*. London; New York: RoutledgeCurzon.

Dimitrov, Martin. 2008. "The Resilient Authoritarians." *Current History*, Vol. 107, No. 705, pp. 24–29.

2013. "Vertical Accountability in Communist Regimes: The Role of Citizen Complaints in Bulgaria and China." In Martin Dimitrov (ed.) *Why Communism Did Not Collapse: Understanding Authoritarian Regime Resilience in Asia and Europe.* New York: Cambridge University Press, pp. 276–302.

2015. "Internal Government Assessments of the Quality of Governance in China." *Studies in Comparative International Development,* Vol. 50, No. 1, pp. 50–72.

Distelhorst, Greg, and Yue Hou. 2017. "Constituency Service under Nondemocratic Rule: Evidence from China." *The Journal of Politics,* Vol. 79, No. 3, pp. 1024–1040.

Dobson, W. J. 2013. *The Dictator's Learning Curve: Inside the Global Battle for Democracy.* New York: Anchor.

Earl, Jennifer. 2003. "Tanks, Tear Gas, and Taxes: Toward a Theory of Movement Repression." *Sociological Theory,* Vol. 21, No. 1, pp. 44–68.

2011. "Political Repression: Iron Fists, Velvet Gloves, and Diffuse Control." *Annual Review of Sociology,* Vol. 37, pp. 261–284.

Earl, Jennifer and Sara A. Soule. 2006. "Seeing Blue: A Police-Centered Explanation of Protest Policing." *Mobilization: An International Journal,* Vol. 11, No. 2, pp. 145–164.

Earl, Jennifer, Sara A. Soule, and John D. McCarthy. 2003. "Protests under Fire? Explaining the Policing of Protest." *American Sociological Review,* Vol. 68, No. 4, pp. 581–606.

Edin, Maria. 2003. "State Capacity and Local Agent Control in China: CCP Cadre Management from a Township Perspective." *The China Quarterly,* Vol. 173, pp. 35–52.

Elfstrom, Manfred and Sarosh Kuruvilla. 2014. "The Changing Nature of Labor Unrest in China." *Industrial and Labor Relations Review,* Vol. 67, No. 2, pp. 453–480.

Erie, Matthew S. 2016. *China and Islam: The Prophet, the Party, and Law.* New York: Cambridge University Press.

Estlund, Cynthia. 2017. *A New Deal for China's Workers?* Cambridge: Harvard University Press.

Fahmy, Hazem. 2012. "An Initial Perspective on 'The Winter of Discontent': The Root Causes of the Egyptian Revolution." *Social Research,* Vol. 79, No. 2, pp. 349–376.

Fewsmith, Joseph. 2016. "The Challenges of Stability and Legitimacy." In Robert S. Ross and Jo Inge Bekkevold (eds.) *China in the Era of Xi Jinping: Domestic and Foreign Policy Challenges.* Washington, D.C.: Georgetown University Press, pp. 92–114.

Fillieule, Olivier and Fabien Jobard. 1998. "The Policing of Protest in France: Toward a Model of Protest Policing." In Donatella Della Porta and Herbert Reiter (eds.) *Policing Protest: The Control of Mass Demonstrations in Western Democracies.* Minneapolis: University of Minnesota Press, pp. 70–90.

Fisher, Richard. 2010. *China's Military Modernization: Building for Regional and Global Reach.* Stanford: Stanford University Press.

Fjelde, Hanne and Håvard Hegre. 2014. "Political Corruption and Institutional Stability." *Studies in Comparative International Development,* Vol. 49, No. 3, pp. 267–299.

Francisco, Ronald A. 1995. "The Relationship between Coercion and Protest: An Empirical Evaluation in Three Coercive States." *The Journal of Conflict Resolution*, Vol. 39, No. 2, pp. 263–282.

2005. "The Dictator's Dilemma." In Christian Davenport, Hank Johnston, and Carol Mueller (eds.) *Repression and Mobilization*. Minneapolis: University of Minnesota Press, pp. 58–81.

Franklin, James C. 2009. "Contentious Challenges and Government Responses in Latin America." *Political Research Quarterly*, Vol. 62, No. 4, pp. 700–714.

2015. "Persistent Challengers: Repression, Concessions, Challenger Strength, and Commitment in Latin America." *Mobilization: An International Journal*, Vol. 20, No. 1, pp. 61–80.

Freedom House. 2015. *The Politburo's Predicament: Confronting the Limitations of Chinese Communist Party Repression*. Washington, D.C.: Freedom House.

Friedman, Eli. 2013. "Insurgency and Institutionalization: The Polanyian Countermovement and Chinese Labor Politics." *Theory and Society*, Vol. 42, No. 3, pp. 295–327.

2014. *Insurgency Trap: Labor Politics in Postsocialist China*. Ithaca: Cornell University Press.

Fu, Diana. 2016. "Disguised Collective Action in China." *Comparative Political Studies*, Vol. 50, No. 4, pp. 499–527.

2017. *Mobilizing without the Masses: Control and Contention in China*. Cambridge: Cambridge University Press.

Fu, Diana, and Greg Distelhorst. 2018. "Grassroots Participation and Repression under Hu Jintao and Xi Jinping." *The China Journal*, Vol. 79, pp. 100–122.

Gallagher, Mary E. 2005. "Use the Law As Your Weapon!": Institutional Change and Legal Mobilization in China." In Neil J. Diamant, Stanley B. Lubman, and Kevin J. O'Brien (eds.) *Engaging the Law in China: State, Society, and Possibilities for Justice*. Stanford: Stanford University Press, pp. 55–83.

2017. *Authoritarian Legality in China: Law, Workers, and the State*. New York: Cambridge University Press.

Gallagher, Mary E. and Jonathan K. Hanson. 2013. "Authoritarian Survival, Resilience, and the Selectorate Theory." In Martin Dimitrov (ed.) *Why Communism Did Not Collapse: Understanding Authoritarian Regime Resilience in Asia and Europe*. New York: Cambridge University Press, pp. 185–204.

Gamson, William A. 1990. *The Strategy of Social Protest*. Belmont: Wadsworth.

Gandhi, Jennifer. 2008. *Political Institutions under Dictatorship*. New York: Cambridge University Press.

Gandhi, Jennifer and Adam Przeworski. 2006. "Cooperation, Cooptation, and Rebellion under Dictatorships." *Economics & Politics*, Vol. 18, No. 1, pp. 1–26.

2007. "Authoritarian Institutions and the Survival of Autocrats." *Comparative Political Studies*, Vol. 40, No. 11, pp. 1279–1301.

Gartner, Scott Sigmund and Patrick M. Regan. 1996. "Threat and Repression: The Non-Linear Relationship between Government and Opposition Violence." *Journal of Peace Research*, Vol. 33, No. 3, pp. 273–287.

Geddes, Barbara. 1999. "What Do We Know About Democratization after Twenty Years?" *Annual Review of Political Science*, Vol. 2, pp. 115–144.

2003. *Paradigms and Sand Castles: Research Design in Comparative Politics*. Ann Arbor: University of Michigan Press.

Gilley, Bruce. 2003. "The Limits of Authoritarian Resilience." *Journal of Democracy*, Vol. 14, No. 1, pp. 18–26.

Giugni, Marco G. and Florence Passy. 1998. "Contentious Politics in Complex Societies: New Social Movements between Conflicts and Cooperation." In Marco Giugni, Doug McAdam and Charles Tilly (eds.) *From Contention to Democracy*. Lanham: Rowman & Littlefield Publishers, pp. 81–108.

Gladney, Dru. 2004. *Dislocating China: Muslims, Minorities, and Other Subaltern Subjects*. Chicago: University of Chicago Press.

Goldstein, Robert R. 1978. *Political Repression in Modern America: 1870 to the Present*. Cambridge: Schenkman.

Goldstone, Jack A. 2003. "Introduction: Bridging Institutionalized and Noninstitutionalized Politics." In Jack A. Goldstone (ed.) *States, Parties, and Social Movements*. New York: Cambridge University Press, pp. 1–24.

　　2004. "More Social Movements or Fewer? Beyond Political Opportunity Structures to Relational Fields." *Theory and Society*, Vol. 33, No. 3, pp. 333–365.

Goldstone, Jack A. and Charles Tilly. 2001. "Threat (And Opportunity): Popular Action and State Response in the Dynamics of Contentious Action." In Ronald Aminzade, Jack A. Goldstone, Doug McAdam, Elizabeth J. Perry, Sidney Tarrow, William H. Sewell, and Charles Tilley (eds.) *Silence and Voice in the Study of Contentious Politics*. New York: Cambridge University Press, pp. 179–194.

Goodwin, Jeff. 2001. *No Other Way Out: States and Revolutionary Movements, 1945–1991*. New York: Cambridge University Press.

Greitens, Sheena Chestnut. 2016. *Dictators and Their Secret Police: Coercive Institutions and State Violence*. New York: Cambridge University Press.

　　2017. "Rethinking China's Coercive Capacity: An Examination of PRC Domestic Security Spending, 1992–2012." *The China Quarterly*, Vol. 232, pp. 1002–1025.

Guo, Xuezhi. 2012. *China's Security State: Philosophy, Evolution, and Politics*. New York: Cambridge University Press.

Gurr, Ted Robert. 1986. "The Political Origins of State Violence and Terror: A Theoretical Analysis." In Michael Stohl and George Lopez (eds.) *Governmental Violence and Repression: An Agenda for Research*. New York: Greenwood Press, pp. 45–71.

Haggard, Stephan and Robert R. Kaufman. 2016. *Dictators and Democrats: Masses, Elites, and Regime Change*. Princeton: Princeton University Press.

Han, Enze. 2010. "Boundaries, Discrimination, and Interethnic Conflict in Xinjiang, China." *International Journal of Conflict and Violence*, Vol. 4, No 2, pp. 172–184.

　　2013. *Contestation and Adaptation: The Politics of National Identity in China*. New York: Oxford University Press.

Hann, Chris. 2011. "Smith in Beijing, Stalin in Urumchi: Ethnicity, Political Economy, and Violence in Xinjiang, 1759–2009." *Focaal – Journal of Global and Historical Anthropology*, Vol. 60, pp. 108–123.

Hassid, Jonathan. 2008. "Controlling the Chinese Media: An Uncertain Business." *Asian Survey*, Vol. 48, No. 3, pp. 414–430.

Hastings, Justin V. 2005. "Perceiving a Single Chinese State: Escalation and Violence in Uighur Protests." *Problems of Post-Communism*, Vol. 52, No. 1, pp. 28–38.

　　2011. "Charting the Course of Uyghur Unrest." *The China Quarterly*, No. 208, pp. 893–912.

He, Baogang and Mark E. Warren. 2011. "Authoritarian Deliberation: The Deliberative Turn in Chinese Political Development." *Perspectives on Politics*, Vol. 9, No. 2, pp. 269–289.

He, Baogang and Stig Thøgersen. 2010. "Giving the People a Voice? Experiments with Consultative Authoritarian Institutions in China." *Journal of Contemporary China*, Vol. 19, No. 66, pp. 675–692.

Heilmann, Sebastian. 2008. "Policy Experimentation in China's Economic Rise." *Studies in Comparative International Development*, Vol. 43, No. 1, pp. 1–26.

2011. "Policy-Making through Experimentation: The Formation of a Distinctive Policy Process." In Sebastian Heilmann and Elizabeth J. Perry (eds.) *Mao's Invisible Hand: The Political Foundations of Adaptive Governance in China*. Cambridge: Harvard University Asia Center, pp. 62–101.

Heilmann, Sebastian and Elizabeth J. Perry. 2011. "Embracing Uncertainty: Guerrilla Policy Style and adaptive Governance in China." In Sebastian Heilmann and Elizabeth J. Perry (eds.) *Mao's Invisible Hand: The Political Foundations of Adaptive Governance in China*. Cambridge: Harvard University Asia Center, pp. 1–29.

Helmke, Gretchen and Steven Levitsky. 2004. "Informal Institutions and Comparative Politics: A Research Agenda." *Perspectives on Politics*, Vol. 2, No. 4, pp. 725–740.

2006a. "Introduction." In Gretchen Helmke and Steven Levitsky (eds.) *Informal Institutions and Democracy: Lessons from Latin America*. Baltimore: Johns Hopkins University, pp. 1–30.

2006b. "Conclusion." In Gretchen Helmke and Steven Levitsky (eds.) *Informal Institutions and Democracy: Lessons from Latin America*. Baltimore: Johns Hopkins University, pp. 274–284.

Hess, David and Brian Martin. 2006. "Backfire, Repression, and the Theory of Transformative Events." *Mobilization: An International Journal*, Vol. 11, No. 1, pp. 249–267.

Hess, Steve. 2016. "Sources of Authoritarian Resilience in Regional Protest Waves: The Post Communist Colour Revolutions and 2011 Arab Uprisings." *Government and Opposition: An International Journal of Comparative Politics*, Vol. 51, No. 1, pp. 1–29.

Heurlin, Christopher. 2016. *Responsive Authoritarianism in China: Land, Protests, and Policy Making*. New York: Cambridge University Press.

Hierman, Brent. 2007. "The Pacification of Xinjiang: Uighur Protest and the Chinese State, 1988–2002." *Problems of Post-Communism*, Vol. 54, No. 3, pp. 48–62.

Hillman, Ben. 2014. *Patronage and Power: Local State Networks and Party-State Resilience in Rural China*. Stanford: Stanford University Press.

2016. "Introduction: Understanding the Current Wave of Conflict and Protest in Tibet and Xinjiang." In Ben Hillman and Gray Tuttle (eds.) *Ethnic Conflict and Protest in Tibet and Xinjiang: Unrest in China's West*. New York: Columbia University Press, pp. 1–17.

Ho, Peter. 2007. "Embedded Activism and Political Change in a Semiauthoritarian Context." *China Information*, Vol. 21, No. 2, pp. 187–209.

Ho, Peter and Richard Louis Edmonds. 2007. "Perspectives of Time and Change: Rethinking Embedded Environmental Activism in China." *China Information*, Vol. 21, No. 2, pp. 331–344.

Holbig, Heike. 2009. "Ideological Reform and Political Legitimacy in China: Challenges in the Post-Jiang Era." In Gunter Schubert and Thomas Heberer (eds.) *Regime Legitimacy in Contemporary China: Institutional Change and Stability.* London: Routledge, pp. 13–34.

Holland, Alisha C. 2015. "The Distributive Politics of Enforcement." *American Journal of Political Science,* Vol. 59, No. 2, pp. 357–371.

2016. "Forbearance." *American Political Science Review,* Vol. 110, No. 2, pp. 232–246.

Howard, Philip N. and Muzammil M. Hussain. 2013. *Democracy's Fourth Wave?: Digital Media and the Arab Spring.* New York: Oxford University Press.

Howell, Jude. 2011. "Civil Society in China." In Michael Edwards (ed.) *The Oxford Handbook of Civil Society.* New York: Oxford University Press, pp. 159–170.

Hu, Lianhe, Hu Angang, He Shenghong, and Guo Yong. 2009. *Report of Social Stability in Contemporary China (Dangdai zhongguo shehui wending wenti baogao).* Beijing Red Flag Press.

Huggins, Martha K. 2010. "Systemic Police Violence in Brazil." In Joseph B. Kuhns and Johannes Knutsson (eds.) *Police Use of Force: A Global Perspective.* Santa Barbara: Praeger, pp. 52–62.

Human Rights Watch. 2002. *Dangerous Meditation – China's Campaign Against Falungong.* New York: Human Rights Watch.

2005. *Devastating Blows Religious Repression of Uighurs in Xinjiang.* New York: Human Rights Watch.

2009. *'We Are Afraid to Even Look for Them' – Enforced Disappearances in the Wake of Xinjiang's Protests.* New York: Human Rights Watch.

2015. *World Report 2015: China (Events of 2014).* New York: Human Rights Watch.

Hung, Ho-fung. 2007. "Changes and Continuities in the Political Ecology of Popular Protest: Mid-Qing China and Contemporary Resistance." *China Information,* Vol. 21, No. 2, pp. 299–329.

2011. *Protest with Chinese Characteristics: Demonstrations, Riots, and Petitions in the Mid-Qing Dynasty.* New York: Columbia University Press.

Huntington, Samuel P. 1991. *The Third Wave: Democratization in the Late Twentieth Century.* Norman and London: University of Oklahoma Press.

Hurst, William. 2004. "Collective Action by Chinese Laid-Off Workers: The Importance of Regional Political Economy." *Studies in Comparative International Development,* Vol. 39, No. 2, pp. 94–120.

2008. "Mass Frames and Worker Protest." In Kevin J. O'Brien (ed.) *Popular Protest in China.* Cambridge: Harvard University Press, pp. 71–87.

International Crisis Group. 2011a. *Popular Protest in North Africa and the Middle East (IV): Tunisia's Way.* Middle East/North Africa Report No. 106. Brussels: International Crisis Group.

2011b. *Popular Protest in North Africa and the Middle East (I): Egypt Victorious?* Middle East/North Africa Report No. 101. Brussels: International Crisis Group.

Johnson, Thomas. 2013. "The Health Factor in Anti-Waste Incinerator Campaigns in Beijing and Guangzhou." *The China Quarterly,* Vol. 214, pp. 356–375.

Johnston, Hank. 2011. *States and Social Movements.* Cambridge: Polity Press.

2012. "State Violence and Oppositional Protest in High-Capacity Authoritarian Regimes." *International Journal of Conflict and Violence,* Vol. 6, No. 1, pp. 55–74.

Jumet, Kira D. 2017. *Contesting the Repressive State: Why Ordinary Egyptians Protested during the Arab Spring*. New York: Oxford University Press.

Junker, Andrew. 2014a. "Follower Agency and Charismatic Mobilization in Falun Gong." *Sociology of Religion*, Vol. 75, No. 3, pp. 418–441.

2014b. "The Transnational Flow of Tactical Dispositions: The Chinese Democracy Movement and Falun Gong." *Mobilization: An International Journal*, Vol. 19, No. 3, pp. 329–350.

Karklins, Rasma. 1987. "The Dissent/Coercion Nexus in the USSR." *Studies in Comparative Communism*, Vol. 20, No. 3, pp. 321–341.

Keith, Ronald C. and Zhiqiu Lin. 2003. "The 'Falun Gong Problem': Politics and the Struggle for the Rule of Law in China." *The China Quarterly*, No. 175, pp. 623–642.

Kennedy, John James. 2009a. "Maintaining Popular Support for the Chinese Communist Party: The Influence of Education and the State-Controlled Media." *Political Studies*, Vol. 57, pp. 517–536.

2009b. "Legitimacy with Chinese Characteristics: 'Two Increases, One Reduction.'" *Journal of Contemporary China*, Vol. 18, No. 60, pp. 391–395.

Kerkvliet, Benedict J. Tria. 2010. "Governance, Development, and the Responsive–Repressive State in Vietnam." *Forum for Development Studies*, Vol. 37, No. 1, pp. 33–59.

Khatib, Lina and Ellen Lust. 2014. "Introduction. Reconsidering Activism in the Arab World: Arab Uprisings and Beyond." In Lina Khatib and Ellen Lust (eds.) *Taking to the Streets: The Transformation of Arab Activism*. Baltimore: Johns Hopkins University Press, pp. 1–21.

King, Gary, Jennifer Pan, and Margaret E Roberts. 2013. "How Censorship in China Allows Government Criticism but Silences Collective Expression." *American Political Science Review*, Vol. 107, No. 2, pp. 1–18.

Koopmans, Ruud. 1995. *Democracy from Below: New Social Movements and the Political System in West Germany*. Boulder: Westview.

2004. "Protest in Time and Space: The Evolution of Waves of Contention." In David A. Snow, Sarah A. Soule, and Hanspeter Kriesi (eds.) *The Blackwell Companion to Social Movements*. Malden: Blackwell Publishing, pp. 19–46.

Koopmans, Ruud and Dieter Rucht. 2002. "Protest Event Analysis." In Bert Klandermans and Suzanne Staggenborg (eds.) *Methods in Social Movement Research*. Minneapolis: University of Minnesota Press, pp. 231–259.

Kubik, Jan. 1994. *The Power of Symbols against the Symbols of Power: The Rise of Solidarity and the Fall of State Socialism in Poland*. University Park: Pennsylvania State University Press.

Kurzman, Charles. 1996. "Structural Opportunity and Perceived Opportunity in Social-Movement Theory: The Iranian Revolution of 1979." *American Sociological Review*, Vol. 61, pp. 153–170.

2004. *The Unthinkable Revolution in Iran*. Cambridge: Harvard University Press.

Landry, Pierre F. 2008. *Decentralized Authoritarianism in China: The Communist Party's Control of Local Elites in the Post-Mao Era*. New York: Cambridge University Press.

Landry, Pierre F., Deborah Davis, and Shiru Wang. 2010. "Elections in Rural China: Competition Without Parties." *Comparative Political Studies*, Vol. 43, No. 6, pp. 763–790.

Lauth, Hans-Joachim. 2000. "Informal Institutions and Democracy." *Democratization*, Vol.7, No. 4, pp. 21–50.

Lee, Ching Kwan. 2002. "From the Specter of Mao to the Spirit of the Law: Labor Insurgency in China." *Theory and Society*, Vol. 31, No. 2, pp. 189–228.

2007. *Against the Law: Labor Protests in China's Rustbelt and Sunbelt*. Berkeley: University of California Press.

Lee, Ching Kwan and Yonghong Zhang. 2013. "The Power of Instability: Unraveling the Microfoundations of Bargained Authoritarianism in China." *American Journal of Sociology*, Vol. 118, No. 6, pp. 1475–1508.

Legewie, Joscha. 2016. "Racial Profiling and Use of Force in Police Stops: How Local Events Trigger Periods of Increased Discrimination." *American Journal of Sociology*, Vol. 122, No. 2, pp. 379–424.

Lei, Ya-Wen. 2016. "Freeing the Press: How Field Environment Explains Critical News Reporting in China." *American Journal of Sociology*, Vol. 122, No. 1, pp. 1–48.

Levitsky, Steven and Lucan A. Way. 2002. "The Rise of Competitive Authoritarianism." *Journal of Democracy*. Vol. 13, No. 2, pp. 51–65.

2010. *Competitive Authoritarianism: Hybrid Regimes After the Cold War*. New York: Cambridge University Press.

Levitsky, Steven and Maria Victoria Murillo. 2009. *Annual Review of Political Science*. Vol. 12, pp. 115–133.

Li, Cheng. 2012. "The End of the CCP's Resilient Authoritarianism? A Tripartite Assessment of Shifting Power in China." *The China Quarterly*, Vol. 211, pp. 595–623.

Li, Lianjiang. 2008. "Political Trust and Petitioning in the Chinese Countryside." *Comparative Politics*, Vol. 40, No. 2, pp. 209–226.

Li, Lianjiang, Mingxing Liu, and Kevin J. O'Brien. 2012. "Petitioning Beijing: The High Tide of 2003–2006." *The China Quarterly*, Vol. 210, pp. 313–334.

Li, Yao. 2013. "Fragmented Authoritarianism and Protest Channels: A Case Study of Resistance to Privatizing a Hospital." *Journal of Current Chinese Affairs*, Vol. 42, No. 2, pp. 195–224.

2017. "A Zero-Sum Game? Repression and Protest in China." *Government and Opposition: An International Journal of Comparative Politics*, doi:10.1017/gov.2017.24.

Liebman, Benjamin L. 2007. "China's Courts: Restricted Reform." *The China Quarterly*, No. 191, pp. 620–638.

2011. "The Media and the Courts: Towards Competitive Supervision?" *The China Quarterly*, No. 208, pp. 833–850.

2013. "Malpractice Mobs: Medical Dispute Resolution in China." *Columbia Law Review*, Vol. 113, No. 1, pp. 181–264.

Lipsky, Michael. 1970. "Introduction." In Michael Lipsky (ed.) *Law and Order: Police Encounters*. New York: Aldine Publishing Company, pp. 1–7.

Liu, Xiaobo. 1992. *The Monologues of a Doomsday's Survivor (Mori xingcunzhe de zibai)*. Taiwan: China Times Publishing Company. *In Chinese*.

Long, Scott. 2012. "Regression Models for Nominal and Ordinal Outcomes." In Henning Best and Christof Wolf (eds.) *The SAGE Handbook of Regression Analysis and Causal Inference*. London: SAGE Publications Ltd, pp. 173–204.

Lorentzen, Peter L. 2013. "Regularizing Rioting: Permitting Public Protest in an Authoritarian Regime." *Quarterly Journal of Political Science*, Vol. 8, pp. 127–158.

2017. "Designing Contentious Politics in Post-1989 China." *Modern China*, Vol. 43, No. 5, pp. 459–493.

Lu, Xueyi, Li Peilin, and Chen Guanjing. 2012. *Blue Book of Chinese Society of 2013: Analysis and Forecast of Chinese Society* (Zhongguo shehui lanpishu 2013: zhongguo shehui xingshi fenxi yu yuce). Beijing: Social Sciences Academic Press. *In Chinese.*

Lu, Yao, and Ran Tao. 2017. "Organizational Structure and Collective Action: Lineage Networks, Semiautonomous Civic Associations, and Collective Resistance in Rural China." *American Journal of Sociology*, Vol. 122, No. 6, pp. 1726–1774.

Lubman, Stanley B. 1999. *Bird in a Cage: Legal Reform in China after Mao*. Stanford: Stanford University Press.

Luehrmann, Laura M. 2003. "Facing Citizen Complaints in China, 1951–1996." *Asian Survey*, Vol. 43, No. 5, pp. 845–866.

Luo, Qiangqiang, Joel Andreas, and Yao Li. 2017. "Grapes of Wrath: Twisting Arms to Get Villagers to Cooperate with Agribusiness in China." *The China Journal*, Vol. 77, pp. 27–50.

Lust-Okar, Ellen. 2005. *Structuring Conflict in the Arab World: Incumbents, Opponents and Institutions*. Cambridge; New York: Cambridge University Press.

2006. "Elections under Authoritarianism: Preliminary Lessons from Jordan." *Democratization*, Vol. 13, No. 3, pp. 456–471.

2008. "Taking Political Participation Seriously." In Ellen Lust-Okar and Saloua Zerhouni (eds.) *Political Participation in the Middle East and North Africa*. Boulder: Lynne Rienner Publishers, pp. 1–11.

Lynch, Marc. 2012. *The Arab Uprising: The Unfinished Revolutions of the New Middle East*. New York: Public Affairs.

Ma, Yuan. 2014. "'Normalization' and Informal Governance in Preserving Stability at the Grassroots" (Jiceng weiwen shijian zhong de "guifanhua" xingtai yu feizhengshi zhili). *Journal of Public Administration*, No. 6, pp. 67–87. *In Chinese.*

Machiavelli, Niccolò. 1532 (1988). *Machiavelli: The Prince*. Quentin Skinner and Russell Price (eds.). New York: Cambridge University Press.

Mackerras, Colin. 2004. "What Is China? Who Is Chinese? Han-Minority Relations, Legitimacy, and the State." In Peter Hays Gries and Stanley Rosen (eds.) *State and Society in 21st-Century China: Crisis, Contention, and Legitimation*. New York: RoutledgeCurzon, pp. 216–234.

2012. "Causes and Ramifications of the Xinjiang July 2009 Disturbances." *Sociology Study*, Vol. 2, No. 7, pp. 496-510.

Magaloni, Beatriz. 2006. *Voting for Autocracy: Hegemonic Party Survival and Its Demise in Mexico*. New York: Cambridge University Press.

2008. "Credible Power-Sharing and the Longevity of Authoritarian Rule." *Comparative Political Studies*, Vol. 41, No. 4–5, pp. 715–741.

Magaloni, Beatriz and Ruth Kricheli. 2010. "Political Order and One-Party Rule." *Annual Review of Political Science*, Vol. 13, pp. 123–143.

Malesky, Edmund and Paul Schuler. 2010. "Nodding or Needling: Analyzing Delegate Responsiveness in an Authoritarian Parliament." *American Political Science Review*, Vol. 104, No. 3, pp. 482–502.

Manion, Melanie. 2015. *Information for Autocrats: Representation in Chinese Local Congresses*. Cambridge: Cambridge University Press.

2017. "'Good Types' in Authoritarian Elections." *Comparative Political Studies*, Vol. 50, No. 3, pp. 362–394.

Mann, Michael. 2012. *The Sources of Social Power (Volume 2): The Rise of Classes and Nation-States, 1760–1914* (2nd edition). New York: Cambridge University Press.

McAdam, Doug. 1982. *Political Process and the Development of Black Insurgency, 1930–1970.* Chicago: University of Chicago Press.

1983. "Tactical Innovation and the Pace of Insurgency." *American Sociological Review,* Vol. 48, No. 6, pp. 735–754.

McAdam, Doug and Hilary S. Boudet. 2012. *Putting Social Movements in Their Place: Explaining Opposition to Energy Projects in the United States, 2000–2005.* New York: Cambridge University Press.

McAdam, Doug, Robert Sampson, Simon Weffer, and Heather MacIndoe. 2005. "There Will Be Fighting in the Streets: The Distorting Lens of Social Movement Theory." *Mobilization: An International Journal,* Vol. 10, No. 1, pp. 1–18.

McAdam, Doug, Sidney G. Tarrow, and Charles Tilly. 2001. *Dynamics of Contention.* New York: Cambridge University Press.

McCarthy, John and Clark McPhail. 1998. "The Institutionalization of Protest in the United States." In David S. Meyer and Sidney Tarrow (eds.) *The Social Movement Society: Contentious Politics for a New Century.* Lanham: Rowman & Littlefield Publishers, pp. 83–110.

McPhail, Clark, David Schweingruber, and John D. McCarthy. 1998. "Protest Policing in the United States, 1960–1995." In Donatella Della Porta and Herbert Reiter (eds.) *Policing Protest: The Control of Mass Demonstrations in Western Democracies.* Minneapolis: University of Minnesota Press, pp. 49–69.

Meng, Jianzhu. 2008. "Thoroughly Study and Practice the Scientific Outlook on Development; Be Loyal Guards of the Party and Close Friends of the Masses" (Shenru xuexi shijian kexue fazhanguan, zuodangde zhongchengweishi he renminqunzhong de tiexinren). *Qiushi,* No. 21, pp. 15–18. *In Chinese.*

Meng, Tianguang, Jennifer Pan, and Ping Yang. 2017. "Conditional Receptivity to Citizen Participation." *Comparative Political Studies,* Vol. 50, No. 4, pp. 399–433.

Mertha, Andrew C. 2008. *China's Water Warriors: Citizen Action and Policy Change.* Ithaca: Cornell University Press.

Meyer, David S. 2015. *The Politics of Protest: Social Movements in America* (2nd edition). New York: Oxford University Press.

Meyer, David S. and Sidney Tarrow. 1998. "A Movement Society: Contentious Politics for a New Century." In David S. Meyer and Sidney Tarrow (eds.) *The Social Movement Society: Contentious Politics for a New Century.* Lanham: Rowman & Littlefield Publishers, pp. 1–28.

Michelson, Ethan. 2008. "Justice from Above or Below? Popular Strategies for Resolving Grievances in Rural China." *The China Quarterly,* Vol. 193, pp. 43–64.

Miller, Michael K. 2015. "Elections, Information, and Policy Responsiveness in Autocratic Regimes." *Comparative Political Studies,* Vol. 48, No. 6, pp. 691–727.

Millward, James. 2004. *Violent Separatism in Xinjiang: A Critical Assessment.* Policy Studies 6. Washington, D.C.: East-West Center Washington.

2007. *Eurasian Crossroads: A History of Xinjiang.* New York: Columbia University Press.

2009. "Introduction: Does the 2009 Urumchi Violence Mark a Turning Point?" *Central Asian Survey,* Vol. 28, No. 4, pp. 347–360.

Minzner, Carl F. 2006. "Xinfang: An Alternative to Formal Chinese Legal Institutions." *Stanford Journal of International Law,* Vol. 42, No. 1, pp. 103–179.

2011. "China's Turn against Law." *The American Journal of Comparative Law*, Vol. 59, pp. 935–984.

Moss, Dana M. 2014. "Repression, Response, and Contained Escalation under 'Liberalized' Authoritarianism in Jordan." *Mobilization: An International Journal*, Vol. 19, No. 3, pp. 489–514.

Moustafa, Tamir. 2007. *The Struggle for Constitutional Power: Law, Politics, and Economic Development in Egypt*. New York: Cambridge University Press.

2014. "Law and Courts in Authoritarian Regimes." *Annual Review of Law and Social Science*, Vol. 10, No. 1, pp. 281–299.

Nathan, Andrew J. 2003. "Authoritarian Resilience." *Journal of Democracy*, Vol. 14, No. 1, pp. 6–17.

2013. "China at the Tipping Point? Foreseeing the Unforeseeable." *Journal of Democracy*, Vol. 24, No. 1, pp. 20–25.

Naughton, Barry J. and Dali L. Yang. 2004. "Holding China together: Introduction." In Barry J Naughton and Dali L. Yang (eds.) *Holding China together: Diversity and National Integration in the Post-Deng Era*. New York: Cambridge University Press, pp. 1–25.

Noakes, Stephen and Caylan Ford. 2015. "Managing Political Opposition Groups in China: Explaining the Continuing Anti-Falun Gong Campaign." *The China Quarterly*, No. 223, pp. 658–679.

North, Douglass C. 1990. *Institutions, Institutional Change and Economic Performance*. New York: Cambridge University Press.

Oberschall, Anthony. 1996. "Opportunities and Framing in the Eastern European Revolts of 1989." In Doug McAdam, John McCarthy and Mayer Zald (eds.) *Comparative Perspectives in Social Movements*. New York: Cambridge University Press, pp. 93–121.

O'Brien, Kevin J. 1996. "Rightful Resistance." *World Politics*, Vol. 49, No. 1, pp. 31–55.

2003. "Neither Transgressive nor Contained: Boundary-Spanning Contention in China." *Mobilization: An International Journal*, Vol. 8, No. 1, pp. 51–64.

O'Brien, Kevin J. and Lianjiang Li. 2004. "Suing the Local State: Administrative Litigation in Rural China." *The China Journal*, Vol. 51, pp. 75–96.

2005. "Popular Contention and Its Impact in Rural China." *Comparative Political Studies*, Vol. 38, No. 3, pp. 235–259.

2006. *Rightful Resistance in Rural China*. New York: Cambridge University Press.

O'Brien, Kevin J. and Rongbin Han. 2009. "Path to Democracy? Assessing Village Elections in China." *Journal of Contemporary China*, Vol. 18, No. 60, pp. 359–378.

O'Brien, Kevin J. and Yanhua Deng. 2015a. "The Reach of the State: Work Units, Family Ties and 'Harmonious Demolition.'" *The China Journal*, Vol. 74, pp. 1–17.

2015b. "Repression Backfires: Tactical Radicalization and Protest Spectacle in Rural China." *Journal of Contemporary China*. Vol. 24, No. 93, pp. 457–470.

O'Donnell, Guillermo and Philippe C. Schmitter. 1986. *Transitions from Authoritarian Rule: Tentative Conclusions about Uncertain Democracies*. Baltimore: Johns Hopkins University Press.

Oliver, Pamela and Daniel Myers. 1999. "How Events Enter the Public Sphere: Conflict, Location, and Sponsorship in Local Newspaper Coverage of Public Events." *American Journal of Sociology*, Vol. 105, No. 1, pp. 38–87.

Olzak, Susan. 1992. *The Dynamics of Ethnic Competition and Conflict.* Stanford: Stanford University Press.

Olzak, Susan, Maya Beasley, and Johan Olivier. 2003. "The Impact of State Reforms on Protest against Apartheid in South Africa." *Mobilization: An International Quarterly*, Vol. 8, No. 1, pp. 27–50.

Opp, Karl-Dieter and Wolfgang Roehl. 1990. "Repression, Micromobilization, and Political Protest." *Social Forces*, Vol. 69, No. 2, pp. 521–547.

Ownby, David. 2008. *Falun Gong and the Future of China.* New York: Oxford University Press.

Palmer, David A. 2007. *Qigong Fever: Body, Science, and Utopia in China.* New York: Columbia University Press.

Pei, Minxin. 2006. *China's Trapped Transition: The Limits of Developmental Autocracy.* Cambridge: Harvard University Press.

2012. "Is CCP Rule Fragile or Resilient? *Journal of Democracy*, Vol. 23, No. 1, pp. 27–41.

2016. *China's Crony Capitalism.* Cambridge: Harvard University Press.

Penny, Benjamin. 2012. *The Religion of Falun Gong.* Chicago: University of Chicago Press.

Perry, Elizabeth J. 2001. "Challenging the Mandate of Heaven: Popular Protest in Modern China." *Critical Asian Studies*, Vol. 33, No. 2, pp. 163–180.

2002a. "Introduction." *Challenging the Mandate of Heaven: Social Protest and State Power in China.* Armonk: M.E. Sharpe, pp. ix–xxx.

2002b. "Contradictions under Socialism: Shanghai's Strike Wave of 1957." *Challenging the Mandate of Heaven: Social Protest and State Power in China.* Armonk: M.E. Sharpe, pp. 206–237.

2007. "Studying Chinese Politics: Farewell to Revolution?" *The China Journal*, Vol. 57, pp. 1–23.

2008. "Chinese Conceptions of 'Rights': From Mencius to Mao – and Now." *Perspectives on Politics*, Vol. 6, No. 1, pp. 37–50.

2010. "Popular Protest: Playing by the Rules." In Joseph Fewsmith (ed.) *China Today, China Tomorrow: Domestic Politics, Economy, and Society.* Lanham: Rowman & Littlefield Publishers, pp. 11–28.

2012. "The Illiberal Challenge of Authoritarian China." *Taiwan Journal of Democracy*, Vol. 8, No. 2, pp. 3–15.

2014. "Growing Pains: Challenges for a Rising China." *Daedalus*, Vol. 143, No. 2, pp. 5–13.

Pfaff, Steven, and Guobin Yang. 2001. "Double-Edged Rituals and the Symbolic Resources of Collective Action: Political Commemorations and the Mobilization of Protest in 1989." *Theory and Society*, Vol. 30, pp. 539–589.

Potter, Pitman. 1999. "The Chinese Legal System: Continuing Commitment to the Primacy of State Power." *The China Quarterly*, No. 159, pp. 673–683.

Przeworski, Adam. 1991. *Democracy and the Market: Political and Economic Reforms in Eastern Europe and Latin America.* New York: Cambridge University Press.

Punch, Maurice. 2010. *Shoot to Kill: Police Accountability, Firearms and Fatal Force.* Bristol: Policy Press.

Qi, Peng and Wang Zexu. 2013. "Thoughts on Strategies to Handle Mass Incidents by Law in the Transition Period" (Zhuanxingqi quntixing shijian falü zhili celue sikao). *Legal System and Society*, No. 8, pp. 81–86. *In Chinese.*

Rasler, Karen. 1996. "Concessions, Repression, and Political Protest in the Iranian Revolution." *American Sociological Review*, Vol. 61, No. 1, pp. 132–152.

Reilly, James. 2012. *Strong Society, Smart State: The Rise of Public Opinion in China's Japan Policy*. New York: Columbia University Press.

Reny, Marie-Eve. 2018. "Compliant Defiance: Informality and Survival among Protestant House Churches in China." *Journal of Contemporary China*, Vol. 27, No. 111, pp. 472–485.

Reny, Marie-Eve and William Hurst. 2013. "Social Unrest." In Chris Ogden (ed.) *Handbook of China's Governance and Domestic Politics*. New York: Routledge, pp. 210–220.

Repnikova, Maria. 2017. *Media Politics in China: Improvising Power under Authoritarianism*. New York: Cambridge University Press.

Rigger, Shelley. 2014. "Taiwan's Democratization and Mainland China's Future." In Kate Xiao Zhou, Shelley Rigger, and Lynn T. White III (eds.) *Democratization in China, Korea, and Southeast Asia?* New York: Routledge, pp. 36–50.

Ritter, Emily Hencken and Courtenay R. Conrad. 2016. "Preventing and Responding to Dissent: The Observational Challenges of Explaining Strategic Repression." *American Political Science Review*, Vol. 110, No. 1, pp. 85–99.

Robertson, Graeme B. 2011. *The Politics of Protest in Hybrid Regimes: Managing Dissent in Post-communist Russia*. New York: Cambridge University Press.

Van Rooij, Benjamin. 2010. "The People vs. Pollution: Understanding Citizen Action against Pollution in China." *Journal of Contemporary China*, Vol. 19, No. 63, pp. 55–77.

Rootes, Christopher. 2004. "Environmental Movements." In David A. Snow, Sarah A. Soule and Hanspeter Kriesi (eds.) *The Blackwell Companion to Social Movements*. Malden: Blackwell Publishing, pp. 608–640.

Saich, Tony. 2000. "Negotiating the State: The Development of Social Organization in China." *The China Quarterly*, No. 161, pp. 124–141.

2007. "Citizens' Perceptions of Governance in Rural and Urban China." *Journal of Chinese Political Science*, Vol. 12, No. 1, pp. 1–28.

2011. "Citizens' Perceptions of Adequate Governance: Satisfaction Levels Among Rural and Urban Chinese." In Everett Zhang, Arthur Kleinman, and Tu Weiming (eds.) *Governance of Life in Chinese Moral Experience: The Quest for an Adequate Life*. London: Routledge, pp. 199–214.

2016. "State-Society Relations in the People's Republic of China Post-1949." *Governance and Public Policy in China*, Vol. 1, No. 1, pp. 1–57.

Schubert, Gunter. 2008. "One-Party Rule and the Question of Legitimacy in Contemporary China: Preliminary Thoughts on Setting up a New Research Agenda." *Journal of Contemporary China*, Vol. 17, No. 54, pp. 191–204.

Scott, James C. 1976. *The Moral Economy of the Peasant: Rebellion and Subsistence in Southeast Asia*. New Haven: Yale University Press.

1985. *Weapons of the Weak: Everyday Forms of Peasant Resistance*. New Haven: Yale University Press.

1990. *Domination and the Arts of Resistance: Hidden Transcripts*. New Haven: Yale University Press.

Seidman, Gay. 2009. "Armed Struggle in the South African Anti-Apartheid Movement." In Jeff Goodwin and James M. Jasper (eds.) *The Social Movements Reader: Cases and Concepts* (2nd edition). Malden: Wiley-Blackwell, pp. 279–294.

Selden, Mark and Elizabeth J. Perry. 2010. "Introduction: Reform and Resistance in Contemporary China." In Elizabeth J. Perry and Mark Selden (eds.) *Chinese Society: Change, Conflict and Resistance* (3rd edition). London; New York: Routledge, pp. 1–30.

Shambaugh, David. 2008. *China's Communist Party: Atrophy and Adaptation*. Berkeley: University of California Press.

    2016. *China's Future*. Cambridge: Polity Press.

Shi, Fayong. 2008. "Social Capital at Work: The Dynamics and Consequences of Grassroots Movements in Urban China." *Critical Asian Studies*, Vol. 40, No. 2, pp. 233–262.

Shi, Fayong and Yongshun Cai. 2006. "Disaggregating the State: Networks and Collective Resistance in Shanghai." *The China Quarterly*, Vol. 186, pp. 314–332.

Shi, Tianjian. 2001. "Cultural Impact on Political Trust: A Comparison of Mainland China and Taiwan." *Comparative Politics*, Vol. 33, No. 4, pp. 401–420.

    2015. *The Cultural Logic of Politics in Mainland China and Taiwan*. New York: Cambridge University Press.

Shock, Kurt. 2005. *Unarmed Insurrections: People Power Movements in Nondemocracies*. Minneapolis: University of Minnesota Press.

Shue, Vivienne. 1991. "Powers of State, Paradoxes of Dominion." in Kenneth Lieberthal, Joyce Kallgren, Roderick MacFarquhar, and Frederic Wakeman (eds.) *Perspectives on Modern China: Four Anniversaries*. Armonk: M.E. Sharpe, pp. 205–225.

Siavelis, Peter. 2006. "Accommodating Informal Institutions and Chilean Democracy." In Gretchen Helmke and Steven Levitsky (eds.) *Informal Institutions and Democracy: Lessons from Latin America*. Baltimore: Johns Hopkins University, pp. 33–55.

Skocpol, Theda. 1979. *States and Social Revolutions: A Comparative Analysis of France, Russia and China*. Cambridge: Cambridge University Press.

Slater, Dan. 2010. *Ordering Power: Contentious Politics and Authoritarian Leviathans in Southeast Asia*. New York: Cambridge University Press.

Slater, Dan, and Sofia Fenner. 2011. "State Power and Staying Power: Infrastructural Mechanisms and Authoritarian Durability." *Journal of International Affairs*, Vol. 65, No. 1, pp. 14–29.

Soule, Sarah A. and Christian Davenport. 2009. "Velvet Glove, Iron Fist, or Even Hand? Protest Policing in the United States, 1960–1990." *Mobilization: An International Journal*, Vol. 14, No. 1, pp. 1–22.

Spires, Anthony J. 2011. "Contingent Symbiosis and Civil Society in an Authoritarian State: Understanding the Survival of China's Grassroots NGOs." *American Journal of Sociology*, Vol. 117, No. 1, pp. 1–45.

Stern, Rachel E. 2014. "The Political Logic of China's Environmental Courts." *The China Journal*, Vol. 72, pp. 53–75.

Stern, Rachel E. and Jonathan Hassid. 2012. "Amplifying Silence: Uncertainty and Control Parables in Contemporary China." *Comparative Political Studies*, Vol. 45, No. 10, pp. 1230–1254.

Stern, Rachel E. and Kevin J. O'Brien. 2011. "Politics at the Boundary: Mixed Signals and the Chinese State." *Modern China*, Vol. 38, No. 2, pp. 174–198.

Stockmann, Daniela. 2013. *Media Commercialization and Authoritarian Rule in China*. Cambridge; New York: Cambridge University Press.

Stockmann, Daniela and Mary E. Gallagher. 2011. "Remote Control: How the Media Sustain Authoritarian Rule in China." *Comparative Political Studies*, Vol. 44, No. 4, pp. 436–467.

Su, Yang and Xin He. 2010. "Street as Courtroom: State Accommodation of Labor Protest in South China." *Law & Society Review*, Vol. 44, No. 1, pp. 157–184.

Svolik, Milan W. 2012. *The Politics of Authoritarian Rule*. New York: Cambridge University Press.

Tang, Wenfang. 2005. *Public Opinion and Political Change in China*. Stanford: Stanford University Press.

2016. *Populist Authoritarianism: Chinese Political Culture and Regime Sustainability*. New York: Oxford University Press.

Tanner, Murray Scot. 2002a. "The Institutional Lessons of Disaster: Reorganizing the People's Armed Police after Tiananmen." In James C. Mulvenon (ed.) *The People's Liberation Army as Organization*. Washington, D.C.: RAND, pp. 587–635.

2002b. *Torture in China: Calls for Reform from within China's Law Enforcement System*. Prepared Statement to Accompany Testimony Before the Congressional-Executive Committee on China. Washington, D.C.: Congressional-Executive Committee on China.

2004. "China Rethinks Unrest." *The Washington Quarterly*, Vol. 27, No. 3. pp. 137–156.

2009. "How China Manages Internal Security Challenges and Its Impact on PLA Missions." In *Beyond the Strait: PLA Missions Other than Taiwan*. Carlisle: Strategic Studies Institute, pp. 39–98.

Tanner, Murray Scot and Eric Green. 2007. "Principals and Secret Agents: Central versus Local Control Over Policing and Obstacles to 'Rule of Law' in China." *The China Quarterly* No. 191, pp. 644–670.

Tarrow, Sidney G. 2011. *Power in Movement: Social Movements and Contentious Politics* (3rd edition). New York: Cambridge University Press.

Tarrow, Sidney and Charles Tilly. 2007. "Contentious Politics and Social Movements." In Carles Boix and Susan C. Stokes (eds.) *The Oxford Handbook of Comparative Politics*, pp. 435–460. Oxford: Oxford University Press.

Teets, Jessica. 2013. "Let Many Civil Societies Bloom: The Rise of Consultative Authoritarianism in China." *The China Quarterly*, No. 213, pp. 19–38.

2014. *Civil Society under Authoritarianism: The China Model*. New York: Cambridge University Press.

Terrone, Antonio. 2016. "Propaganda in the Public Square: Communicating State Directives on Religion and Ethnicity to Uyghurs and Tibetans in Western China." In Ben Hillman and Gray Tuttle (eds.) *Ethnic Conflict and Protest in Tibet and Xinjiang: Unrest in China's West*. New York: Columbia University Press, pp. 40–59.

Thaxton, Ralph. 2016. *Force and Contention in Contemporary China: Memory and Resistance in the Long Shadow of the Catastrophic Past*. New York, NY: Cambridge University Press.

Thompson, E. P. 1971. "The Moral Economy of the English Crowd in the Eighteenth Century." *Past and Present*, No. 50, pp. 76–136.

1974. "Patrician Society, Plebeian Culture." *Journal of Social History*. Vol. 7, No. 4, pp. 382–405.

Thornton, Patricia. 2010. "The New Cybersects: Popular Religion, Repression and Resistance." In Elizabeth J. Perry and Mark Selden (eds.) *Chinese Society: Change, Conflict and Resistance* (3rd edition). London; New York: Routledge, pp. 215–238.

Tilly, Charles. 1978. *From Mobilization to Revolution*. New York: Random. House.
    1984. "Social Movements and National Politics." In Charles Bright and Susan Hard-
        ing (eds.) *Statemaking and Social Movements: Essays in History and Theory*. Ann
        Arbor: University of Michigan Press, pp. 297–317.
    1995. *Popular Contention in Great Britain 1758–1834*. Cambridge: Harvard Univer-
        sity Press.
    2003. *The Politics of Collective Violence*. New York: Cambridge University Press.
    2006. *Regimes and Repertoires*. Chicago: University of Chicago Press.
    2008. *Contentious Performances*. New York: Cambridge University Press.
Tilly, Charles and Sidney Tarrow. 2007. *Contentious Politics*. New York: Oxford
    University Press.
Tomba, Luigi. 2014. *The Government Next Door: Neighborhood Politics in Urban
    China*. Ithaca: Cornell University Press.
Tong, James. 2009. *Revenge of the Forbidden City: The Suppression of the Falungong in
    China, 1999–2005*. New York: Oxford University Press.
    2012. "Banding after the Ban: The Underground Falungong in China, 1999–2011."
        Journal of Contemporary China, Vol. 21, No. 78, pp. 1045–1062.
Tong, Xin. 2006. "The Persisting Socialist Cultural Tradition" (Yanxu de shehuizhuyi
    wenhua chuantong). *Sociological Studies*. No. 1, pp. 59–76. *In Chinese*.
Tong, Yanqi and Shaohua Lei. 2013. *Social Protests in Contemporary China,
    2003–2010: Transitional Pains and Regime Legitimacy*. Abingdon; New York:
    Routledge.
Trejo, Guillermo. 2012. *Popular Movements in Autocracies: Religion, Repression, and
    Indigenous Collective Action in Mexico*. New York: Cambridge University Press.
Truex, Rory. 2016. *Making Autocracy Work: Representation and Responsiveness in
    Modern China*. New York: Cambridge University Press.
    2018. "Focal Points, Dissident Calendars, and Preemptive Repression." *Journal of
        Conflict Resolution* doi: 10.1177/0022002718770520.
Tsai, Kellee S. 2007. *Capitalism without Democracy: The Private Sector in Contempor-
    ary China*. Ithaca: Cornell University Press.
    2013. "Cause or Consequence? Private-Sector Development and Communist Resili-
        ence in China." In Martin Dimitrov (ed.) *Why Communism Did Not Collapse:
        Understanding Authoritarian Regime Resilience in Asia and Europe*. New York:
        Cambridge University Press, pp. 205–234.
    2016. "Adaptive Informal Institutions," in Tulia Falleti, Orfeo Fioretes, and Adam
        Sheingate (eds.) *Oxford Handbook of Historical Institutionalism*. New York:
        Oxford University Press, pp. 270–287.
Tsai, Lily L. 2007. *Accountability Without Democracy: Solidary Groups and Public
    Goods Provision in Rural China*. New York: Cambridge University Press.
Tsang, Steve. 2009. "Consultative Leninism: China's New Political Framework," *Jour-
    nal of Contemporary China*, Vol. 18, No. 62, pp. 865–880.
Tsinghua University. 2010. "Achieving Long-Term Stability through the Institutional-
    ization of Interest Expression" (Yi liyi biaoda zhiduhua shixian shehui de changzhi
    jiuan). Report by Research Group on Social Development, Department of Soci-
    ology. *In Chinese*. Beijing: Tsinghua University.
Ulfelder, Jay. 2005. "Contentious Collective Action and the Breakdown of Authoritar-
    ian Regimes." *International Political Science Review*, Vol. 26, No. 3, pp. 311–334.

United Nations. 2014. *Concluding Observations on the Third to Fifth Periodic Reports of United States of America*. Report by Convention against Torture and Other Cruel, Inhuman or Degrading Treatment or Punishment. New York: United Nations.

U.S. Department of Health and Human Services. 2014. *Results from the 2013 National Survey on Drug Use and Health: Summary of National Findings*. Washington, D.C.: U.S. Department of Health and Human Services.

Vairel, Frédéric. 2011. "Protesting in Authoritarian Situations: Egypt and Morocco in Comparative Perspective." In Joel Beinin and Frédéric Vairel (eds.) *Social Movements, Mobilization, and Contestation in the Middle East and North Africa*. Stanford: Stanford University Press, pp. 27–42.

Waddington, P.A.J. 1998. "Controlling Protest in Contemporary Historical and Comparative Perspective." In Donatella Della Porta and Herbert Reiter (eds.) *Policing Protest: The Control of Mass Demonstrations in Western Democracies*. Minneapolis: University of Minnesota Press, pp. 117–140.

Walder, Andrew G. 2004. "The Party Elite and China's Trajectory of Change." *China: An International Journal*, Vol. 2, No. 2, pp. 189–209.

——— 2009a. "Unruly Stability: Why China's Regime Has Staying Power." *Current History*, Vol. 108, No. 719, pp. 257–263.

——— 2009b. "Political Sociology and Social Movement." *Annual Review of Sociology*, Vol. 35, pp. 393–412.

Wallace, Jeremy L. 2014. *Cities and Stability: Urbanization, Redistribution, and Regime Survival in China*. New York: Oxford University Press.

Wang, Juan. 2012. "Shifting Boundaries between the State and Society: Village Cadres as New Activists in Collective Petition." *The China Quarterly*, Vol. 211, pp. 697–717.

——— 2015. "Managing Social Stability: The Perspective of a Local Government in China." *Journal of East Asian Studies*, Vol. 15, No. 1, pp. 1–25.

Wang, Yuhua. 2014. "Coercive Capacity and the Durability of the Chinese Communist State." *Communist and Post-Communist Studies*, Vol. 47, pp. 13–25.

Wang, Yuhua and Carl Minzner. 2015. "The Rise of the Security State." *The China Quarterly*, Vol. 222, pp. 339–359.

Wang, Zhengxu. 2006. "Explaining Regime Strength in China." *China: An International Journal*, Vol. 4, No. 2, pp. 217–237.

Weiner, Myron. 1971. "Political Participation: Crisis of the Political Process." In Leonard Binder and Joseph La Palombara (eds.) *Crises and Sequences in Political Development*. Princeton: Princeton University Press, pp. 159–204.

Weller, Robert. 2012. "Responsive Authoritarianism and Blind-Eye Governance in China." In Nina Bandelj and Dorothy J. Solinger (eds.) *Socialism Vanquished, Socialism Challenged: Eastern Europe and China, 1989–2009*. New York: Oxford University Press, pp. 83–102.

Whyte, Martin King. 2010. *Myth of the Social Volcano: Perceptions of Inequality and Distributive Injustice in Contemporary China*. Stanford: Stanford University Press.

Williams, Kristian. 2015. *Our Enemies in Blue: Police and Power in America* (3rd edition). Chico: AK Press.

Wintrobe, Ronald. 1998. *The Political Economy of Dictatorship*. Cambridge, New York: Cambridge University Press.

Wong, Stan Hok-wui and Minggang Peng. 2015 "Petition and Repression in China's Authoritarian Regime: Evidence from a Natural Experiment." *Journal of East Asian Studies*, Vol. 15, No. 1, pp. 27–67.

World Bank. 2005. *Waste Management in China: Issues and Recommendations*. Washington, D.C.: World Bank.

Wright, Teresa. 2004. "Contesting State Legitimacy in the 1990s: The China Democracy Party and the China Labor Bulletin." In Peter Hays Gries and Stanley Rosen (eds.) *State and Society in 21st-century China: Crisis, Contention, and Legitimation*. New York: RoutledgeCurzon, pp. 123–140.

2010. *Accepting Authoritarianism: State-Society Relations in China's Reform Era*. Stanford: Stanford University Press.

Xie, Yue. 2012. "The Political Logic of Weiwen in Contemporary China." *Issues and Studies*, Vol. 48, No. 3, pp. 1–41.

2013. "Rising Central Spending on Public Security and the Dilemma Facing Grassroots." *Journal of Current Chinese Affairs*, Vol. 42, No. 2, pp. 79–109.

Yan, Xiaojun. 2016. "Patrolling Harmony: Pre-Emptive Authoritarianism and the Preservation of Stability in W County." *Journal of Contemporary China*, Vol. 25, No. 99, pp. 406–421.

Yang, Dali L. 2004. *Remaking the Chinese Leviathan: Market Transition and the Politics of Governance in China*. Stanford: Stanford University Press.

2007. "China's Long March to Democracy." *Journal of Democracy*, Vol. 18, No. 3, pp. 58–64.

Yang, Guobin and Craig Calhoun. 2007. "Media, Civil Society, and the Rise of a Green Public Sphere in China." *China Information*, Vol. 21, No. 2, pp. 211–236.

Yao, Yusheng. 2013. "Village Elections and Their Impact: An Investigative Report on a Northern Chinese Village." *Modern China*, Vol. 39, No. 1, pp. 37–68.

Youwei. 2015. "The End of Reform in China: Authoritarian Adaptation Hits a Wall." *Foreign Affairs*, Vol. 94, No. 3, pp. 2–7.

Yu, Jianrong. 2004. "Institutional Defects of Xinfang System and Its Political Outcomes" (Xinfang de zhidu queshi jiqi zhengzhi houguo). *Phoenix Weekly*, Vol. 165, No. 32. *In Chinese*.

2005. "Critique of China's Petition System" (Zhongguo xinfang zhidu pipan). *China Reform*, Issue 2. *In Chinese*.

2007. "China's Disturbances and Governance Crisis" (Zhongguo de saoluan shijian yu guanzhi weiji). *Teahouse for Sociologists*, 1, pp. 26–37. *In Chinese*.

Zhang, Mingjun and Chen Peng. 2012. "Analytical Reports of Typical Mass Incidents in China in 2011" (2011 niandu zhongguo shehui dianxing quntixing shijian fenxi baogao). *China Social and Public Security Research Reports*, Vol. 1, pp. 1–29. In Chinese.

2014. "Analytical Reports of Typical Mass Incidents in China in 2013" (2013 niandu zhongguo shehui dianxing quntixing shijian fenxi baogao). *China Social and Public Security Research Reports*, Vol. 5, pp. 1–12. In Chinese.

2015. "Analytical Reports of Typical Mass Incidents in China in 2014" (2014 niandu zhongguo shehui dianxing quntixing shijian fenxi baogao). *China Social and Public Security Research Reports*, Vol. 6, pp. 1–10. In Chinese.

Zhang, Mingjun and Liu Xiaoliang. 2017. "Analytical Report on Mass Incidents in China in 2016 (2016 nian zhongguo shehui quntixing shijian fenxi baogao)." *China Social and Public Security Research Reports*, Vol. 10, pp. 3–18. *In Chinese*.

Zhang, Shengqian. 2006. "On Legal Countermeasures to Deal with Mass Incidents" (Lun quntixing shijian chuzhi de falü duice). *Journal of Hubei University of Police*, Vol. 92, No. 5, pp. 58–61. *In Chinese.*

Zhao, Dingxin. 2001. *The Power of Tiananmen*. Chicago: University of Chicago Press.

2010. "Authoritarian Regime and Contentious Politics." In Kevin T. Leicht and Craig C. Jenkins (eds.) *Handbook of Politics: State and Society in Global Perspective*. New York: Springer, pp. 459–476.

2012. "Will Revolution Take Place in China Today? (Dangjin zhongguo huibuhui fasheng geming)" *Twenty-First Century*, Vol. 134, pp. 4–16. *In Chinese.*

Zhao, Yuezhi and Sun Wusan. 2007. "Public Opinion Supervision: Possibilities and Limits of the Media in Constraining Local Officials." In Elizabeth J. Perry and Merle Goldman (eds.) *Grassroots Political Reform in Contemporary China*. Cambridge: Harvard University Press, pp. 300–326.

Zheng, Yongnian. 2015. "The Institutionalization of the Communist Party and the Party System in China." In Allen Hicken and Erik Martinez Kuhonta (eds.) *Party System Institutionalization in Asia: Democracies, Autocracies, and the Shadows of the Past*. New York: Cambridge University Press, pp. 162–188.

Zhi. 2014. *Record of the Shining Hospital Takeover* (Guangliang yiyuan guishu jishi; 2nd edition), unpublished manuscript. *In Chinese.*

Zhou, Kai and Xiaojun Yan. 2014. "The Quest for Stability: Policing Popular Protest in the People's Republic of China." *Problems of Post-Communism*, Vol. 61, No. 3, pp. 3–17.

Zweig, David. 2010. "To the Courts or to the Barricades? Can New Political Institutions Manage Rural Conflict?" In Elizabeth J. Perry and Mark Selden (eds.) *Chinese Society: Change, Conflict and Resistance* (3rd edition). London; New York: Routledge, pp. 123–147.

Index

(continued from p. iii)

Christian Davenport, *How Social Movements Die: Repression and Demobilization of the Republic of New Africa*

Christian Davenport, *Media Bias, Perspective, and State Repression*

Gerald F. Davis, Doug McAdam, W. Richard Scott, and Mayer N. Zald, *Social Movements and Organization Theory*

Donatella della Porta, *Clandestine Political Violence*

Donatella della Porta, *Where Did the Revolution Go?: Contentious Politics and the Quality of Democracy*

Mario Diani, *The Cement of Civil Society: Studying Networks in Localities*

Nicole Doerr, *Political Translation: How Social Movement Democracies Survive*

Barry Eidlin, *Labor and the Class Idea in the United States in Canada*

Todd A. Eisenstadt, *Politics, Identity, and Mexico's Indigenous Rights Movements*

Diana Fu, *Mobilizing without the Masses: Control and Contention in China*

Daniel Q. Gillion, *The Political Power of Protest: Minority Activism and Shifts in Public Policy*

Marco Giugni and Maria Grasso *Street Citizens: Protest Politics and Social Movement Activism in the Age of Globalization*

Jack A. Goldstone, editor, *States, Parties, and Social Movements*

Jennifer Hadden, *Networks in Contention: The Divisive Politics of Climate Change*

Michael T. Heaney and Fabio Rojas, *Party in the Street: The Antiwar Movement and the Democratic Party after 9/11*

Tamara Kay, *NAFTA and the Politics of Labor Transnationalism*

Neil Ketchley, *Egypt in a Time of Revolution: Contentious Politics and the Arab Spring*

Yao Li, *Playing by the Informal Rules: Why the Chinese Regime Remains Stable despite Rising Protests*

Joseph Luders, *The Civil Rights Movement and the Logic of Social Change*

Doug McAdam and Hilary Boudet, *Putting Social Movements in Their Place: Explaining Opposition to Energy Projects in the United States, 2000–2005*

Doug McAdam, Sidney Tarrow, and Charles Tilly, *Dynamics of Contention*

Holly J. McCammon, *The U.S. Women's Jury Movements and Strategic Adaptation: A More Just Verdict*

Olena Nikolayenko, *Youth Movements and Elections in Eastern Europe*

Sharon Nepstad, *Religion and War Resistance and the Plowshares Movement*

Kevin J. O'Brien and Lianjiang Li, *Rightful Resistance in Rural China*

Silvia Pedraza, *Political Disaffection in Cuba's Revolution and Exodus*

Héctor Perla Jr., *Sandinista Nicaragua's Resistance to US Coercion*

Federico M. Rossi, *The Poor's Struggle for Political Incorporation: The Piquetero Movement in Argentina*

Chandra Russo, *Solidarity in Practice: Moral Protest and the US Security State*

Eduardo Silva, *Challenging Neoliberalism in Latin America*

Erica S. Simmons, *Meaningful Resistance: Market Reforms and the Roots of Social Protest in Latin America*

Sarah Soule, *Contention and Corporate Social Responsibility*

Sherrill Stroschein, *Ethnic Struggle, Coexistence, and Democratization in Eastern Europe*

Yang Su, *Collective Killings in Rural China during the Cultural Revolution*

Sidney Tarrow, *The Language of Contention: Revolutions in Words, 1688–2012*